Shotguns

Pictured are three of the 8 of 8 Winchester Model 21 Grand American sets produced with 20, 28, and 410 gauge barrels. Only four of the planned eight sets were ever built. They are valued today at $80,000 each. (Courtesy Dave Riffle. Photo by Dennis Adler)

Shotguns

By Dennis Adler
Foreword by R.L. Wilson

CHARTWELL
BOOKS, INC.

Featuring Shotguns From The Dave Riffle, Gary Reynolds,
And U.S. Repeating Arms Company Collections

This edition published in 2006 by
CHARTWELL BOOKS
A division of BOOK SALES, INC.
114 Northfield Avenue
Edison, New Jersey 08837

Published by arrangement with Dennis Adler who is represented by International Transactions, Inc. of New York, USA

Designed by Keith Betterley

ISBN-13: 978-0-7858-2108-3
ISBN-10: 0-7858-2108-2

Printed in China

To Jeanne for uttering those prophetic words:

"Maybe we should start collecting Winchesters..."

Foreword
By R.L. Wilson

In the study and appreciation of American history, and in understanding the crucial role played by firearms in that extraordinary saga, the two most famous gunmakers are Colt and Winchester. Their products are so much in demand that they indisputably hold the title of the Blue Chips of gun collecting.

And while a notable amount of literature on these marques has appeared in print, much of it from the period of post-World War II, there are still major categories which demand focused books. Such works are in response not only to the "need to know" from students, historians and collectors, but also are a powerful reflection of the ever-expanding explosion of interest in the magical world of firearms.

In *Winchester Shotguns*, Dennis Adler does a great service to all those keen on Winchester arms and accessories – and to the company itself. This title fills a distinct void, and does it superbly.

As in his previous firearms books, Dennis captures the beauty, craftsmanship, technology and romance of his subject not only with richly-worded text, but in magnificent color photographs. The study of arms is a highly visual, and technical, pursuit. Having the objects sitting on a page, as if they are on the reader's desk, is a true delight. Few photographers can equal those images of excellence. And no one today can match his combination of skill, aptitude and artistry at doing *both* text and photographs.

This foreword presents an opportunity not only to recognize those special Adler touches, but also to comment on the synergy between the world of firearms, and that of the automobile. So many enthusiasts in the realm of cars are also keen on guns – and vice versa. And no other author has achieved so much in both fields. Further, with his relative youth, there is no doubt much, much more to come from Dennis Adler.

Among the Winchester enthusiasts who are also collectors, keen on both fine guns and great cars – consider the following: publisher Robert E, Petersen, Hunting World founder Robert M. Lee, editor/publisher David E. Davis, and gunmakers William B. Ruger, Sr. and Jr. Even though he did not have the time or opportunity to become a "car crank," Theodore Roosevelt not only loved his Winchesters (primarily rifles), but he was the first President of the United States to ride in an automobile.

Crossing the fine line between the gun and the automobile, Dennis Adler is doing both worlds a greatly appreciated service. It is my pleasure, and honor, to take the same considerable degree of enjoyment in reading *Winchester Shotguns*, as I do in devouring the Dennis Adler series on exotic and historic automobiles, as well as his previously published firearms volumes.

And I join with thousands of others in looking forward to more from the Adler word machine, and cameras!

– R.L.W.

Preface and Acknowledgements

Collecting can get you into a whole lot of trouble. Some 30 years ago I found myself drawn to Smith & Wesson revolvers. Many thousands of dollars later I realized there were more enticing S&W models out there than I could ever afford. Segue. I started collecting Broomhandle Mausers. Many, many thousands of dollars later I realized there were more enticing Broomhandle models out there than I could ever afford. Segue. I started collecting Colt cap-and-ball revolvers. Of course, by now I was writing books about them, the first titled *Colt Blackpowder* published in 1998 by Steve Fjestad and Blue Book Publications. Four more books followed on black powder arms. Segue. Post Civil War cartridge conversion revolvers were next and another book, this one titled *Metallic Cartridge Conversions*, published in 2002.

Winchesters, of course, were always on my mind but as the reader can tell from my previous collecting habits and books, my interests were focused entirely on historic handguns. Then I bought a Winchester Model 101 Super Pigeon, followed by a 1901 lever-action shotgun and a Model 1897 pump, and as the late Ronald Reagan liked to say, "Well, there he goes again." I finally got smart though; this time Jeanne, my very supportive, gun collecting better half and I were in it together, and I already had a book deal! So, here I go again.

It is interesting that a full color coffee table-style book has never been done on Winchester shotguns. My good friend and colleague R.L. Wilson has written many of the definitive books on the Winchester Repeating Arms Co., including the consummate history

The author with his 12-gauge Winchester Model 21 Skeet gun.

iv

published in 1991 by Random House, *Winchester – An American Legend*. But even Larry never delved into the complete history of the shotguns built in New Haven as a standalone book. As always, whenever I have asked him why a book hasn't been done on a given subject of my interest, his standard reply has been, "Why don't you write one?" Thus inspired once again, *Winchester Shotguns* is the result.

As with all of my previous firearms books, and automotive history books, there are countless people behind the scenes who contribute a great deal of time and without whose help most of my books would not have been possible.

Within the world of firearms collecting there are many who specialize in specific makes and models. Among Winchester collectors, Dave Riffle has earned a place as both a respected Winchester collector and dealer with a penchant for the Model 12 and Model 21. His collection makes up a considerable portion of this book. My thanks to Dave for helping bring this one to life and for allowing me to move in with him and upset his entire house for a week with a studio.

Then there are collectors who have a passion for just one model, and make it a life's-goal to acquire every variation and year of manufacture produced. I know of an automotive enthusiast who only collects American cars built in 1957. He's got a warehouse full. Another who only collects Lincolns, and the list goes on. Among Winchester collectors, few have more Model 1897 pump-action shotguns than Gary Reynolds, who allowed me to photograph the finest examples in his collection. What you will see in the chapter covering the legendary Model 1893, Model 1897, Model 97, and riot and trench gun variations, represents one of the finest assemblages of historic Winchesters ever published.

Last, and certainly not least, how could one do a book on Winchester shotguns without going to the source, the U.S. Repeating Arms Co. and the home of Winchester in New Haven, Connecticut? While the Cody Firearms Museum in Cody, Wyoming is the cultural center of Winchester history, the heart and soul of Winchester is still in New Haven, not far from the original buildings erected by Oliver Winchester in the mid 19th century. It is here that the history of Winchester has been preserved with representative examples of nearly every model produced, as well as experimental models never put into production. A studio was once again built and the history of Winchester shotguns recorded in the very room where the finest collection in the world resides. My thanks to Lee Harris of Winchester for allowing me not only to visit the private company collection in New Haven but to photograph everything from a Model 1879 double hammer gun to the latest camouflaged Super X2. To say we couldn't have done it without you Lee would be an understatement.

Even with all that, we still couldn't get every gun we wanted to photograph. Fortunately, we have yet another ally in Patrick Hogan, President of the Rock Island Auction Company in Moline, Illinois, and Greg Martin, President of Greg Martin Auctions in San Francisco, California.

Both Rock Island and Greg Martin Auctions offer some of the world's finest Winchester shotguns each year, among countless other historic arms. They also have first class photographic departments to record the images used in the beautiful Rock Island and Greg Martin auction catalogs. Greg and Patrick have filled in the gaps with a handful of models that were simply unavailable to photograph, giving this book representative examples of nearly every Winchester shotgun ever produced.

Finally, there was one more Model 1879 we needed, the only example extant chambered in 16 gauge and Brian Merz of Merz Antique Guns in Fergus Falls, Minnesota, came up with the photo to complete our Introduction on the British-built Winchester double hammer guns. And of course my friends Mark McNeely and Chuck Ahern at Allegheny Trade Co. in Duncansville, Pennsylvania, pitched in with antique Winchester shell boxes, brass shells and an early Model 1897 for use as photo props. Thanks guys, as always.

To Jeanne, Larry, Lee, and all the collectors and auction companies who participated in the creation of this first ever full-color history of Winchester shotguns, I offer my humble thanks and appreciation. Segue.

—**Dennis Adler**

vi

Contents

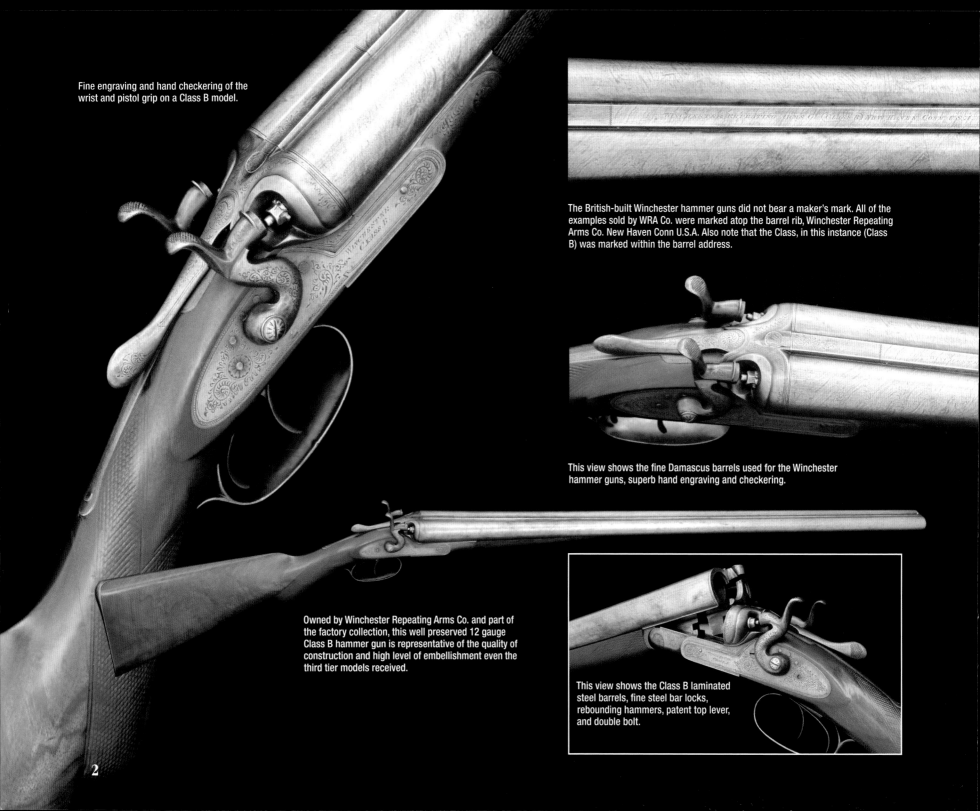

Fine engraving and hand checkering of the wrist and pistol grip on a Class B model.

The British-built Winchester hammer guns did not bear a maker's mark. All of the examples sold by WRA Co. were marked atop the barrel rib, Winchester Repeating Arms Co. New Haven Conn U.S.A. Also note that the Class, in this instance (Class B) was marked within the barrel address.

This view shows the fine Damascus barrels used for the Winchester hammer guns, superb hand engraving and checkering.

Owned by Winchester Repeating Arms Co. and part of the factory collection, this well preserved 12 gauge Class B hammer gun is representative of the quality of construction and high level of embellishment even the third tier models received.

This view shows the Class B laminated steel barrels, fine steel bar locks, rebounding hammers, patent top lever, and double bolt.

Introduction
The First Winchester Shotguns
Model 1879

Oliver Fisher Winchester was born November 30, 1810, and died on December 10, 1880. In his life he went from a New England farm boy to a world-renowned industrialist and entrepreneur. In addition to his role in building the Winchester Repeating Arms Company, he was a generous patron of Yale University, a founder of the Yale National Bank and the New Haven Water Company, and was elected Lieutenant Governor of Connecticut in 1866. The New Haven Palladium eulogized him as "an eminent citizen, to whose public spirit and private enterprise [New Haven] is indebted for much of her present prosperity...the great establishment which he organized, and to which he gave his name, stands to-day as a monument to the great ability and enterprise which marked his whole business career." (Photo courtesy R.L. Wilson)

It has been said that Colt's .45 Peacemaker and the Winchester Model 1873 lever action rifle were "The Guns That Won The West," and that may be true, but there was nothing on the American frontier that could disperse a mob, settle an argument, or dispense swift justice faster than a shotgun.

Throughout the 1860s and 1870s, Winchester built an unrivaled reputation with its famed lever-action rifles, just as Colt had established itself as an American icon in the 1850s with its single action revolvers. But the most affordable, practical, and easiest to handle firearm on the American frontier, either for self-defense or hunting, was a double barrel shotgun. The simple shotgun in the hands of farmers, frontier women, sons and daughters, lawmen, and the lawless, might not have been the gun that won the west, but it was most certainly the gun that settled it.

Both Colt, in Hartford, Connecticut, and its closest competitor, E. Remington & Sons, in Ilion, New York, offered their own brand of shotguns beginning in the 1870s, while Winchester, preferring to concentrate on improving and expanding its line of rifles, continued to import side-by-side shotguns from Great Britain well into the 1880s and sell them under the Winchester name.

Oliver Winchester had established the New Haven Arms Co. of New Haven, Connecticut, in 1857 to perfect the design and manufacturing of the Volcanic repeating rifle and pistol, the fundament of the first Winchester lever action model. The Volcanics, offered in both pistol and rifle versions, were never highly successful and Oliver Winchester continually sought to improve them. Inventor-gunmaker Benjamin Tyler Henry, Winchester's plant superintendent, finally took the Volcanic's design to task at Oliver Winchester's behest, but eventually started over, and three years later, in 1860, gave Winchester the repeater he had sought to build, the first successful, magazine-fed, breech-loading, lever-action rifle. Patented October 16, 1860, it was to become known as the Henry rifle.

To Oliver Winchester's fortune the start of the Civil War in 1861 made the Henry, which went into production in 1862, one of the most admired and feared weapons in the hands of U.S. troops, and one

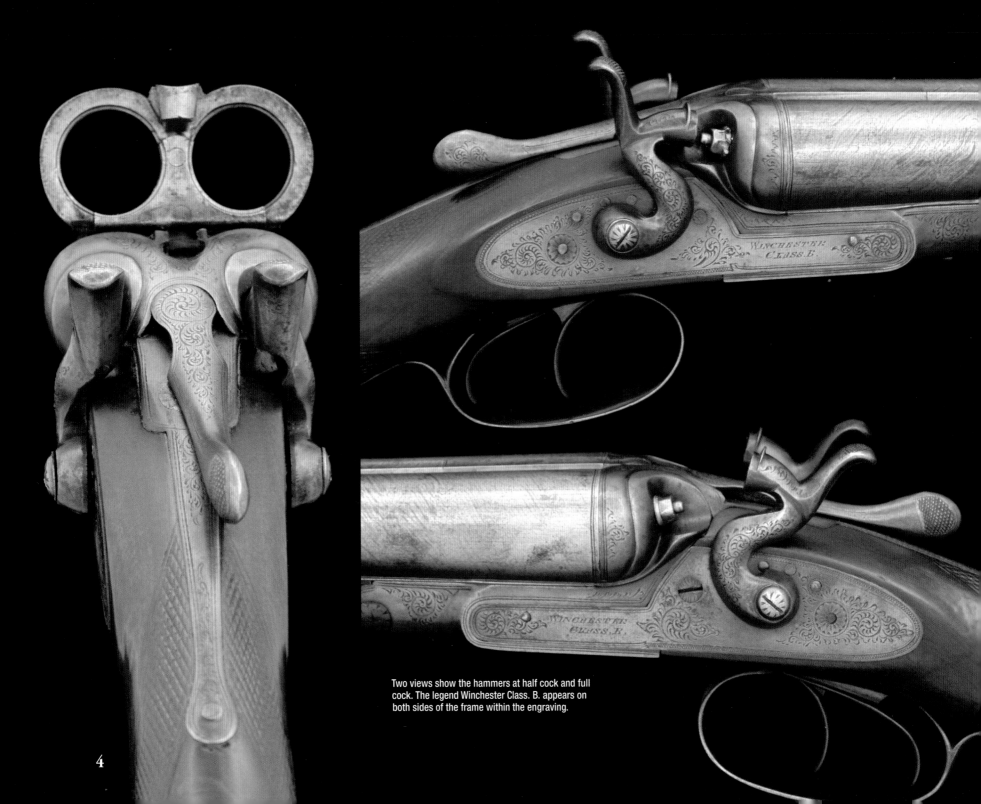

Two views show the hammers at half cock and full cock. The legend Winchester Class. B. appears on both sides of the frame within the engraving.

4

of the most coveted prizes for any Confederate soldier. Ironically, the U.S. War Department didn't purchase Henry rifles for the Federal Troops in any significant number, instead individual soldiers and units purchased them at their own expense. The Army simply had too many different types of rifles and ammunition in its arsenal, and no one, except those in the field, recognized the value of the 16-shot, .44 rimfire Henry repeater.

Regarded as less than ideal for combat because of the Henry's open follower slot on the lower side of the magazine tube, and its propensity to jamming if not carefully maintained, in a fight the Henry was worth a dozen soldiers armed with single shot percussion U.S. Rifled Muskets. The Rebels on the receiving end began calling the Henry that "Damned Yankee rifle you can load on Sunday and shoot all week." During the War Between the States, soldiers armed with Henry lever-action rifles decided many a skirmish.

By 1866 the Henry design had been further improved and Oliver Winchester had renamed his venture the Winchester Repeating Arms Company. The Winchester lever-action rifle of the late 1860s was an unparalleled success, easily the greatest advance in firearms design since Samuel Colt had received his patent for the single action revolver.

For Winchester, however, the manufacturing of shotguns was initially of secondary concern and beginning in 1879, only then did the New Haven arms maker begin importing side-by-side shotguns of exceptional quality built in Birmingham, England. A year earlier, Winchester had imported cheaper grade hammer doubles and sold them through the New York sales depot. Even though they were not marked with the Winchester name, they quickly sold out, encouraging Winchester to import the finer grades in 1879.

The British-built Winchester Model 1879 shotguns were marked atop the barrel rib, Winchester Repeating Arms Co. New Haven Conn U.S.A. The receivers were also marked Winchester and further noted the grade of the model ranging from Class A through Class D and Match Gun, the latter being the top of the line. This same inscription was also included within the address on the barrel rib. The Class B was one of the most popular and those found today in very good condition sell for several thousand dollars. According to the latest *Blue Book of Gun Values*, 26th Edition, a Class A or Match Gun in 95%+ condition can

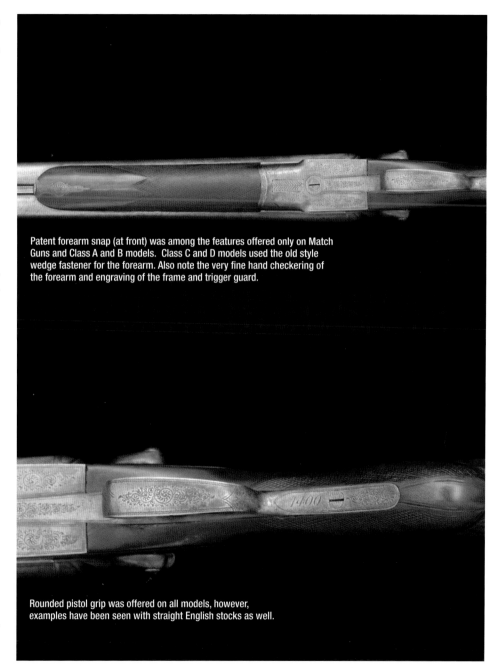

Patent forearm snap (at front) was among the features offered only on Match Guns and Class A and B models. Class C and D models used the old style wedge fastener for the forearm. Also note the very fine hand checkering of the forearm and engraving of the frame and trigger guard.

Rounded pistol grip was offered on all models, however, examples have been seen with straight English stocks as well.

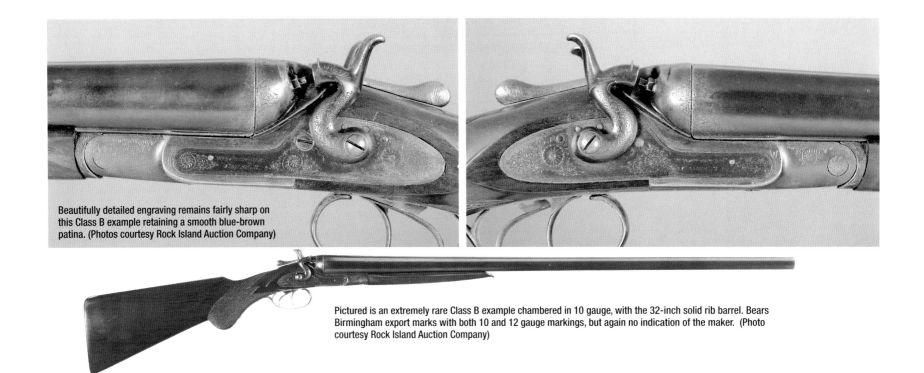

Beautifully detailed engraving remains fairly sharp on this Class B example retaining a smooth blue-brown patina. (Photos courtesy Rock Island Auction Company)

Pictured is an extremely rare Class B example chambered in 10 gauge, with the 32-inch solid rib barrel. Bears Birmingham export marks with both 10 and 12 gauge markings, but again no indication of the maker. (Photo courtesy Rock Island Auction Company)

bring over $4,000. At auction, however, a Match Gun in 95% condition often demands twice that estimate on today's market and it is not unusual to see asking prices of $8,000, nearly 100 times the original retail!

The Model 1879 side-by-sides were double hammer guns with finish and engraving commensurate to grade. Beautiful Damascus barrels, case colored receiver, hammers, break lock, and trigger guard, combined with select walnut stocks and forearms contributed to the Winchester's value and appearance. Fine hand checkering on the forearm and round knob pistol grip stock completed the handsome design. The elegant and highly detailed

hand engraving on the Class B, Class A, and Match Gun made the Winchester doubles popular among sportsmen, while the lesser grades found their way into the hands of settlers, lawmen, and shopkeepers. Known makers of the Winchester double guns were W.C. Scott & Sons (later acquired by the prestigious firm of Holland & Holland), C.G. Bonehill, W.C. McEntree & Co., and Richard Rodman. [1] It is not known which manufacturer made the various guns, as there are no maker's marks. All of these guns, however, bore English proof marks. Some examples of Match Guns and Class A guns also had WRA Co engraved on the trigger guard. [2]

Between 1879 and 1884, when Winchester dis-

continued their importation, it is estimated that 10,000 examples of varying grades were ordered by Winchester agent P.G. Sanford and sold through the company's New York City sales branch, which was the exclusive retailer.

The Winchester catalog of 1879 included an insert describing the five grades of Double Barrel Breech Loading Shotguns. The 1880 catalog listed the retail prices as follows [3]:

Winchester Match Gun $85.00
Class A 70.00
Class B 60.00
Class C 50.00
Class D 40.00

[1] Winchester An American Legend, by R.L. Wilson, 1991 Random House. [2] Winchester Shotguns and Shotshells by Ronald W. Stadt, 1984 Armory Publications [3] The History of Winchester Firearms, 6th Edition, by Thomas Henshaw, 1993 Winchester Press

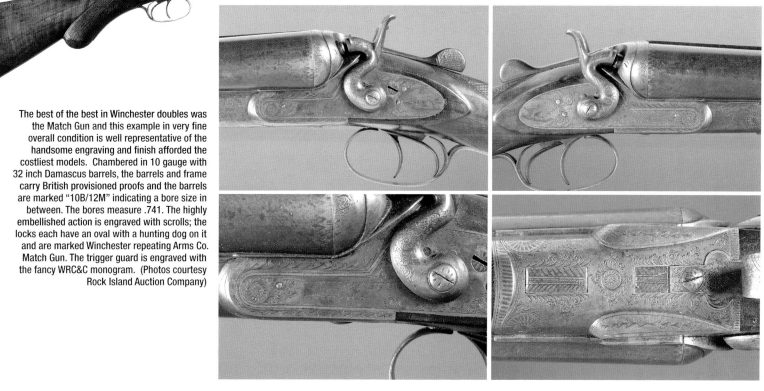

The best of the best in Winchester doubles was the Match Gun and this example in very fine overall condition is well representative of the handsome engraving and finish afforded the costliest models. Chambered in 10 gauge with 32 inch Damascus barrels, the barrels and frame carry British provisioned proofs and the barrels are marked "10B/12M" indicating a bore size in between. The bores measure .741. The highly embellished action is engraved with scrolls; the locks each have an oval with a hunting dog on it and are marked Winchester repeating Arms Co. Match Gun. The trigger guard is engraved with the fancy WRC&C monogram. (Photos courtesy Rock Island Auction Company)

This superb Winchester Match Gun is chambered for 20 gauge shells and fitted with shorter 26-inch Damascus barrels. This example has the maker serial number 2199 on the bottom of the barrel, Birmingham proofs and several sets of initials, which unfortunately do not help identify the maker. Engraving is similar to the 10 gauge model shown. (Photos courtesy Rock Island Auction Company)

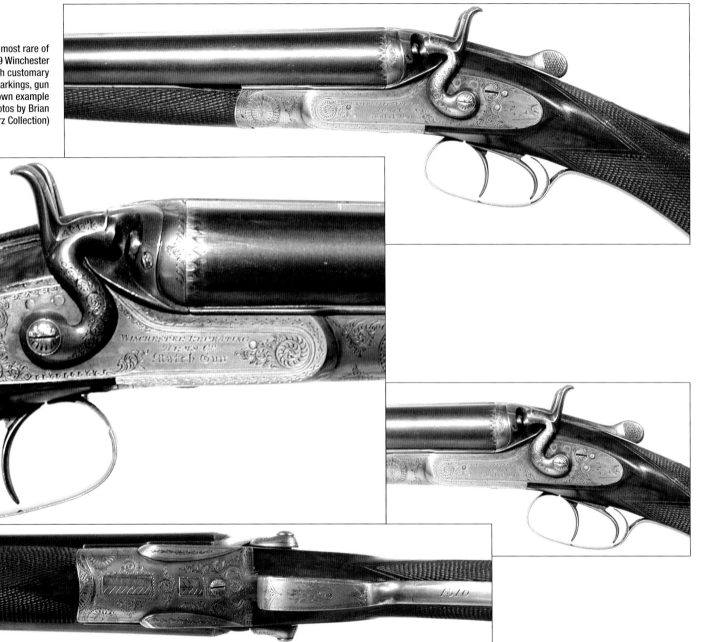

This is by far one of the most rare of all British built Model 1879 Winchester doubles. Embellished with customary Match Gun engraving and markings, gun No. 1310 is the only known example chambered in 16 gauge. (Photos by Brian Merz, courtesy LeRoy Merz Collection)

This assortment of Winchester, Western and Peters shotgun shells illustrate the variety of gauges Winchester had offered over the past 125 years.

The number of shotgun shells displayed on this vintage Winchester cartridge board illustrates how significant a role the shotgun has played in Winchester firearms history.

In addition to the five grades, barrels could be selected in 26-inch, 30-inch and 32-inch lengths and chambered in 10 gauge, 12 gauge, 20 gauge, or 16 gauge. Examples of all three barrel lengths are known.

The 1880 Sales Depot Catalog provided details of the five grades and identified a sixth grade, the Club Gun, which was much like the Class A. As noted in the catalog, the top-of-the-line "Match Gun" featured fine laminated steel barrels, full choke, fine steel bar rebounding locks, Scott's patented top lever, Purdy's Double Bolt, extension rib, solid head

strikers, patent forearm snap, half pistol hand, low hammers, and horn buttplate. Drop of stock was 2-7/8th inches. Pull 14-1/8th. The 12 bore model with 30-inch barrel weighed 7-1/4 to 7-3/4 pounds, whereas the 10 gauge with 32 inch barrel was one pound heavier.

When the directors of the Winchester Repeating Arms Co. decided the time had finally come to develop a shotgun built in New Haven, almost five years had passed since Oliver Fisher Winchester's death on December 10, 1880. Winchester had just celebrated his 70th birthday less

than two weeks before, on November 30th. Under the direction of his son-in-law, Thomas Gray "T.G." Bennett, who succeeded Winchester as president of W.R.A. Co., it was decided that the Connecticut arms maker would not introduce a new double barrel model to compete with Colt and Remington, nor continue importing double hammer guns from Great Britain, rather the inspiration for the first Winchester-built shotgun would come from the company's successful lever-action rifles, and the genius of a Utah gunmaker named John Moses Browning.

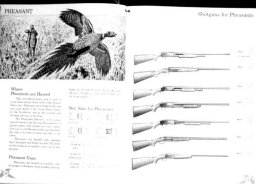
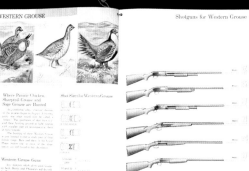

The 1950s marked the highlight of Winchester shotgun history when a great diversity of models in all price ranges made Winchester the world's leader in shotgun manufacturing. This series of images depicts all of the various models offered as shown in the July 15, 1950 Winchester Salesman's Catalog. (Author's collection)

The Winchester Model 1887 lever-action shotgun (bottom) and later 1901 models were nearly identical, however, the color casehardened receiver of the 1887 is far more attractive. Note the rounded pistol grip design.

Chapter One
The Rifleman's Solution
Winchester's Lever Action Shotguns
Model 1887 and 1901

The American West of the 1880s remained pretty much untamed and lawmen in the Southwest often found themselves outnumbered by liquored up cattlemen and unsavory characters that were quick with a six-shooter and short on civility. The side-by-side shotgun was often the great equalizer in more than a few confrontations. A pistolero pressed into a fight with the law might think twice when the barrel of a 10 gauge double was leveled at him, but in a sticky situation, every town sheriff and deputy marshal from the Texas panhandle to California knew they were going to need more than two shots from a scattergun at one time or another.

Now there's an old saw that "God created man, but it was Sam Colt who made them equal." On the Western Frontier of the 1880s that might have been true, but in 1887 John M. Browning and the Winchester Repeating Arms Co. of New Haven, Connecticut, made both lawmen and bad men just a little more equal with the introduction of a six-shot (one in the chamber, five in the magazine) lever-action shotgun chambered in either 12 gauge or 10 gauge. The six-shot 1887 Winchester shotgun was truly the great equalizer.

The Model 1887 was designed by John and Matthew S. Browning of Ogden City, Utah, and patented by the Winchester Repeating Arms Co. on February 16 and July 20, 1886. Winchester had actually purchased the design rights, along with a hand-built model of the Browning lever-action shotgun two years earlier. Browning had designed it specifically at the request of T.G. Bennett, following Winchester's purchase of another Browning design, a lever-action rifle that would become the Model 1886. Ironically, at the time, Browning was more in favor of developing a slide-action model and had been working on the design when Bennett requested a lever-action.[1] Of course, Browning got his wish six years later when Winchester added the Model 1893 slide-action shotgun to its product line.[2]

Introduced in 1887, the Winchester lever-action shotgun was initially available only in 12 gauge but after serial number 22148 an even more powerful 10 gauge version was added. Winchester's 1888 sales catalog described the new lever-action shotgun as follows:

"Sportsmen will find this a strong, serviceable arm. The system contains but sixteen parts in all, and can be readily understood from sectional cuts. The breech block and finger lever form one piece, and move together in opening and closing. The hammer, placed in the breech block, is automatically cocked during the closing motion; but can also be cocked or set at half cock by hand.

"The trigger and finger lever are so adjusted that the trigger cannot be pulled prematurely, and the gun cannot be discharged until closed. The barrel can be examined and cleaned from the breech. The magazine and carrier hold five cartridges, which with one in the chamber, make six at the command of the shooter. Anyone accustomed to shooting can readily shoot double birds with this gun.

"This gun has yet been very little used in public. On the occasion of its first appearance, the gun divided with one other gun the first prize for fifty birds, February 22nd, 1887, at Plainfield, N.J."

As a firearms designer John M. Browning had been associated with Winchester since 1883 when his model for a single-shot rifle, intended to compete

[1] Winchester An American Legend, by R.L. Wilson, 1991 Random House.
[2] Although the John Browning designed Model 1893 and improved Model 1897 are often and mistakenly regarded as America's first pump-action shotguns, the idea was first conceived in Connecticut by Christopher Spencer of Spencer Rifle fame, who designed a pump model c. 1882, and which was successfully marketed by Francis Bannerman Sons of New York from 1884 to approximately 1907 in both 10 and 12 gauge models. Flayderman's Guide to Antique American Firearms, 7th Edition, Krause Publications.

Priced at around $25.00, the Winchester model 1887 lever action shotgun was one of the landmark Winchester designs by John M. Browning.

with the highly successful Sharps, was purchased by the Winchester Repeating Arms Co. This was the beginning of a lengthy on and off relationship with Browning that began to disintegrate in 1902, when Winchester rejected his design for a semi-automatic shotgun. As a result, he took his plans to Farbrique Nationale (F.N.) in Belgium, beginning an affiliation that would establish Browning as a major international arms maker. John Browning, who passed away in 1926, would surely be amused if he knew the company built upon the basis of that rejected shotgun design in 1902 purchased the Winchester Repeating Arms Company in 1997.

During his tenure as an arms designer, Browning's signature could be found on such historic models as the Winchester 1886 lever action rifle, the 1887 and 1901 lever-action shotguns, and 1893 and 1897 pump-action shotguns.

As noted by historian George Madis in *The Winchester Book*, the action on the 1887 shotgun was entirely different from the Winchester lever action rifles and was a variation of the rolling block design, a truly fascinating mechanism to see in action. "While Winchester's rifles utilized a sliding bolt moving toward and away from the chamber, their new shotgun had a bolt which duplicated the arc made by the lever in its movement. As the bolt slides upward into its closed position, a camming action is accomplished by forcing the rear portion of the bolt against the receiver," explained Madis. "With a powder fouled chamber or shells which were oversize, (very common in those days) this was an important feature."

The Model 1887 was offered with a standard rolled steel barrel, as well as a Damascus barrel for an additional $15 to $20. Barrels were full choked unless otherwise specified and Winchester offered cylinder bore and modified choke as an option. The 1887 models had beautifully color casehardened receivers and levers, and barrel lengths of 30-¹/₄ inches in 12 gauge and 32-¹/₄ inches in 10 gauge. Custom barrel lengths were also offered and a short barrel version was available for lawmen, guards, and messengers requiring a lighter, more maneuverable shotgun. Most guard guns had a 22-¹/₄ inch barrel, making the Winchester lever action shotgun one incredibly imposing weapon! Paul Newman brandished a guard gun in the movie *Judge Roy Bean*. Most recently an 1887 with standard length barrel was featured in Tom Selleck's epic remake of *Monte Walsh*.

"According to a lawman in one of the frontier towns," wrote Madis, "Most of the drovers couldn't hold their liquor and were poor shots with pistols when sober. I saw very few cattlemen who were

The town law could get the attention of a rowdy crowd of liquored up cattlemen by discharging a shot from an 1887 guard gun into the air. There were still five more left if that didn't work! Perhaps Winchester literature said it best: "The Winchester lever action 'Riot' gun is made with a 20 inch, rolled steel barrel, cylinder bore barrel, bored expressly to shoot buckshot... They are far superior to a revolver for shooting in the dark, where aim is uncertain, as a buckshot cartridge contains nine bullets to one contained by a revolver cartridge." (Photo by Ron Sirko)

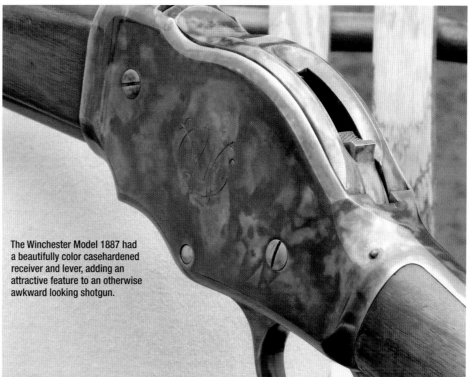

The Winchester Model 1887 had a beautifully color casehardened receiver and lever, adding an attractive feature to an otherwise awkward looking shotgun.

The ornate Winchester Repeating Arms Co. monogram, designed by engraver John Ulrich, was stamped into the left side of every 1887 and 1901 model receiver.

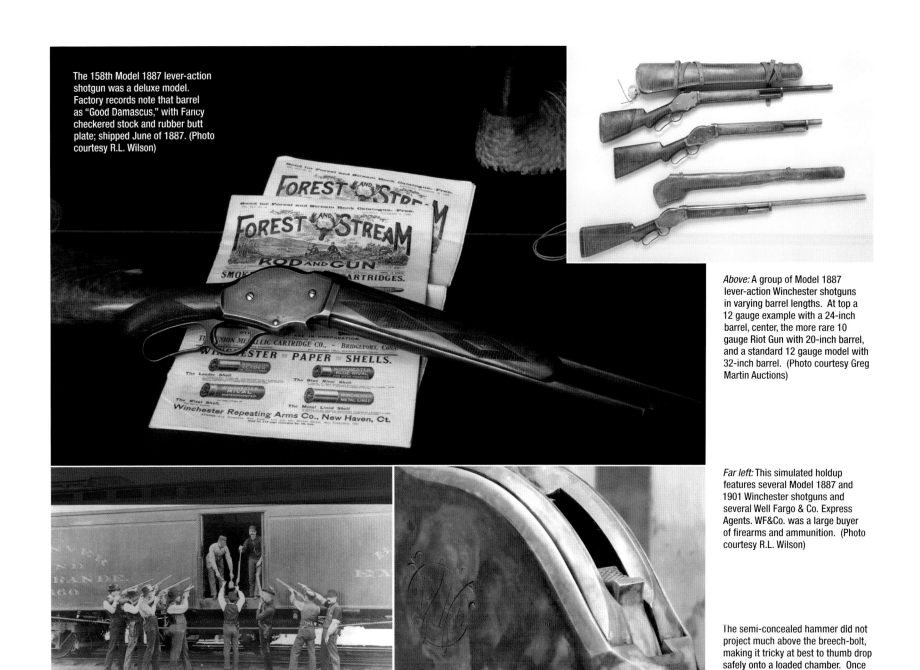

The 158th Model 1887 lever-action shotgun was a deluxe model. Factory records note that barrel as "Good Damascus," with Fancy checkered stock and rubber butt plate; shipped June of 1887. (Photo courtesy R.L. Wilson)

Above: A group of Model 1887 lever-action Winchester shotguns in varying barrel lengths. At top a 12 gauge example with a 24-inch barrel, center, the more rare 10 gauge Riot Gun with 20-inch barrel, and a standard 12 gauge model with 32-inch barrel. (Photo courtesy Greg Martin Auctions)

Far left: This simulated holdup features several Model 1887 and 1901 Winchester shotguns and several Well Fargo & Co. Express Agents. WF&Co. was a large buyer of firearms and ammunition. (Photo courtesy R.L. Wilson)

The semi-concealed hammer did not project much above the breech-bolt, making it tricky at best to thumb drop safely onto a loaded chamber. Once cocked, the 1887 Winchester was ready for business!

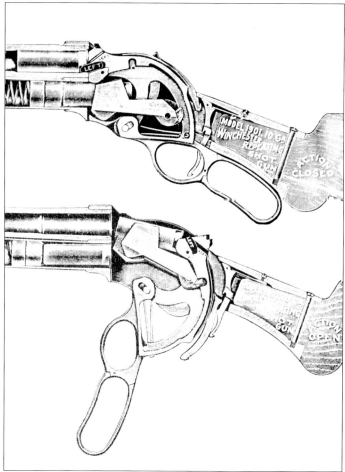

The rolling block-like action of the 1887 followed the arc of the lever in its movement with the internal mechanism dropping down from the receiver. Note the trigger to the rear of the mechanism. The factory illustration shows a cutaway of the working action.

The Winchester name and address were stamped on the bottom tang on 1887 models. On the 1901, this was moved to the top tang.

goods shots. They would just empty their gun in the direction of the target. With a Winchester they were fair shots. A short shotgun was the best to carry since these men had a great deal of respect for what a scattergun could do. Most of them thought a shotgun couldn't miss and had the idea that no one had a chance against a shotgun."

Late in 1897 Winchester added another variation listed as a Riot Gun. Noted the factory, "The Winchester lever action 'Riot' gun is made with a 20 inch, rolled steel barrel, cylinder bore barrel, bored expressly to shoot buckshot... They are far superior to a revolver for shooting in the dark, where aim is uncertain, as a buckshot cartridge contains nine bullets to one contained by a revolver cartridge. The 'Riot' gun has the regular lever action. The magazine holds five cartridges, which, with one in the chamber makes a total of six at the command of the shooter."

A highly distinctive looking design with a profile similar to the Spencer rifle, the identifying characteristics of the 1887 are the Winchester address on the lower tang under the lever, the serial number stamped on the bottom of the receiver, just ahead of the lever, and the gauge "10" or "12" stamped on the top of the barrel, just forward of the receiver, on models with serial numbers around 30,000 and above. Early models also bore the Winchester proof mark, the initials WP surrounded by an oval, on the left side of the barrel adjacent to the gauge stamping.

While the use of factory proof marks were inconsistent, every 1887 model had the ornate Winchester Repeating Arms Co. monogram, designed by engraver John Ulrich, stamped into the left side of the receiver. The standard finish for the barrel and metal surfaces was Winchester bright blue, as shown, although a few examples of the 1887 had bright blue receivers and levers instead of case colors. A handsome browned finish for the barrel was also offered as an option, but is rarely seen today.

The John Browning design was well conceived, sturdy, and capable of handling heavy black powder loads, but it left a couple of things to chance. There was no safety, and the semi-concealed hammer did not project much above the breech-bolt, making it tricky at best to thumb drop safely onto a loaded chamber. Once cocked, the 1887 Winchester was ready for business!

Shouldering the hefty lever gun for an aimed shot revealed a standard brass bead front sight, but once again there were options offered by Winchester. Customers could order nickel silver front sights and a center bead to aid in more rapid sighting. The rear sight was simply a notch in the forward part of the receiver, a holdover from the traditional side-by-side where shooters learned to sight down the centerline of the two barrels. Rounded semi-pistol grip stocks and a generous-sized steel buttplate made the 1887 easier to handle. The factory also provided custom

Among changes between the 1887 and 1901 were a two-piece finger lever on the '01.

Manufactured by The Winchester Repeating Arms Co.
New Haven, Conn. U.S.A. Pat. Feb. 16. 86. July 20. 86. Dec. 14. 86. Aug. 31. 97. MODEL 1901 10 GA.

With the Model 1901 the choke type was stamped on the left side of the barrel near the receiver and proof marks were located on both the barrel and receiver, with address, patent dates and the Model 1901 designation and gauge stamped on the top of the barrel.

checkering on the fore ends and pistol grip and select walnut stocks with varnished finish, but the majority of 1887 models produced had standard oil stained straight grain walnut stocks and fore ends like the examples pictured.

The fore end design of the 1887 is one of the model's most distinctive features. It is of two-piece construction, divided by the barrel and magazine tube and held together with one screw on early models and two on later production. The two series also differed in the type of magazine retainer used. The early examples had a stud secured to the underside of the barrel with a screw holding the retainer cap in place. This was changed around serial number 28,000 and by serial numbers above 30,000 the design changeover had been fully integrated. The improved retainer used a steel band that partially encircled the barrel and was secured by a screw. A second screw passed com-

pletely through the end of the magazine. This later design was carried over to the new Model 1901.

There are a number of minor changes in Model 1887 design and Madis notes that, "Early issues before number 28,000 do not have the small screw forward of the large-headed screw which is located to the right side of the forward part of the frame. The small screw acts as a guide for the right extractor; the large screw acts as a stop for the breech bolt in its forward and downward movement." On earlier models, the 1887 had only a single extractor. Above serial numbers around 28,000 the guns were equipped with two extractors and Winchester advised owners of early models to return their shotguns to the factory where the additional extractor could be fitted at no cost to the customer. Madis further noted that, "Early issues before serial number 46,000 only seldom have the large plug-screw,

Case colors fade and blueing turns to gray but a Winchester Model 1887 or 1901 is still an impressive shotgun, even after nearly 120 years. The Model 1887 at top shows the small screw forward of the large-headed screw at the front of the frame. The small screw was used as a guide for the right extractor. On earlier models, the 1887 had only a single extractor. Above serial numbers around 28,000 the guns were equipped with two extractors.

23

Winchester described the Model 1887 as being a strong, serviceable bird gun for sportsmen, and with the lever-action it offered hunters not only a second follow-up shot, but also four more behind that. This was a decided advantage on the American frontier, where a missed shot could easily mean a missed meal.

which is located on the left side of the frame, while the screw is not present after number 50,000."

Built for black powder shells, the 1887 was discontinued after approximately 64,855 examples had been produced, and replaced by the improved Model 1901 built to withstand the added pressures of smokeless powder shot shells.

In 1900 Winchester advised its sales outlets that the stock of 1887 lever-action models was exhausted and there would be no supplies until late summer. When the new stock of lever-action shotguns became available, they were introduced as the Model 1901.

The January 1902 Winchester catalog described the new Model 1901 as follows:

"The Model 1901 Winchester Lever Action Repeating Shotgun is the only 10 gauge repeater on the market. It is expressly bored to handle either smokeless or black powder, and is particularly well adapted for duck and wildfowl shooting. The gun resembles in outline the original Winchester Lever Action Repeating Shotgun, but differs in detail. It has a tighter breech joint more completely supporting the shell in the chamber. A positive firing pin retractor is provided. The finger lever is made separate from the breech-block and with a finger lever lock. When the action is closed, the gun is locked against opening by this finger lever lock, but is instantly released by a downward pressure on the finger lever.

"The standard gun is made with a 32 inch rolled steel barrel, hardened and browned frame, and pistol grip stock of plain walnut, not checked, finished with a checked steel butt plate. Barrels for this model are bored to shoot close and hard, and no gun will be sent out that does not make a good target. Unless otherwise specified, guns with 32 inch full choke barrels will be sent on all orders; but shorter barrels, or barrels with different styles of bore, either modified choke or full cylinder, will be furnished when so ordered without extra charge. Damascus barrels of different grades, and other extras, can be furnished at prices given below.

"The operation of the Model 1901 Lever Action Repeating Shotgun is simple, and can be easily understood. To load the magazine, throw down the lever and push five cartridges through the carrier into the magazine, placing the sixth in the chamber. The forward and backward motion of the finger lever, which can be executed while the gun is at the shoulder, throws out the empty shell, raises a new cartridge from the magazine and places it in the chamber, and the gun is then ready to be fired"[3]

The Model 1901 was only offered as 10-gauge, and as noted, offered with a standard 32-inch barrel. There were no 'Riot' variations as with the 1887, thus any short-barreled 1901 models were cut down in the field. Built to handle the new smokeless powder cartridges, (the 1887 models were black powder

[3] Winchester Shotguns and Shotshells by Ronald W. Stadt, 1984 Armory Publications.

only) the '01 came with a bright blue receiver, barrel, and lever. The beautiful case colored receiver was discontinued with the 1887, thus the '01 is a little less attractive but no less, if not more desirable today among collectors.

There were subtle changes in the '01's design, particularly in the finger lever, which was now constructed of two pieces, and the addition of a trigger block, which prevented the accidental discharge as the lever was being closed. The choke type was now stamped on the left side of the barrel near the receiver, and the Winchester trademark was moved to the upper tang. Proof marks were consistent, located on both the barrel and receiver, and an address with patent dates and the Model 1901 designation and gauge were added to the top of the barrel:

MANUFACTURED BY THE WINCHESTER REPEATING ARMS CO.
NEW HAVEN, CONN. U.S.A. PAT. FEB. 16. 86. JULY 20. 86 DEC. 14. 86. AUG 31. 97

Between the above markings and the receiver is the model designation: Model 1901, together with the bore size. The price for a standard model was $30.00 in 1902. A fancy stock added another $10.00 and checkering $5.00. "Good" 3 blade Damascus barrels were $15.00 and "Fine" 4 blade barrels $20.00 extra. By 1918 the price of the standard model had increased to $38.00. [4]

Serial numbers for the '01 series began at 64856 and 13,500 examples were produced through 1920. Heftier than a lever action rifle, the Winchester 10 gauge wasn't as agile to lever from the shoulder but was one terrifically effective gun. At ranges of 25 feet, patterns were tight and one can only imagine the deadly accuracy with buckshot. It's no wonder lawmen and guards favored the 1887 and 1901. Unfortunately, Winchester's hope that the legendary reputation of their lever-action rifles would rub off on the shotguns was unrequited. Sales to the public were never brisk, and Winchester itself created stiff competition for the 1887 with the introduction of the John Browning designed 1893 and 1897 slide-action shotguns, one of the most successful designs of both the 19th or 20th century.

Perhaps author Dean K. Boorman said it best in *The History of Winchester Firearms*, "The Model 1887 Shotgun was awkward in appearance...and had limited popularity." Of course, to a desperado looking down the barrel of a 10 gauge lever action shotgun packing six rounds of buckshot, that's understandable.

[4] Ibid

Our special thanks to Roger Kirwin and Old Bedford Village, Bedford, PA, for allowing us to make a great deal of noise and smoke in their historic western setting.

Even in the early 1900s the American West was still the Wild West and when push came to shove lawmen found comfort in brandishing either a 10 gauge Winchester lever-action shotgun or 12 gauge Model 1897 pump over a six-gun.

25

Chapter Two
Winchester Perfects The Slide-Action Shotgun
Model 1893 and Model 1897

John Moses Browning had a better idea.

It wasn't an original idea but he managed to make it his own by designing a slide-action shotgun that eclipsed the notoriety, and for the most part, the memory of earlier slide-action designs. Browning had been developing his slide-action model when T.G. Bennett and the Winchester Repeating Arms Co. requested that he concentrate instead on the design of a lever-action shotgun. Bennett no doubt believed that this would capitalize on the reputation of the New Haven gunmaker's celebrated Model 1873 lever-action rifles. This was not to be the case, however, and in 1893 Winchester added yet another John Browning design to its product line, the slide-action shotgun he had been developing back in 1884.

Browning's design was actually the third slide-action shotgun put into production. The first had been introduced in 1882 by celebrated rifle maker Christopher Miner Spencer and his partner Sylvester Roper, and originally sold by the newly organized Spencer Arms Co., of Windsor, Connecticut. For Spencer, who had gone bankrupt in 1869 due to a military surplus of used Civil War era Spencer rifles flooding the market, this was to be his second and last venture in the firearms field. Spencer's biggest competitor, the Winchester Repeating Arms Company, acquired the assets of his first company in 1869 and subsequently discontinued manufacture of the Spencer rifle. Christopher

Spencer's triumphant return lasted until 1889, when once again facing bankruptcy, he sold out to Francis Bannerman Sons of New York, who successfully manufactured and marketed the Spencer slide-action shotgun until around 1907, in both a 10-gauge solid frame model and in 12-gauge solid frame and takedown versions.

The Spencer slide-action shotgun may have "inspired" John Browning, but it did not influence his overall design. Spencer had, in part, based his shotgun on the action of the Spencer rifle, which was loaded at the breech. One shell could be inserted into the barrel of the Spencer shotgun in this same fashion by sliding the forearm halfway back, which dropped the block, exposing the breech. A double set trigger then allowed the shooter to cock the action after returning the slide lever to its forward position. With a full movement of the forearm, the Spencer functioned as a slide-action shotgun, ejecting a spent shell directly upward from the breech, removing a fresh round from the magazine tube, loading it into the chamber and cocking the internal hammer as the action slide was returned forward. The Spencer was also the very first "hammerless" slide-action shotgun and the only pump action shotgun ever manufactured that utilized a vertical rather than horizontal movement of the breech block. It was a rugged, hefty looking design with a handsome color casehardened frame and Damascus

It was to become the most successful exposed hammer shotgun of the 19th and 20th centuries. The Winchester Model 1897 was offered in a variety of configurations from Field Grade to deluxe Black Diamond Pigeon Grade. Pictured from top to bottom, a pair of Model 1897 "Trench" guns, a Black Diamond Pigeon Gun, Black Diamond Trap gun with custom engraving and gold inlay, a custom engraved 1897, a second Black Diamond Trap gun with custom engraving and gold inlay, a "Fancy Finished" 1897 with checked straight stock and forearm, and a Model 97 takedown "Riot" gun. (Gary Reynolds Collection)

John M. Browning designed the first Winchester slide-actions shotguns, the Model 1893. Pictured are an example with hand-checkered stock, standard Model 1893 and a rarely seen model, an 1893 "Riot" gun. (Gary Reynolds Collection)

finish barrel. Unfortunately, with only about 20,000 examples produced, it became little more than a footnote in the history of the American shotgun.

The Spencer was followed by another slide-action design, this one introduced in 1892, and patented by Andrew Burgess and the Burgess Gun Co., of Buffalo, New York. The Burgess design took a completely different approach. Rather than using the forearm to activate the slide mechanism, an iron sleeve was fitted over the wrist of the stock which set the bolt and breech into motion by sliding the pistol grip rearward.[1] Neither design, however, was as elegant in its proportions or as easy to operate as Browning's 1893.

Since the 1887 lever-action shotguns were not discontinued, and would in fact be improved upon and replaced by the Model 1901 (which remained in production until 1920), the 1893 slide-action shotgun was not regarded as a successor. It was brought out to compete with the Spencer and Burgess, while at the same time complementing Winchester's new slide-action .22 caliber rimfire Model 1890 rifle. As a footnote, Winchester purchased the Burgess Gun Co. in 1899 and withdrew the Burgess slide-action shotgun from the market!

The Browning design, Patent No. 441390 granted in November 1890, and subsequently purchased by Winchester, was, in a word, handsome, if such physical attributes can be applied to a firearm. Like Winchester's Model 1890 slide-action rifle, the 1893 had an exposed hammer. The shotgun utilized side ejection, the stock had a trim wrist, bold rounded pistol grip, adapted from the Model 1887, and very clean, elegant lines through the receiver, barrel, magazine, and forearm. It had the look of a fine sporting arm.

The general specifications were for a plain wood stock with pistol grip and a choice of either 30-inch or 32-inch full-choke rolled steel barrels. Modified choke or cylinder bore barrels were furnished on special order, as were Damascus barrels at additional cost. Additional cost factory options

[1] *Flayderman's Guide to Antique American Firearms 7th Edition, by Norm Flayderman, 1998, Krause Publications.*

The Model 1893 arrived just as the days of the Old West were winding down, but it was certainly a welcomed addition to the gun rack of many a frontier town lawman. Designed for black powder shells, brass cased shot shells were the most reliable. (Model 1893 courtesy of Mike Clark, Collector's Firearms, Houston, Texas)

29

Two very fine examples of deluxe Model 1893 Winchesters, the top example with a hand-checkered stock, and the bottom a rare Black Diamond model with checkered straight stock and checkered deluxe forearm. This example has exceptionally fine "fancy" wood. (Gary Reynolds Collection)

Black Diamond models were fitted with hand-checkered forearms.

30

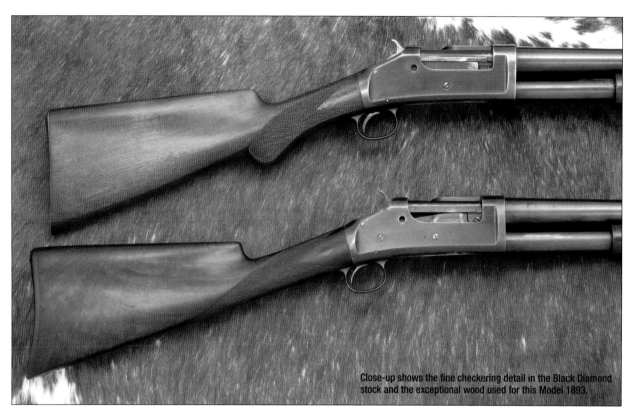

Close-up shows the fine checkering detail in the Black Diamond stock and the exceptional wood used for this Model 1893.

included fancy wood, checkering, and engraving, though such examples are rare. Chambered only for 12 gauge, 2-5/8 in shells, the tubular magazine held 5 rounds.

Factory markings were more elaborate than on the 1887 shotguns. Serial numbers were stamped on the underside of the receiver near the forward end and barrels were stamped with two lines:

MANUFACTURED BY WINCHESTER REPEATING ARMS. CO.
NEW HAVEN. CONN. U.S.A. MODEL 1893. PAT. NOV. 25. 1890.

The top of the barrel was also stamped with the gauge marking "12" near the receiver. Later models have a second patent date on the lower line "& DEC. 6. 1892." This began at about serial number 12300. Also at the appear-ance of the second marking Winchester began stamping the slide rods with:

WINCHESTER
MODEL 1893

The June 1893 catalog described the Winchester Repeating Shotgun Model 1893 as follows:

"This gun is operated by a sliding forearm below the barrel. It is locked by the closing motion and can be unlocked only by pushing forward the firing pin, which may be done by the hammer or by finger. When the hammer is down, the backward and forward motion of the sliding forearm unlocks and opens the breech, ejects the cartridge or fired shell and replaces it with a fresh cartridge.

Underside of 1893 shows serial number location on the frame.

MANUFACTURED BY THE WINCHESTER REPEATING ARMS CO.
NEW HAVEN. CONN. U S A MODEL 1893. PAT. NOV. 25. 1890.

12

Close-up of Model 1893 barrel shows the
manufacturer's two-line address and gauge.

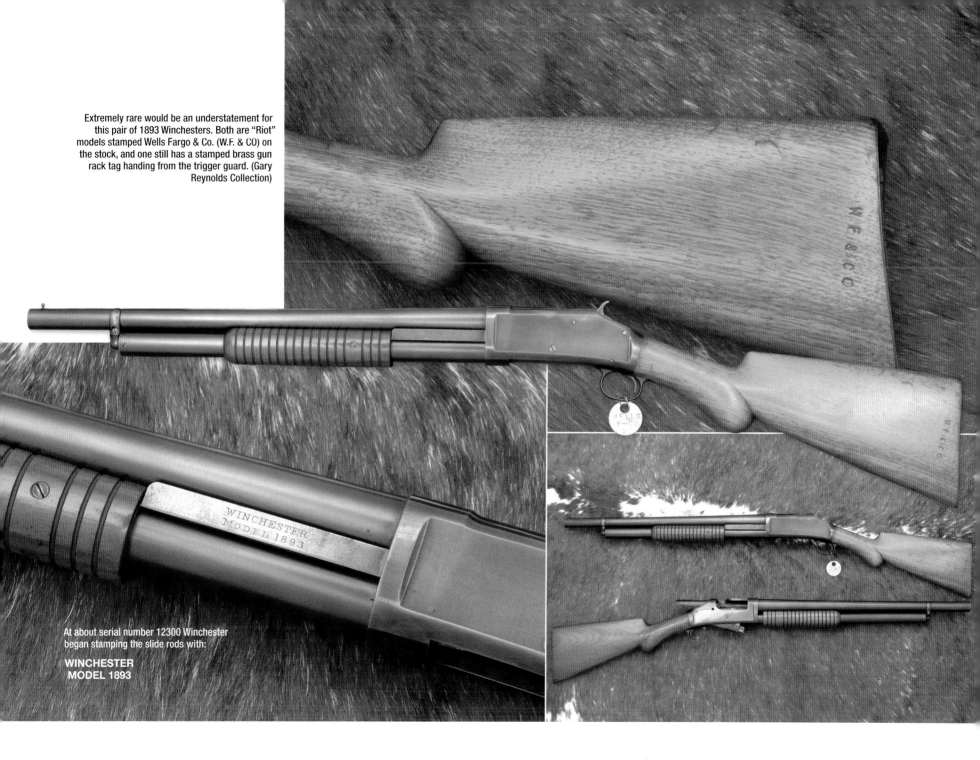

Extremely rare would be an understatement for this pair of 1893 Winchesters. Both are "Riot" models stamped Wells Fargo & Co. (W.F. & CO) on the stock, and one still has a stamped brass gun rack tag handing from the trigger guard. (Gary Reynolds Collection)

At about serial number 12300 Winchester began stamping the slide rods with:

**WINCHESTER
MODEL 1893**

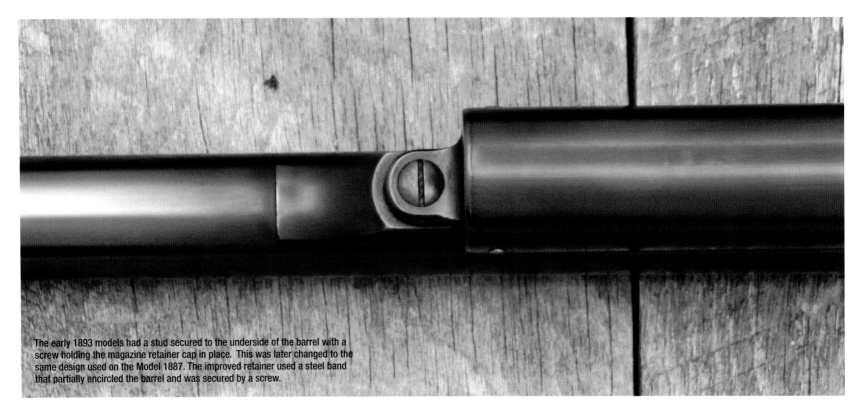

The early 1893 models had a stud secured to the underside of the barrel with a screw holding the magazine retainer cap in place. This was later changed to the same design used on the Model 1887. The improved retainer used a steel band that partially encircled the barrel and was secured by a screw.

"The construction of the arm is such that the hammer cannot fall or the firing pin strike the cartridge until the breech block is in place and locked fast. The trigger touches the sear only when the gun is closed—that is, the hammer cannot be let down except when the gun is locked. Having closed the gun and set the hammer at half-cock, it is locked both against opening and pulling the trigger. While the hammer stands at the full-cock notch, the gun is locked against opening.

"To open the gun, lift the hammer to full cock and push forward the firing pin, pulling back the action slide." [2]

That rather lengthy description was accompanied by a distinctive sound produced by the back and forth motion of the slide mechanism chambering a shell – a two-step metallic beat – a fearsome, unmistakable noise. Even today, the sound of a slide-action shotgun being racked into battery is often enough to deter the average person without a shot ever being fired!

For those who did shoulder the Model 1893, either as defensive or offensive weapon, or for the task to which most sportsmen believed it was best suited, hunting birds, the 6-shot, slide-action Winchester was a high watermark in firearms history. The John Browning design established a framework, the fundamentals of which have remained in use for well over a century.

The Browning design was the wellspring for the modern pump shotgun. The Model 1893 introduced the horizontal sliding breech bolt with attached extractor. It used, as did the Spencer, an opening at the bottom of the receiver to load the magazine but also permitted loading with the action closed, thereby allowing a shooter to reload while the gun was kept ready for action.

The Model 1893 was not without its faults, however. Like the Model 1887, the Model 1893 was designed for use with black powder shot shells, and the advent of smokeless powder, which became popular in the 1890s, was caus-

[2] The History of Winchester Firearms 1866-1992 Sixth Edition by Thomas Henshaw, Winchester Press, New Win Publishing Co., Clinton, N.J.

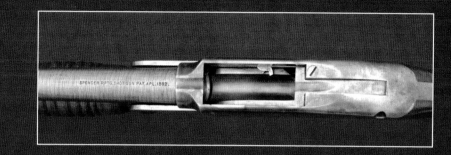

Patented in 1882, the Spencer was not only the world's first slide-action shotgun, but the first hammerless design, predating the Winchester Model 1912 by 30 years, and the Browning-designed Model 1893 slide-action shotgun by 11 years. The Spencer design allowed one shell to be inserted into the barrel at the breech by sliding the forearm halfway back, which dropped the block. A double set trigger then allowed the shooter to cock the action after returning the slide lever to its forward position. With a full movement of the forearm, the Spencer functioned as a slide-action shotgun, ejecting a spent shell directly upward, removing a fresh round from the magazine, loading it into the chamber and cocking the internal hammer as the action slide was returned forward. The Spencer was the only pump action shotgun ever manufactured that utilized a vertical rather than horizontal movement of the breech block. The example shown bears the F. Bannerman manufacturer's markings and legend Model 1890. Also note the April 1882 patent date on top of the barrel. (Author's Collection)

Model 1893 serial numbers were stamped on the bottom of the frame near the barrel.

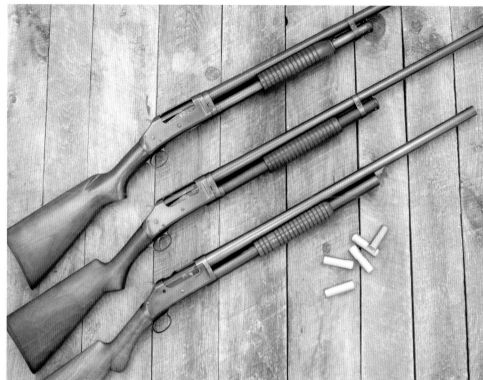

There are three variations (excluding deluxe models) of the Model 1897 and Model 97 stock. The earliest examples have the round pistol grip carried over from the Model 1893. Later models have a half pistol grip. The other variation in stock design is the comb, which can be either straight or fluted. Pictured are a Model 1893, Model 1897, and Model 97, top.

The early forearm design of the Model 1897 was the same as the 1893 (pictured at bottom) with 17 grooves and a screw on either side of the forearm securing it to the slide mechanism. Field Grade examples of the 1897 had a round forearm with 18 semi-circular grooves and new design precluding the use of screws. Another variation of Field Grade models was a "flat bottom" forearm with 14 grooves (on the sides only, top example), which was put into production in 1947.

Here and facing page: These views of an 1893 (bottom) and 1897 clearly show the significant design change made in the top of the frame. Note how far back the bolt comes when the slide is open. Just imagine your thumb in the wrong place.

ing no end to breakage from the higher pressures smokeless powder generated. Winchester withdrew its first slide-action model from the market early in 1897 after about 34,050 had been made.

By the time Winchester retired the Model 1893 the design had undergone seven major improvements and 21 minor changes. The Model 1897 was the end result featuring a redesigned ejection system with the upper part of the receiver closed and the shells ejected straight out from the side. This was the most distinctive visual difference. Serial numbers for the Model 1897 picked up where the Model 1893 left off, thus Model 1897 serial numbers begin around 34051.[3]

With a slightly longer receiver ruggedly built to withstand the pressures generated by smokeless powder, the Model 1897 could chamber both the old 2-5/8 inch black powder and the new 2-3/4 inch smokeless shells. Aside from the new receiver design the Model 1897 had the same general appearances as its predecessor. Initially, only solid frame models were available but in 1898 Winchester added a 12 gauge takedown model, followed by a 16 gauge takedown version in

1900. The 1898 models were the world's first takedown pump shotguns. Initially there were 10 design changes between the 1893 and 1897:

1. Top of cartridge ejection opening in frame made straight
2. Spring placed on inside of action handle encircling the magazine
3. Release pin and plunger (for action side lock)
4. New firing pin lock put in breech block
5. Friction spring put in under cartridge guide
6. Collar put inside of magazine to keep spring and follower from coming out
7. Screw put in receiver to hold magazine from turning
8. Receiver holding bolt made shorter
9. Butt stock made longer. Drop changed, and outside shape changed slightly
10. Top of breech block made straight

[3] Production figures vary. According to George Madis in "The Winchester Book," production ended at 32,800. Henshaw states 34,050 in "The History of Winchester Firearms."

Design changes in the left side of the frame between the 1893 and 1897 are shown in this view. Also the later style half pistol grip stock compared to the 1893 and early 1897 round pistol grip stock.

40

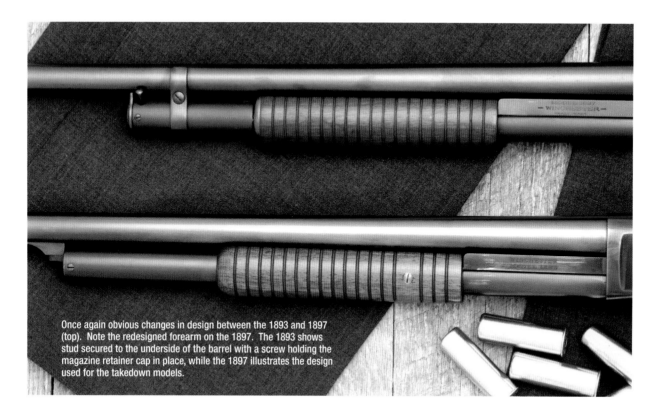

Once again obvious changes in design between the 1893 and 1897 (top). Note the redesigned forearm on the 1897. The 1893 shows stud secured to the underside of the barrel with a screw holding the magazine retainer cap in place, while the 1897 illustrates the design used for the takedown models.

At about serial number 47000 three additional changes were made and a "C" prefix was placed over the serial number. (Model 1893 shotguns without an alphabetical prefix were built prior to September 1894. An "A" was added above serial numbers starting with 23000 and the last Model 1893s, built in January 1897, had a "B" prefix, which was carried over to the first models in the 1897 series).

Changes within the "C" prefix models:
1. A small wire was put into the receiver and connected to the action slide lock release pin, to hold it from coming out when the gun was taken apart.
2. The receiver was made 1-$\frac{1}{2}$ hundredths thicker on each side. This was thought best due to the increased cuts on the inside.
3. The action side lock spring was changed.

Although it had been well received, there had been more than enough problems with the Model 1893 breaking under the stresses of smokeless powder shells, and suffering minor malfunctions even with black powder shells, that in 1897 Winchester offered to exchange any Model 1893 returned to the factory for a brand new Model 1897, free of charge! The number of Model 1893 shotguns returned is unknown.

Throughout the Model 1897's long production history continual improvements were made, which included a flat-ended magazine plug on "D" guns, and slightly deeper 5/16th inch wide grooves on the receiver ring, beginning with "E" prefix models. Prior to the "E" guns, cartridge stops were fastened with screws through the receiver sides and shells were difficult to release from the magazine for unloading – most shooters worked them through the action. This was changed by fastening the cartridge stops with screws through the bottom of the action and providing buttons, which could be used to retract the cartridge stops. In *The Winchester Book,* author George Madis noted that during the first 12 years of production Winchester made 37 major and 52 minor changes to the Model 1897's design.

One feature that Model 1897 owners quickly became familiar with was

Two variations of high grade Model 1897s: a Black Diamond with checkered half pistol grip stock, and a straight or English style stock with checkering.

Two styles of hand checkered forearms. Also note the Model 97 barrel markings including bore and choke.

the new "inertia lock" which kept the action locked until the chambered round had been fired. Operation of the new system was described in Winchester sales literature as follows:

"Under the slide handle, and acting against the stop of the magazine, is placed a spring. When the gun is closed, this spring pushes against the upper end of the action slide, and presses it toward the stock. A lever is hung in the carrier-block, when the slide handle is pressed forward, a spring in the rear end of the lever forces the forward end of the lever out and it catches against the notch in the action slide. When the hammer stands at full cock, the rear end of the lever is forced outward and its notched forward end holds the slide fast. When the hammer stands at half cock, the same occurs. But when the hammer has fallen, the spring which lies under the rear end of the lever forces the forward end of the lever toward the center of the gun. The spring under the slide handle, however, still holds the forward end of the lever in place, and the gun cannot be opened until a slight forward motion of the slide handle releases the lever. Thereupon it may be opened by pulling back the slide handle. In firing, the recoil of the gun gives the slight forward motion to the slide handle, releases the lever, and enables the immediate opening of the gun.

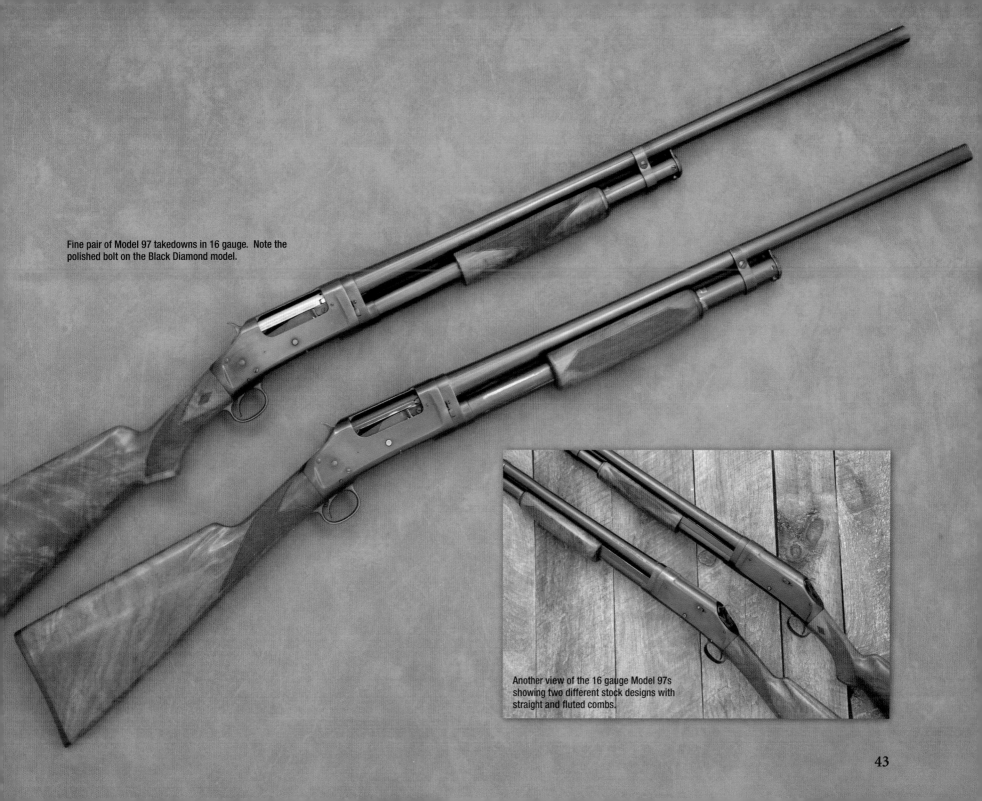

Fine pair of Model 97 takedowns in 16 gauge. Note the polished bolt on the Black Diamond model.

Another view of the 16 gauge Model 97s showing two different stock designs with straight and fluted combs.

43

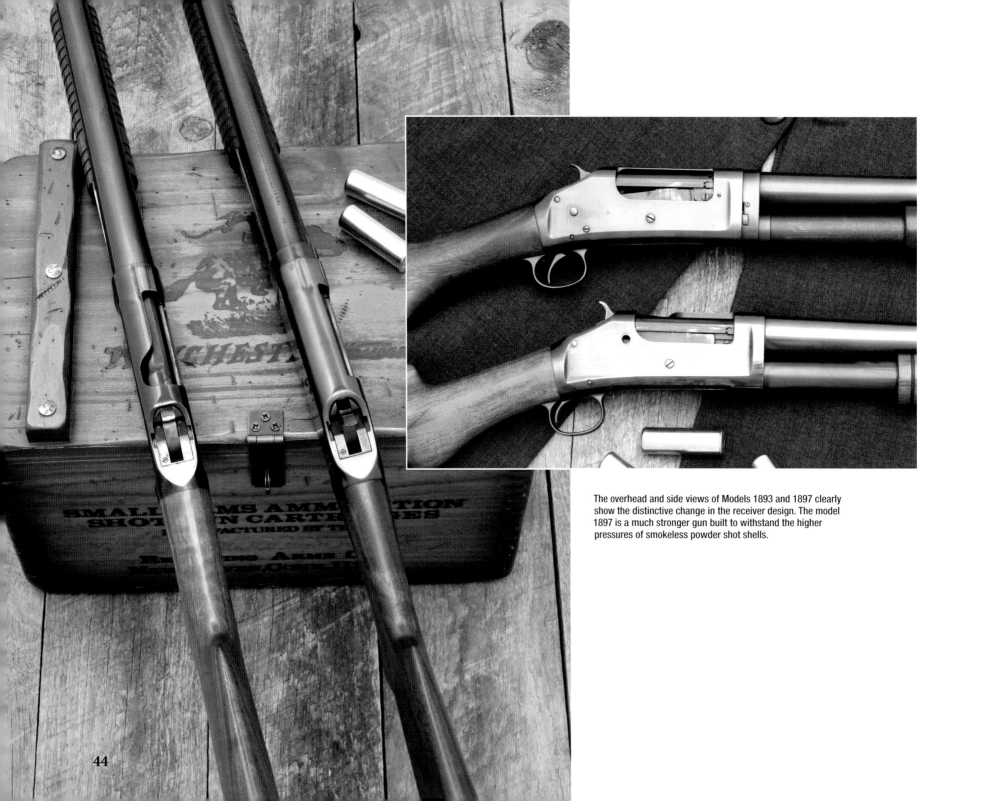

The overhead and side views of Models 1893 and 1897 clearly show the distinctive change in the receiver design. The model 1897 is a much stronger gun built to withstand the higher pressures of smokeless powder shot shells.

"To open the gun at full cock, a button upon the right hand side must be pressed. This throws off the recoil lock and allows the gun to come open by making a slight forward push of the slide handle. When the hammer has fallen without exploding the cartridge, it will be necessary to push forward the slide handle before the gun can be pulled opened. At half cock the gun is locked against firing and opening." [4]

This was probably the most important passage in the Winchester sales literature. In the hands of the inexperienced, opening the action on a Model 1897 can be frustrating. What it all boils down to is this: In order to open the action on a Model 1897, the hammer should be down, and then the forearm pushed slightly forward to release the lock, after which the forearm can be easily pulled back to open the action. The procedure is the same if the hammer is at full cock after pressing the side release. What the Winchester literature never mentioned, however, is that the breech bolt comes back well over the wrist of the stock when you open the action, and if you don't watch your hand position, the leading edge of the breech bolt will cut the top of your thumb knuckle! Voice of experience.

The Model 1897 slide-action Winchester shotgun was offered in a greater variety of grades than its predecessor, beginning with standard or Field Grade (1897-1957 in 12 and 16 gauge, the latter last offered in 1950), followed by Trap (1897-1931 in 12 and 16 gauge), Special Trap Grade (1931-1939 in 12 and 16 gauge), Tournament Grade (1910-1931 in 12 gauge only), Standard Trap Gun (1931-1939 in 12 and 16 gauge), and deluxe Pigeon Gun (1897-1939 in 12 and 16 gauge). Between 1897 and 1913 Winchester also offered a "Fancy Finished" gun with a checked grip and forearm, 4 blade Damascus barrel, fancy walnut stock, and checked rubber buttplate. First listed for $62.00, it was last offered in Catalog No. 78, January 1913. In addition, the 1897 was available as a "Brush" gun with a short 26-inch cylinder bore choke barrel and 4-shot magazine (1897-1931), and "Riot" gun with a 20-inch cylinder choke barrel (1898-1935 with takedown version added in 1921), which became eminently popular with lawmen, prison guards, and police, not to mention those on the wrong side of the law.

By the time America entered WWI there was yet another version of the Model 1897, the "Trench" gun with a 20-inch cylinder choke barrel, perforated steel cooling sleeve and bayonet lug. As noted by author Bruce N. Canfield in the May 2004 issue of *American Rifleman*, "…the first procure-

[4] "Winchester Shotguns and Shotshells" by Ronald W. Stadt, 1984 Armory Publications, Tacoma, Washington.

This close-up shows the serial number placement on solid frame and takedown models. Note that takedown models have the serial numbers on both the frame and barrel assembly.

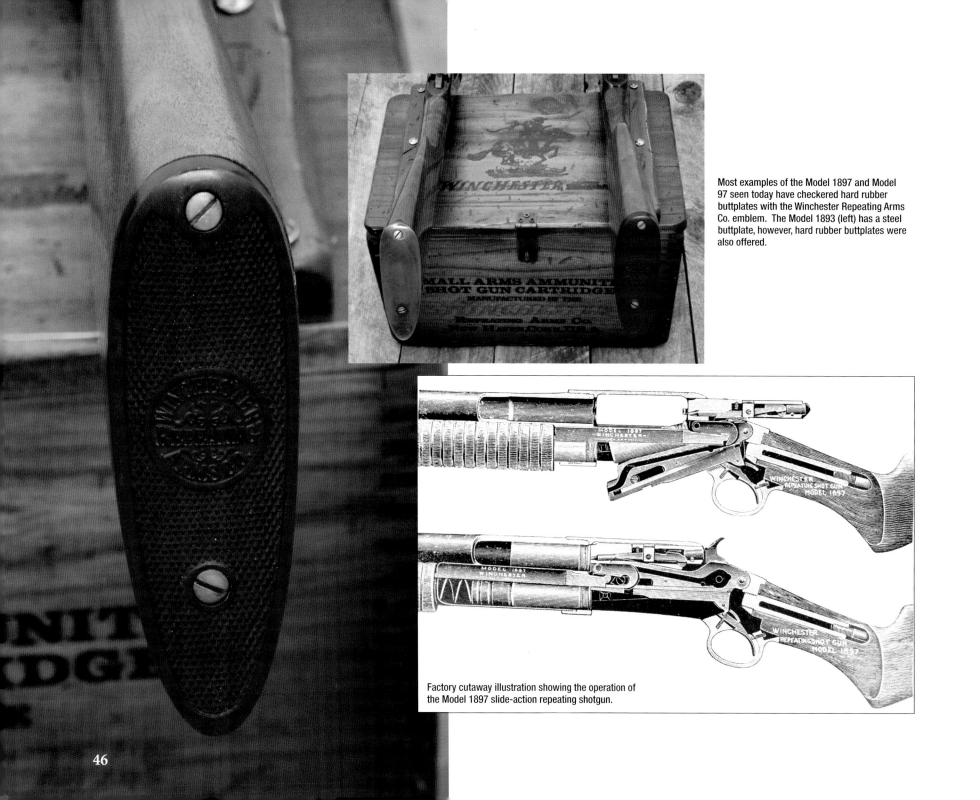

Most examples of the Model 1897 and Model 97 seen today have checkered hard rubber buttplates with the Winchester Repeating Arms Co. emblem. The Model 1893 (left) has a steel buttplate, however, hard rubber buttplates were also offered.

Factory cutaway illustration showing the operation of the Model 1897 slide-action repeating shotgun.

MODEL 97 ACTION

Factory cutaway illustration and factory cutaway Model 1897 display gun. (Gary Reynolds Collection)

Factory cutaway sample gun and Model 1897 illustrating the bolt and action closed and open.

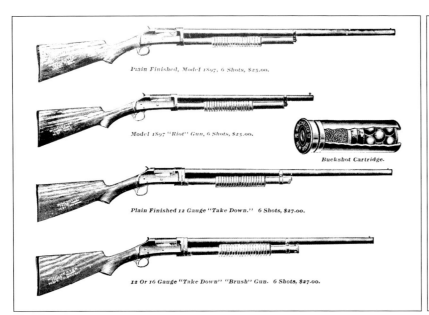

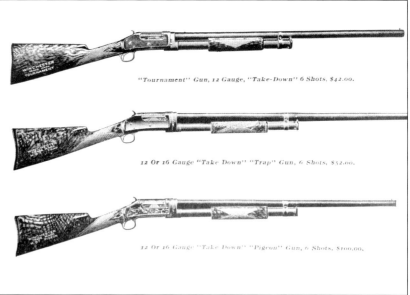

Pages from the 1916 Winchester sales catalog illustrate the different grades offered for the Model 1897 and retail prices. The values have increased just slightly in 90 years!

ment of shotguns specifically for combat use by the U.S. military did not occur until the dawn of the 20th century. Circa 1900, the U.S. Army purchased an estimated 200 Winchester Model 1897 slide-action repeating shotguns for use in the on-going 'pacification' campaigns in the Philippine Islands following the Spanish-American War of 1898.

"When the United States entered World War I in the spring of 1917…many of the senior officers of the American Expeditionary Force (AEF), including Gen. [John] Pershing, had previously served in the Philippines and had first hand knowledge of the effectiveness of the shotgun. It was soon recognized that they possessed much potential both for offensive and defensive trench warfare. The U.S. Army Ordnance Department was ordered to evaluate which shotgun would best suit the troops deploying to France. The consensus was that the Winchester Model 1897 would be the logical choice."

The specifications for a military model, however, were for a version of the 1897 that did not yet exist. The Army asked Winchester to make the 1897 without a disconnector, meaning it could be fired repeatedly by holding down the trigger and rapidly manipulating the slide; the shotgun version of fanning a

revolver. This feature, however, created a problem. The rapid firing of six rounds caused the barrel to heat up, and since the military Model 1897 was affixed with an M1917 "U.S. Enfield" rifle bayonet, a soldier in close-quarters battle (CQB) could not wield a bayonet mounted to a barrel that was too hot to hold. Another alteration was required – the addition of a ventilated metal handguard over the top of the barrel, thus allowing a soldier to grasp the gun by the handguard and forearm. The Springfield Armory worked in conjunction with W.R.A. Co. on the design of both the handguard and bayonet adaptor assembly since Winchester was already producing the majority of M1917 bayonets. These were stamped at the hilt with a W inside a circle.[5]

Winchester delivered 19,196 "Trench" guns to the U.S. military and throughout the war it is estimated that as many as 25,000 were manufactured. A takedown version of the "Trench" gun was also produced beginning in 1921. The military versions remained in production until 1935 and also saw action in WWII.

The standard barrel length for 12 gauge models was 30-inches with full choke, whereas the lighter 16 gauge models had a 28-inch barrel. The longest barrel length offered by Winchester for 12 gauge shotguns was 32-inches, and

[5] "Give Us More Shotguns – American Trench Guns In The Great War" by Bruce N. Canfield, American Rifleman Volume 152, No. 5, May 2004
[6] The 16 gauge was introduced in 1900 with 2-5/8th inch chambers. This was changed to 2-3/4 inch in 1931.

Nearly 100 years old, this original and still working Model 1897 Winchester is an early example with the rounded pistol grip stock carried over from the Model 1893. It is pictured with a Model 1877 Colt .41 caliber double action revolver. (Model 1897 courtesy of Mark McNeely and Chuck Ahern of Allegheny Trade Co., Duncansville, PA.)

This example bears the second style slide rod marking, which began around serial No. 52000.

Brass shot shells were popular because they were less susceptible to the elements than paper shells. Note the slide release button toward the rear of the frame on this Model 1897. This was used to unlock the slide when the hammer was fully cocked. This view also shows the carrier in its lowered position allowing a new shell to spring from the magazine into the carrier's upper surface. Pushing the slide handle forward would then draw the bolt forward thus chambering the new round.

50

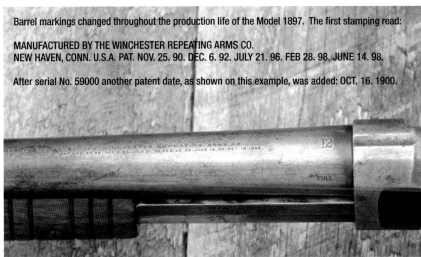

Barrel markings changed throughout the production life of the Model 1897. The first stamping read:

MANUFACTURED BY THE WINCHESTER REPEATING ARMS CO.
NEW HAVEN, CONN. U.S.A. PAT. NOV. 25. 90. DEC. 6. 92. JULY 21. 96. FEB 28. 98. JUNE 14. 98.

After serial No. 59000 another patent date, as shown on this example, was added: OCT. 16. 1900.

30 inches for 16 gauge models (beginning in 1930). Barrels for the 12 gauge were also available in 28 inch and 26 inch lengths, and 26 inches for 16 gauge.[6]

Chokes could be ordered Full, Modified, or Cylinder bore, as well as Winchester No. 1 and No. 2 Skeet (beginning July 1940), improved modified (3/4 choke), and improved cylinder (1/4 choke beginning October 1939). Damascus barrels with 3 blade and 4 blade sights were available at extra cost but were discontinued in 1914. [7]

The standard tubular magazine for both Model 1893 and Model 1897 shotguns had a capacity of 5 shells plus one in the chamber. For bird hunting, however, a Presidential Proclamation signed February 2, 1935 by Franklin Delano Roosevelt, based on the recommendation of the United States Biological Survey, required that the capacity of any automatic loading or repeating shotgun used in shooting migratory birds be limited to three shots; two in the magazine and one in the chamber. In 1935 Winchester thus began supplying a special shape wood magazine plug to reduce magazine capacity to two shells. One of these plugs was included in each carton containing a Model 97. [8]

The Model 1897 and later Model 97 Winchesters were offered with superb

[7] "The History of Winchester Firearms 1866-1992 Sixth Edition," by Thomas Henshaw, 1993 Winchester Press.
[8] Ibid

Picured right: The average Model 1897 weighed 7-1/2 pounds. The 12 gauge with 30-inch barrel tipped the scales at 7 lbs. 14 oz. The short 20-inch barrel "Riot" gun was 12 oz lighter. Fitted with the 28-inch barrel the 12 gauge weighed 7 lbs. 8 oz, the same as the 16 gauge model with 28-inch barrel. Pictured (left to right) Model 1897 in 12 gauge with 32-inch barrel, 16 gauge with 28-inch barrel, and a Model 97 in 12 gauge with 30-inch barrel. (Author's collection)

Later barrel markings and absence of Model 97 markings on the slide rod indicate that this example was built after production passed 950,000.

factory engraving, and the top-of-the-line Pigeon Grade guns came with beautifully embellished hunting scenes on both sides of the receiver and engraving around the frame. The bolt on high-end models was also engraved and marked **Trap Gun** or **Pigeon Gun**. These fine examples also had fancy grain walnut stocks and forearms, and the finest models, designated as "Black Diamond Grade," had special fitting and finishing of the action.

Conrad F. Ulrich and his brother John, who worked almost exclusively for the Winchester factory, created many of the popular engraving patterns used on Trap and Pigeon guns, which featured dogs, hunters, and game birds. Deluxe examples by John Ulrich incorporated these themes within highly detailed scrollwork. Ulrich rarely signed his work, and then only in a discrete J. ULRICH or just the initials JU. In a 1953 letter written to master engraver Alvin A. White, Ulrich's son, Leslie B. Ulrich, also a Winchester engraver, noted that his father generally used letters no greater then 1/16 inch and signed his work on the lower tang. [9]

There were standard cataloged engraving patterns for Winchester arms as well as custom engraving to order. In the 1897 *Highly Finished Arms* catalog the cost of engraving was an additional $6 to Winchester. One can only imagine what the Ulrichs would think today if they knew the value collectors have placed on Winchester shotguns bearing their work!

There are a number of distinguishing characteristics among Model 1897 and Model 97 shotguns, the most distinctive being stocks and forearms. Pigeon guns had the finest wood, either straight (English) stocks or pistol grip stocks with fine checkering, and distinctively checkered forearms of either rounded or semi-beavertail design. Field Grade examples had a round forearm with 18 semi-circular grooves. Another variation for Field Grade models was a "flat bottom" forearm with 14 grooves (on the sides only), which was put into production in 1947. Both are commonly seen today.

There are three variations (excluding deluxe models) of the Model 1897 and

[9] "Winchester Engraving" by R.L. Wilson, 1989 Beinfeld Publishing.

Note the letter "D" is stamped above the serial number on the first Model 97 shown. This indicates that it is fitted with the flat-ended magazine plug. The second gun bears the letter "E" and a serial number over 1 million, very near the end of production.

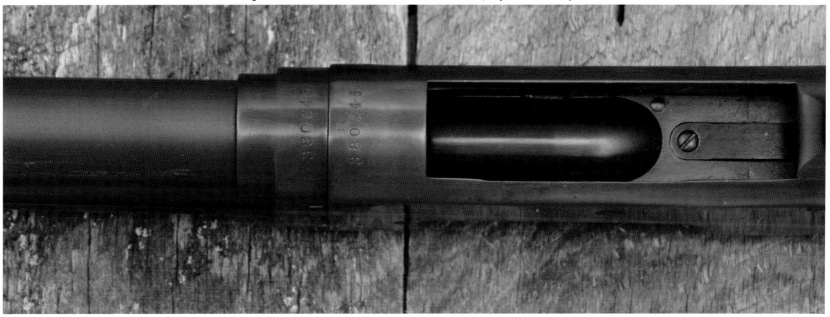

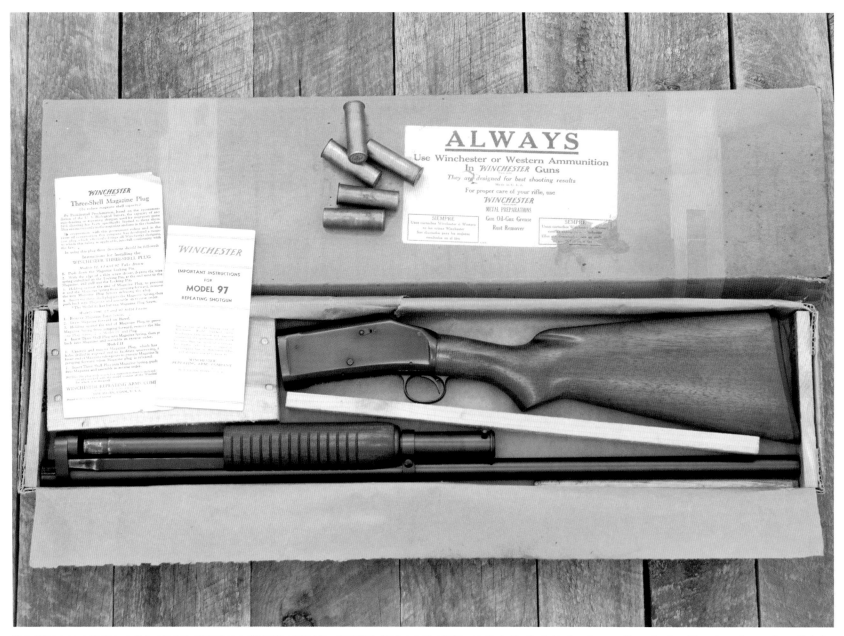

Something every collector would love to find, a brand new, still in the original box, Model 97. Produced after 1947, as indicated by the flat bottom forearm, the packaging still used wood separations. Note the included instructions for installing the three shot wood plug in the magazine. (Gary Reynolds Collection)

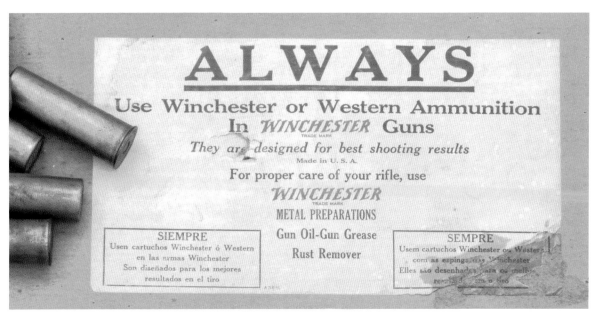

Since 1931 Winchester had been owned by Olin Industries, which also manufactured Western ammunition, thus the recommendation on the Model 97 box lid to use only Winchester or Western ammunition and Winchester cleaning products. Yes, there was packaged advertising even in the 1950s. Brass cartridges are vintage WWI used in Model 1897 "Trench" Guns.

Model 97 stock. The earliest examples have the round pistol grip carried over from the Model 1893. Later models have a half pistol grip and in 1947 the wood for Field Grade and "Riot" guns was changed to full pistol grip. The other variation in stock design is the comb, which can be either straight or fluted. On most examples, checkered hard rubber buttplates with the Winchester logo are seen, although steel buttplates were standard. Some examples are also seen with Winchester recoil pads, although this practice is not correct to the period.

Another distinguishing characteristic of Model 1897 shotguns was the model stamping on the slide rods, which changed no less than five times throughout production. The earliest examples were marked:

WINCHESTER

MODEL 1897

At around serial No. 52000 it was changed to:

MODEL 1897

— WINCHESTER —

At numbers near 231000 the factory added the word TRADE MARK under Winchester.

Production of the Model 1897 was, in a word, prolific, and by serial numbers near 352000 a new marking was introduced:

MODEL 1897

— WINCHESTER —

REG. IN U.S. PAT. OFF.

The last variation, though rarely seen, began after production passed serial No. 485000:

MODEL 1897

— WINCHESTER —

REG. IN U.S. PAT. OFF. & FGN

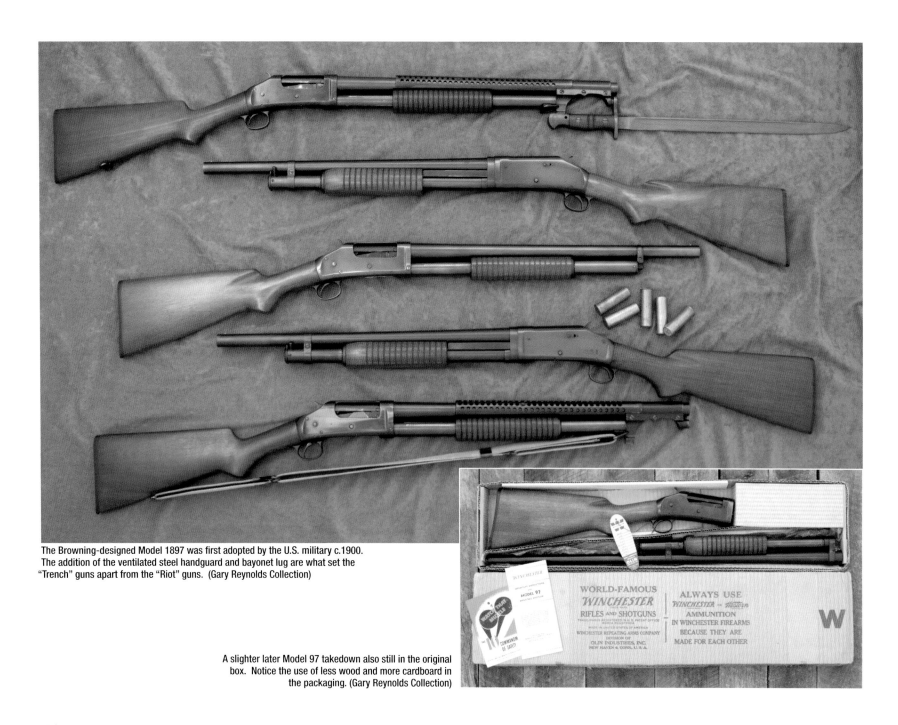

The Browning-designed Model 1897 was first adopted by the U.S. military c.1900. The addition of the ventilated steel handguard and bayonet lug are what set the "Trench" guns apart from the "Riot" guns. (Gary Reynolds Collection)

A slighter later Model 97 takedown also still in the original box. Notice the use of less wood and more cardboard in the packaging. (Gary Reynolds Collection)

A pair of Model 97 "Riot" guns showing both the earlier round forearm and later flat bottom forearm. The top example is a solid frame model, the bottom a takedown. Notice the different style magazine retainers, the solid frame uses a steel band that partially encircles the barrel and is secured by a screw, while the takedown uses a steel band that encircles the magazine and has a rotating retainer. This same design was used on Model 12 and Model 42 takedown versions.

Detail shot of the two different style Model 97 forearms and magazine retainers.

57

Most, but not all "Trench" guns were stamped with US and the Ordnance Department flaming bomb emblem. This also applied to "Riot" guns (pictured) purchased by the military c. 1900. Notes Bruce N. Canfield, "It is likely that those ["Trench" guns] without markings were purchased by the government during WWI, but the war ended before the guns could be issued, thus they were not stamped with the US and flaming bomb markings." (Gary Reynolds Collection)

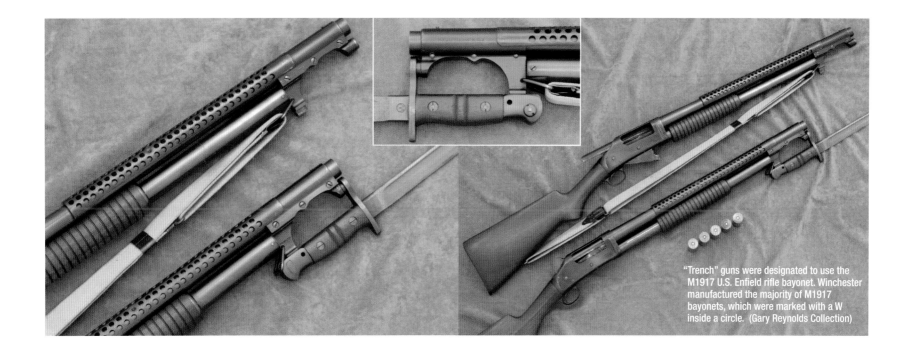

"Trench" guns were designated to use the M1917 U.S. Enfield rifle bayonet. Winchester manufactured the majority of M1917 bayonets, which were marked with a W inside a circle. (Gary Reynolds Collection)

After production exceeded half a million the slide rods were no longer marked.

Barrel markings also changed throughout the production life of the Model 1897. The first stamping read:

MANUFACTURED BY THE WINCHESTER REPEATING ARMS CO.
NEW HAVEN, CONN. U.S.A. PAT. NOV. 25. 90. DEC. 6. 92. JULY 21. 96. FEB 28. 98. JUNE 14. 98.

After serial No. 59000 another patent date was added, OCT. 16. 1900.

The choke was marked on the left rear of the barrel, and the gauge stamped on top of the barrel. This changed at approximately serial No. 230300 after which the gauge marking was moved to the barrel marking on 12 gauge shotguns, and after approximately serial No. 242000 on 16 gauge models. When production passed 500,000 a new stamping was used on the left side of the barrel:

MODEL 97 — WINCHESTER — 12 GA. FULL
— TRADE MARK —

The MANUFACTURED BY stamping was moved to the right side of the barrel and DEC. 25. 06. July 5. 10 added to the patent dates.

Note that at this point in time, c. 1918, Winchester refers to the slide-action shotgun as the Model 97. This remained the barrel stamping until production passed 950,000 after which a new marking was used:

MADE IN NEW HAVEN. CONN. — WINCHESTER — MODEL 97-12 GA. — 2 — CHAM.
U.S. OF AMERICA — TRADE MARK — FULL

The Model 1897 and Model 97 were the most popular shotguns of the late 19th and early 20th centuries, remaining in production long after the improved Model 12 was introduced.

In 1951, John M. Olin, president of Winchester and Olin Industries, which included Western ammunition, was presented with serial number 1,000,000. Winchester continued to build the Model 97 until 1957, by which time production had reached 1,024,700. That's a success story.

Embellishments were the hallmark of Winchester's top-of-the-line models. The Winchester Custom Shop and artisans such as John and Conrad Ulrich engraved the finest examples. (Gary Reynolds Collection)

The underside of the frame and trigger guard also received the engraver's touch!

Beautiful and highly detailed engraving of the Pigeon Gun featured bird-hunting scenes on both sides of the frame; a quail shooting scene on the right and live bird shooting scene on the left. Four-leaf clover and rose were standard patterns, presumably for good luck. Pigeon Guns also had a pigeon engraved on the flat behind the hammer. The top of the frame was embellished and the barrels matted. This was a made-to-order gun which first listed for $100. Note the PAT. APPLIED FOR stamping on the new Model 1897 ejection system.

A very early Model 1897 Pigeon Gun, serial number 46701, engraved in the white. This was the standard engraving pattern established for the Winchester factory engraved Pigeon Gun. Note the unusual forearm on this early example, which still uses a retaining screw. (Gary Reynolds Collection)

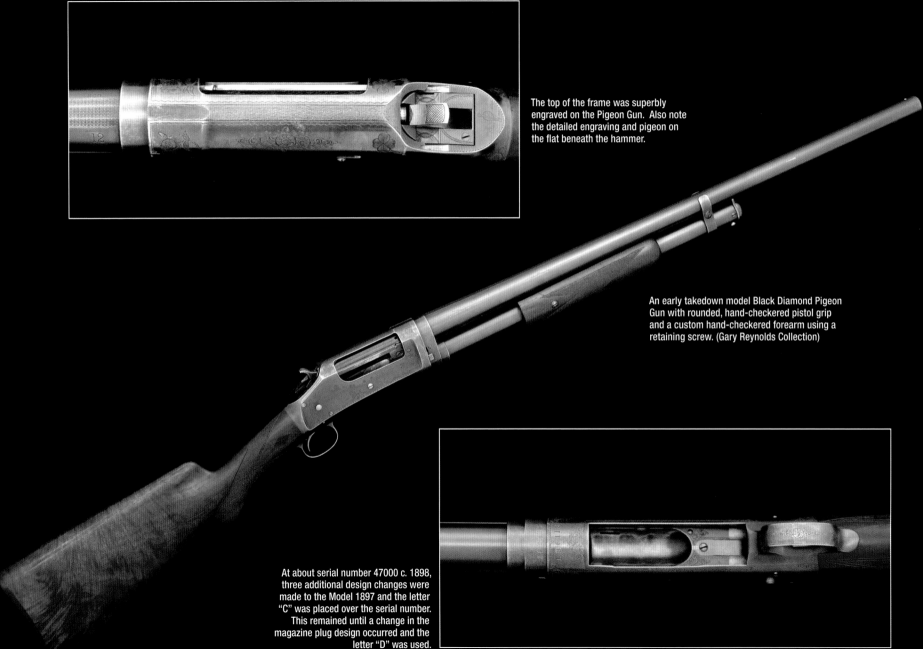

The top of the frame was superbly engraved on the Pigeon Gun. Also note the detailed engraving and pigeon on the flat beneath the hammer.

An early takedown model Black Diamond Pigeon Gun with rounded, hand-checkered pistol grip and a custom hand-checkered forearm using a retaining screw. (Gary Reynolds Collection)

At about serial number 47000 c. 1898, three additional design changes were made to the Model 1897 and the letter "C" was placed over the serial number. This remained until a change in the magazine plug design occurred and the letter "D" was used.

Once again the beautiful Pigeon Gun engraving pattern. You have to wonder what the dog on the right panel is thinking as he looks back at two more birds dropping while he is still retrieving the first! The engraved breech block is marked Pigeon Gun, however, after 1926 Pigeon Gun was not always engraved on the breech block. R.L. Wilson notes the intricacies of the engraving pattern in *Winchester Engraving*: "Interesting early depiction of live pigeon shooting, using the so-called boxed birds. Release lines are attached to the small table at right at which the operator sits, flags mark the outer extremity of the shooting ring, and a pointer is held by the handler for retrieving dead birds, five of which are at the shooter's feet." (Gary Reynolds Collection)

Detail shot shows the fine hand checkering of this Pigeon Gun forearm.

63

Produced c.1897 thus unique cased pair of Black Diamond Model 1897s, serial numbers 288808 and 288809 have 30-inch matted and fully choked barrels, with standard maker address and patent markings. Profusely scrolled and border engraved the work is accented with gold and platinum inlays. Dogs and game birds within the scrollwork, instead of set in panels, present an unusual treatment. Both examples are signed J. ULRICH forward of the trigger guard, inside the cutout for the cartridge feeding mechanism. Note that each barrel has a brass protective cover at the breech end. (Photos courtesy Greg Martin Auctions)

Winchester custom orders were fitted with straight stocks unless otherwise requested, and were hand checkered.

Here is another Winchester engraving pattern on a Model 1897. Notice the attention paid to screw heads and the fine scrollwork on top of the barrel and around the frame. The left side of the receiver features a panel scene with a pointer surrounded by scrollwork, the right side a panel scene with wild turkeys. The work may be attributed to J. Ulrich. According to owner Gary Reynolds this is conceivably a replacement for an 1893, thus the unusual serial number with an L prefix and 0 prefix above it. (Gary Reynolds Collection)

Magnificent work from the Winchester Custom Shop, the engraving style and gold inlays on this Black Diamond Model 97 Trap Gun are similar to those used by Winchester engravers on the Model 21 Grand Americans. Notice the outstanding use of multiple shades of gold to enhance shading and detail in the hunting dog and quail. (Gary Reynolds Collection)

What sets this particular example apart from any other Winchester Custom Shop Model 97, aside from the exceptional engraving and gold inlays, is the chambering. With a 30-inch Full choke barrel, this is the only Model 97 known to have been chambered in 20 gauge. The panel scenes on the left side of the receiver are reminiscent of early sketches by Conrad F. Urlich and John Urlich. (Gary Reynolds Collection)

This elaborate example with heavy scrollwork and gold inlays, is a Model 1897 Trap Gun chambered in 12 gauge with a 30-inch Modified choke barrel. The Winchester Custom Shop work appears to have been executed in a style reminiscent of J. Urlich, with the dogs and game birds set within the scrollwork, rather than into panels, as in the previous example. (Gary Reynolds Collection)

Once again the selection of extra fancy wood and fine hand checkering distinguish the Winchester Custom Shop's workmanship.

Gold inlaid hunting dogs and quail show exceptional detail, which is achieved through shading and combining different colors of gold. A "D" series model, serial number 251465, this example has the third variation of slide rail markings with the addition of TRADE MARK under – WINCHESTER –.

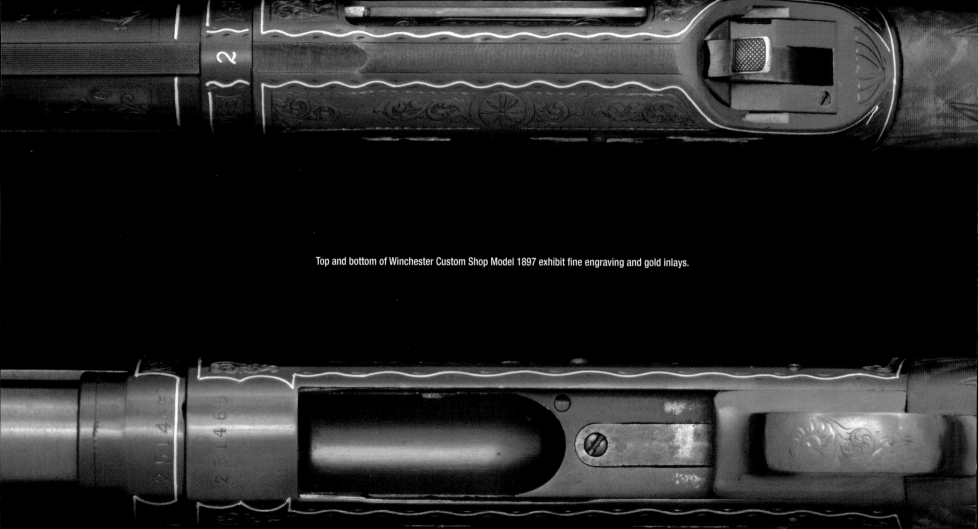

Top and bottom of Winchester Custom Shop Model 1897 exhibit fine engraving and gold inlays.

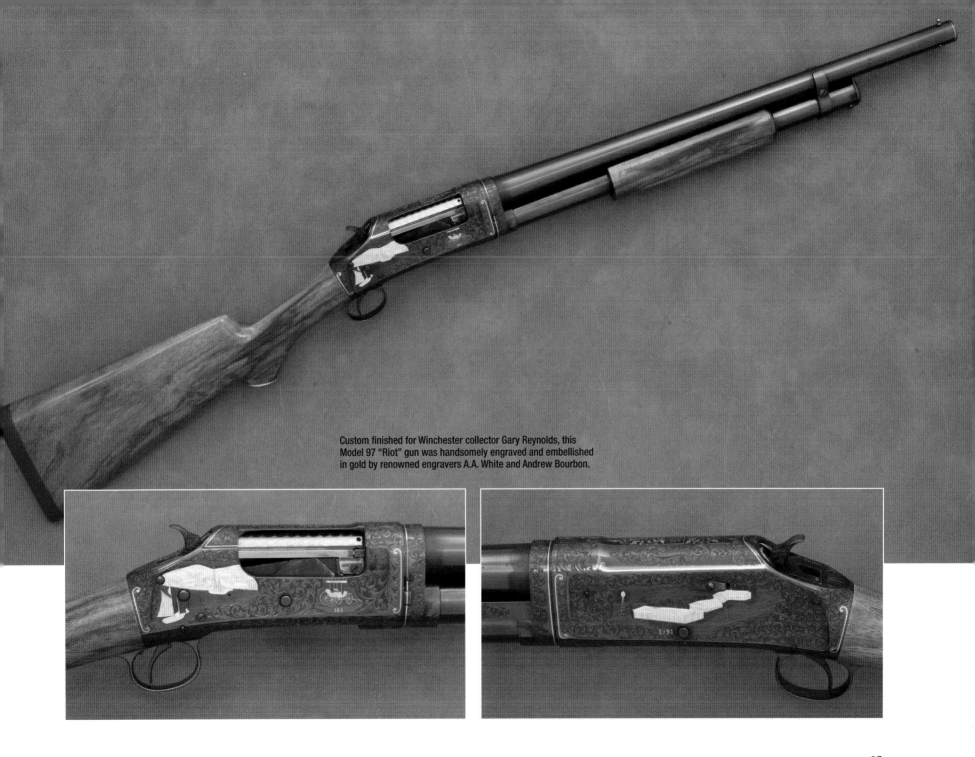

Custom finished for Winchester collector Gary Reynolds, this Model 97 "Riot" gun was handsomely engraved and embellished in gold by renowned engravers A.A. White and Andrew Bourbon.

Pictured with an original 1913 Winchester calendar is the very first Model 1912 shotgun, serial No. 1. This is the 20-gauge model. There is also a serial No. 1 shotgun in 16-gauge and another in 12-gauge. The 1913 calendar was the first major promotional advertising for the Model 1912. The calendar's artist, Robert Robertson, called it, "The Old Man with Chin Whiskers." (Courtesy Dave Riffle)

Chapter Three
Birth of the Modern Slide-action Shotgun
The Model 12

By the dawn of the 20th century Winchester was the most successful manufacturer of rifles and shotguns in America. In the mid 1890s, W.R.A. Co. and John M. Browning had further advanced the design of the Winchester lever action rifle, unveiling the new Model of 1894, destined to become the most famous rifle of all time. The Model 1894, known today as the Model 94, has remained in production for over 100 years.

In 1895 Browning brought New Haven another landmark rifle design, the Model 1895, the first successful box magazine, lever-action repeater ever placed on the market, and another legendary Winchester that is still manufactured to this day. The model 1893 and improved Model 1897 shotguns rounded out an ever-expanding product line that provided sportsmen, explorers, lawmen, the U.S. military, and just plain everyday folks with the greatest selection of rifles and shotguns for hunting and self defense that America had ever known. But there was much more to come.

On August 27, 1901, Winchester delivered its second new shotgun of the 20th century, the improved Model 1901 lever-action repeater. A redesigned and strengthened Model 1887, it was offered only in a hefty 10-gauge version. T.G. Bennett had decided against a 12-gauge 01 to avoid competing with Winchester's new slide-action models. Available in the original 12-gauge and a new 16-gauge takedown version introduced in 1900, the Model 1897 slide-action repeaters had lost none of their sales momentum as the 20th century dawned. By 1902, however, John Browning had a new design waiting in the wings.

Since 1883 W.R.A. Co. had purchased every John M. Browning design, a total of 44 different patents for 31 rifles and 13 shotguns. Of that total the New Haven factory went forward with production on seven different rifles and a trio of shotgun designs between 1885 and 1906, the last being an improved variation of Browning's Model 1890 slide-action .22. The rest of the Browning designs were purchased simply to keep them out of the hands of other arms makers.[1] This was perhaps the catalyst for what led to both a parting of the ways between the Ogden, Utah, arms designer and the creation of Winchester's greatest competitor.

It was, in fact, the design of a shotgun that triggered the estrangement between John Browning and the Winchester Repeating Arms Co. in 1902. The Browning brothers had developed a new, truly innovative, semi-automatic shotgun that required neither a lever nor slide-action device to load the next shell, but fired as quickly as one could pull the trigger! Winchester rejected the design, although the real problem was a disagreement between John Browning and T.G. Bennett. Browning no longer wanted to sell his patents to Winchester outright. Instead Browning wanted (and looking back at the success of his designs, certainly deserved), a royalty from each gun sold. When Bennett's answer was no, Browning took his design for what would become the A5 to Fabrique Nationale (F.N.) in Herstal and Liege, Belgium. The outcome, of course, was perhaps the biggest gaffe in the history of the Winchester Repeating Arms Co. and the whole of the American firearms industry. The Browning F.N. design, introduced in September 1903, went on to eclipse the Model 1897 Winchesters and ultimately force W.R.A. Co. to introduce its own recoil-operated semi-auto shotgun in 1911. Further compounding the problem for Winchester was another competitor, Remington, which in 1905 brought out the Browning design, listed as the Remington Auto-Loading Shotgun Model 11. Versions of both the Remington Model 11 and Browning A5 are still in production to the present day!

[1] 25th Edition Blue Book of Gun Values by S.P. Fjestad, Blue Book Publications, 2004.

Two of the original Model 1912 slide-action Winchesters, the No. 1 gun in 16-gauge (bottom) and No. 1 gun in 20-gauge, (top). The 16-gauge was found in a Little John's auction. The 20-gauge was purchased from a Mr. Bender in Alberta, Canada, whose father had worked for Winchester and opened up their Canadian store. Both have been authenticated as the original first examples built. Somewhere out there, the No. 1 gun in 12-gauge is resting in someone's gun cabinet. Note the design of the first action slide handle (top), which has 13 grooves. The second version on the 16-gauge model (introduced in 1914) has 14 grooves. (Courtesy Dave Riffle)

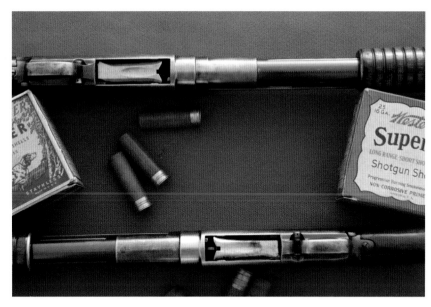

There is, of course, a back-story to the development of many Browning-based Winchester designs. From the onset most were prototypes acquired by T.G. Bennett, which required further development before going into production. While Browning perfected many of his own designs, at Winchester another of the era's greatest firearms inventors, William B. Mason, carried out the majority of work in New Haven.

From 1869 to 1882 Mason had been Samuel Colt's Superintendent of the Armory in Hartford, and was personally responsible for many of Colt's most historic revolvers, including the Richards-Mason cartridge conversions of 1851 and 1861 Navy models, the 1860 Army, and c.1862 Colt .36 caliber pocket pistols. Mason was also responsible for the .44 rimfire 1871-72 Open Top, Colt's Cloverleaf pocket revolver, the landmark Colt Model 1873 Single Action Army, and Colt's improved double action revolvers c. 1881.[2]

Mason's first significant work at Winchester was perfecting the Browning-designed Model 1887 lever-action shotgun. It was

Mason again who finalized John Browning's design for the new Model 1893 slide-action shotgun and designed the improved Model 1897. He also spearheaded the changes and improvements introduced with the Model 1901 lever-action shotgun. During a career that spanned the latter half of the 19th century, and included work for Colt's, Winchester, and Remington, William Mason's name appeared on no less than 125 patents.

In 1885 Mason had taken on an assistant at Winchester, a 23-year old Yale Sheffield Scientific School graduate named Thomas Crossly Johnson. It was to be this team, Mason and Johnson, who would take Winchester into the new century.

Having perfected his skills at Mason's side, T.C. Johnson succeeded his mentor as chief designer following Mason's retirement in the early 1900s. William B. Mason died in 1913 at the age of 76.[3]

Among Mason's accomplishments while at Colt's was his role in the design of Hartford's first hammerless double-barreled shotgun. Mason's experience in this design was not lost

Looking at the underside of the No. 1 20-gauge and No. 1 16-gauge shotguns the serial number stamping can be seen faintly on the underside of the receiver, forward end. Later models also had the serial number on the underside of the receiver extension. The 16-gauge example shows first use of alignment arrows. (Courtesy Dave Riffle)

[2] Metallic Cartridge Conversions by Dennis Adler, Krause Publications, 2002 and A History of the Colt Revolver by Charles T. Haven and Frank A. Belden, Crown Publishers and Bonanza Books, 1940.
[3] Handguns of the World by Edward C. Ezell, 1981 Stackpole Books, 1993 Barnes & Noble, Inc. Stackpole Books

WINCHESTER MODEL 12 TRAP GUN — MONTE CARLO WALNUT STOCK

WINCHESTER MODEL 12 TRAP GUN — HYDRO-COIL MONTE CARLO STOCK (WALNUT COLOR)

WINCHESTER MODEL 12 PIGEON

WINCHESTER MODEL 12 SKEET — WALNUT STOCK

WINCHESTER MODEL 12 SKEET — HYDRO-COIL STOCK (IVORY COLOR)

Winchester Model 12 factory photos display each of the different grades. Photos are from the 1964 press release and also introduce the Hydro-Coil stock. (Photos courtesy U.S. Repeating Arms Co.)

on young Johnson, who later spearheaded the first hammerless Winchester shotguns, the semi-automatic Model 1911 and the most successful shotgun design in history, the Model 1912.

Developed and patented by T.C. Johnson, the Model 1912, upon which design work had begun in 1907, first appeared in the January 1913 Winchester catalog. The new hammerless, takedown model featured a 25-inch round steel barrel, and was initially offered only in 20-gauge. The following year Winchester introduced both 12-gauge and 16-gauge versions.[4]

The Model 1912 was a great stride forward in shotgun design and sportsmen immediately received the new slide-action repeater with open arms. It had taken Johnson a little over three years to perfect the design working through numerous prototypes and more than 50,000 test shots to evaluate and refine the Model 1912's mechanism. On March 29, 1910, T.G. Bennett and T.C. Johnson approved the final design and preparations for production commenced. Twenty-nine months later, the first Model 1912 came off the New Haven assembly line. The example pictured with the 1913 Winchester calendar at the opening of this chapter is serial No. 1, the very first 20-gauge Model 1912 built.

The first deliveries of the Model 1912 to warehouse stock were made on August 30, 1912.[5] The manufacturer's list price was $30.00 for the 20-gauge takedown model with 25-inch nickel steel barrel. An additional $5.00 was charged for orders with a matted rib. Over the years there would be more variations of the Model 1912 (Model 12) than any other Winchester shotgun.

[4] A 12 gauge Riot gun was introduced in 1918 and the 28 gauge was authorized in 1934. Thomas Henshaw, The History of Winchester Shotguns.
[5] Ibid.

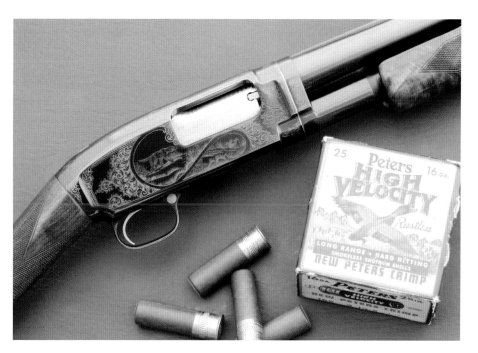

This Model 1912, chambered 16-gauge, was manufactured in 1941 and factory custom engraved by George Ulrich. It is a very early and beautifully engraved example. The Ulrich designs set the pattern for all future engraving; however, this is a far more elaborate design with extra engraving on sides of the receiver and the top. The gun also has a factory gold trigger and engine-turned breech block. (Courtesy Dave Riffle)

The Model 12's Red Headed Cousin
The Winchester Model 25

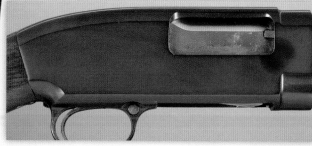

On March 17, 1949, Winchester began shipping a new slide-action shotgun to the factory warehouse, the Model 25, a non-takedown version of the Model 12. Available only in 12-gauge, the solid frame repeater came standard with a 28-inch barrel and a choice of full or modified choke. A shorter 26-inch barrel was also offered with improved cylinder choke. Like the take down Model 12 Field Grade gun, the Model 25 featured a pistol grip stock of American walnut, and 14 groove slide handle.

The model was first listed in the February 2, 1950, price list. Weighing approximately 8 pounds, the Model 25 came with a wooden magazine plug to reduce capacity to two shells for migratory bird hunting. Otherwise the magazine held five folded crimp shells or four rolled crimp shells.

Although priced below the Model 12 Field Grade gun, the Model 25 was not overly successful and in 1954, after 87,937 were produced the model was discontinued.

The Model 25, a non-takedown version of the Model 12, was available only in 12-gauge. The solid frame repeater came standard with a 28-inch barrel and a choice of full or modified choke. Although priced below the Model 12 Field Grade gun, it was not overly successful and in 1954, after 87,937 were produced, the model was discontinued. (Photo courtesy Rock Island Auctions)

Close-up of Ulrich's engraving on the left side of the receiver shows the exceptional detail in the dogs, game bird, and the elegant scrollwork, fine border, and scrolls on top of frame.

76

Later stamping for Winchester Proof Steel barrels shows repositioned Trade Mark and addition of address. Original 1931 design, below, did not have the New Haven address.

MADE IN U.S.A.
WINCHESTER PROOF STEEL —— WINCHESTER —— MOD. 12 – 12 GA.
TRADE MARK

Matting on top of receiver was intended to reduce glare off the metal and aid in sighting. It was also a handsome addition to the Model 12's design.

Following are the general specifications and major changes to the Model 1912:

TYPE

Take down, slide-action repeating shotgun, hammerless, tubular magazine, cross lock safety operated horizontally across front of trigger guard.

STYLES

Standard or Field Gun: First listed in Winchester catalog No. 78, January, 1913.

Tournament Grade: First listed in 1914, discontinued on July 2, 1931, to be succeeded by the Special Trap Grade.

Trap Grade: First listed in 1914, discontinued on July 2, 1931, to be succeeded by the Special Trap Grade.

Riot Gun: Introduced in 1918, last listed in 1963.

Trench Gun: Introduced in 1918, thereafter made on special order only.

Standard Trap Grade: Authorized on December 24, 1930, discontinued on September 15, 1939, to be succeeded by a new style M/12 Trap Gun.

Special Trap Grade: Authorized on December 24, 1930, discontinued on September 15, 1939.

Trap Gun-New Style: A new style of M/12 Trap Gun was authorized on July 21, 1938, discontinued in 1964.

Trap Gun: Ladies and junior Model (20 gauge). This style of Trap Gun was authorized on October 22, 1939, discontinuance authorized on December 31, 1941.

Skeet Gun: Skeet guns with solid raised matted rib barrels were authorized on November 17, 1933. Skeet guns with plain barrels were authorized on January 20, 1937, and last listed in 1947. Skeet Gun, with Cutts compensator attached. This style of Skeet Gun was authorized on August 4, 1938, in 12 gauge; 16 gauge and 20 gauge authorized on February 8, 1939, discontinued in 1940. Guns with Cutts compensator were discontinued in 1954.

Heavy Duck Gun: M/12 Heavy Duck Gun is 12 gauge only, authorized on February 15, 1935, discontinued in 1963.

Pigeon Grade: Pigeon Grade was first listed in 1914, discontinued in 1941. Reintroduced in 1948 and discontinued in 1964. Super Pigeon Grade introduced in 1965.

BARRELS

12 gauge: Plain barrels, 26, 28, 30, and 32-inch, first listed in 1914. Matted barrels, on special order only, first listed in 1914. Solid raised matted rib barrels, 26, 28, 30, and 32-inch, first listed in 1914. Ventilated rib barrels, 30-inch, first listed in 1919. In June 1926, stainless steel barrels were announced as an option for any Winchester shotgun or rifle. They were unsuccessful and discontinued in 1931.

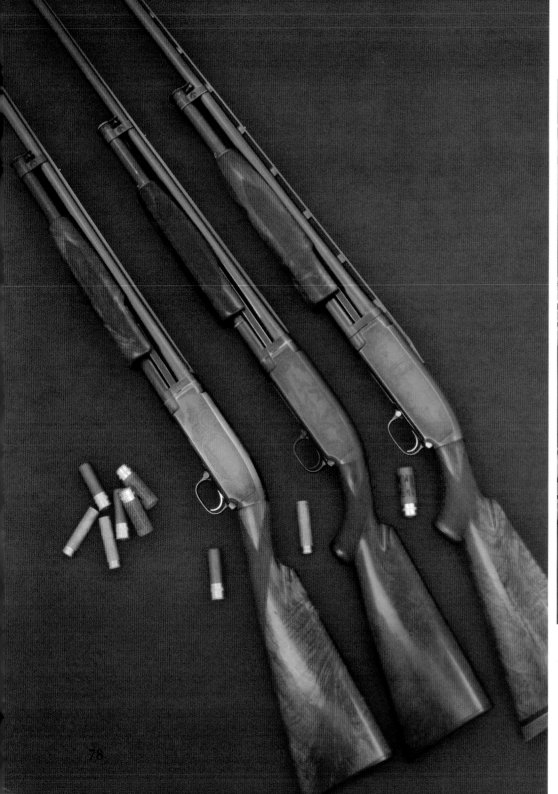

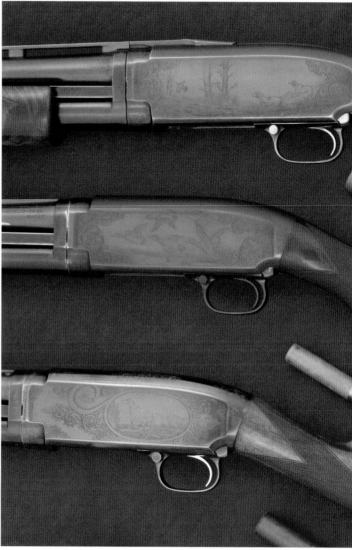

Here are three exceptional examples of engraving by George Ulrich. Top is a 12-gauge, followed by a 16-gauge model, and 28-gauge Black Diamond. The 12-gauge is pattern 12-5, the most elaborate cataloged style. Note the checked, select walnut forearms on all three examples. The 28-gauge Black Diamond has a highly figured straight grip stock and displays new standard Pigeon Grade scene with Number 5 engraving pattern by Ulrich. (Courtesy Dave Riffle)

16 gauge: Plain barrel, 26-inch first listed in 1914, 28-inch first listed about 1927, 30-inch was authorized on November 24, 1930. Matted barrels, special order only, first listed in 1914. Solid raised matted rib barrels, 26-inch first listed in 1914, 28-inch first listed about 1927, 30-inch authorized on November 24, 1930.

20 gauge: Plain barrel, 25-inch, first listed in January 1913. 26-inch barrel, first listed in 1927. 28-inch barrel, first listed in 1927. 30-inch barrel was authorized on November 24, 1930. Matted barrels, on special order only, first listed in January 1913. Solid raised matted rib barrel, 25-inch, first listed in January 1913. The revised edition of the 1935 Winchester catalog noted: "The 25-inch barrel in the M/12, 20 gauge has been made obsolete."

28 gauge: Introduced 1937, discontinued in 1960: Plain barrels, 26-inch and 28-inch, solid raised matted rib barrels, 26-inch and 28-inch.

VENTILATED RIB STYLES

There were six different ventilated rib types from 1919 to 1964. The first style is referred to as the "Two Pin Milled Ventilated Rib," or "Two Pin Duck Bill Ventilated Rib." The "New Winchester Special Ventilated Rib" patented by Simmons and manufactured by Winchester was referred to as the "Round Post, Donut Base Ventilated Rib." This was followed by a third style, also patented by Simmons, and known as the "Round Post Ventilated Rib." There was a final style of the "New Winchester Special Ventilated Rib," known simply as the "Round Post." The last two styles are referred to as "Round Post" New Winchester Special Ventilated Rib, and "Three Pin, Duck Bill Ventilated Rib" respectively. The last version used rectangular supports.

CHOKES

Full choke, modified choke, and cylinder bore. Intermediate chokes-improved modified choke (3/4 choke) and improved cylinder choke (1/4 choke) were authorized on October 29, 1931. Winchester No. 1 Skeet choke and Winchester No. 2 Skeet choke were authorized in 1935.

CHAMBER

12 gauge, 2-3/4-inch shell.
12 gauge Heavy Duck Gun, 3-inch shell. Barrel inscribed. 3" Super-X.
16 gauge, 2-9/16-inch shell. Chambering changed to 2-3/4-inch shell in 1927.
20 gauge, 2-1/2-inch shell. Chambering changed to 2 3/4-inch shell in 1925.
28 gauge, 2-7/8-inch shell, with 2-1/2 inch available on special order.

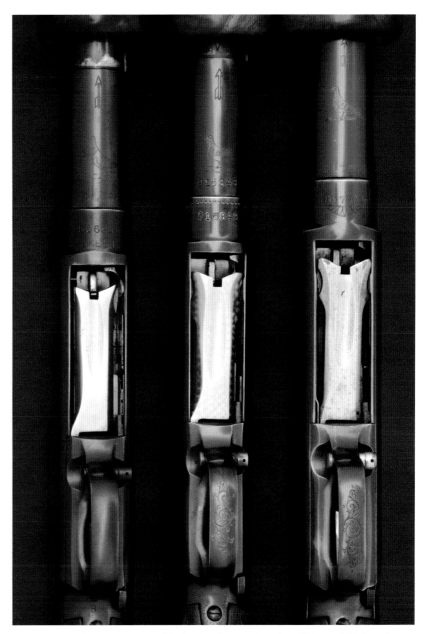

Underside of receivers shows both polished and engine-turned carriers. All three exhibit the roll engraved Pigeon on the underside of the receiver extension.

This trio shows Pigeon Grade Model 12s with the full milled ventilated ribs. Two different styles are shown, "Round Post" and "Three Pin, Duck Bill." (Courtesy Dave Riffle)

STOCKS

Standard or Field Gun

A new style stock was authorized for general use on all Standard or Field Guns on November 6, 1934. This stock is of slightly different dimensions, with a shorter grip than the stock previously used. Made of plain walnut, not checkered, with pistol grip and hard rubber butt plate.

Skeet Gun

The skeet gun stock was used after the introduction of M/12 skeet guns on November 17, 1933. It was the same as the standard or field gun stock, except it was made of selected walnut with checkered stock, full pistol grip, pistol grip cap, and a hard rubber butt plate.

Trap Gun

Trap gun stocks were made of selected walnut with either pistol grip or straight grip and equipped with a rubber recoil pad. Trap gun with Monte Carlo stock was authorized on December 18, 1940.

Heavy Duck Gun

Heavy duck gun stocks were made of plain walnut, not checkered, and equipped with a Winchester rubber recoil pad. A reduction in the length of pull, from 14 inches to 13-5/8 inches, was authorized on January 10, 1936. A change in the drop at heel dimension, from 2-^{1}/$_2$ inches to 2-^{3}/$_8$ inches, was authorized on December 20, 1938. A Hydro-Coil butt stock (to reduce apparent recoil) with matching forearm was available on Model 12 Trap and Skeet Guns during 1964 – ivory color or simulated walnut, regular stock with Skeet Gun, Monte Carlo comb or regular stock with Trap Gun.

SLIDE HANDLES

Standard or Field Gun

Standard shape introduced 1912. Made of plain walnut, 5-inches long, with 13 circular grooves. Second version added c.1914, 5-^{3}/$_4$ inches long with 14 grooves. Third version replaces original styles, c.1919, now 7-inches long with 18 grooves.

Fourth version, c.1947, slightly longer with 11 grooves that stop 3/4th of the way leaving the front plain. In 1955, an all-new action slide handle is introduced, longer, shaped full in the center, and tapered at both ends, with 14 grooves, larger circumference to slide back over the end of the receiver.

Skeet Gun

Extension slide handle, semi-beavertail shape, made of selected walnut, checkered. A new extension slide handle, which is shorter and of a slightly different shape than the older handle, was authorized as standard equipment on December 19, 1934.

Trap Gun

Extension slide handle, semi-beavertail shape, selected walnut, checkered. Note: A special shaped semi-beavertail slide handle was furnished on trap and skeet guns in 12 gauge only, principally on special orders. This handle was larger than the standard slide handle and smaller than the extension handle.

The Pigeon Grade forearms were much larger than those of Field Grade guns. The deisgn allowed for the back of the forearm to slide over the frame (as shown) when a shell was chambered. The larger forearm also gave the shooter a firmer grip and helped improve handling.

Pigeon Grade stocks offered fancy-figured walnut and hand checkering. Pistol grop stocks were the most popular.

Never very popular, it was discontinued in 1934. However it was reinstated, and a few 12 gauge Standard Skeet Guns were sold equipped with this type handle until discontinued on November 1, 1940.

Heavy Duck Gun

Standard shape, made of plain walnut, round with circular grooves, not checkered.

MAGAZINE

Tubular magazine. Capacity, 5 shells. Note: By Presidential Proclamation, signed February 2, 1935, and based on the recommendation of the U. S. Biological Survey, the capacity of any automatic loading or repeating shotgun used in shooting migratory birds is specifically limited to three shots. This means two shells in the magazine and one shell in the chamber. On February 22, 1935, a special shape magazine wood plug was authorized to reduce the magazine capacity to two shells. One of these plugs has been included in each carton containing a M/12 shotgun since that date. The only exception to this was the Heavy Duck Gun, which had the plug inserted in the magazine.

RECEIVERS

Straight-line matting on top of receiver. Receivers sandblasted on the top portion were authorized on February 10, 1939, for use on M/12 skeet and trap guns.

CARTRIDGE GUIDE

A cartridge guide, attached to the ejection side of the carrier, was authorized in 1938. Its purpose is to avoid any possibility of a loaded shell dropping out of the ejector port when short length shells are used.

WEIGHTS

Standard or Field Gun

12 gauge, 30-inch barrel – 7 lbs. 5 oz.
16 gauge, 28-inch barrel – 6 lbs. 9 oz.
20 gauge, 28-inch barrel – 6 lbs. 5 oz.
28 gauge, 26-inch barrel – 7 lbs. 3 oz.

Skeet Gun

12 gauge, 26-inch barrel – 7 lbs. 5 oz.
16 gauge, 26-inch barrel – 6 lbs. 12 oz.
20 gauge, 26-inch barrel – 6 lbs. 11 oz.

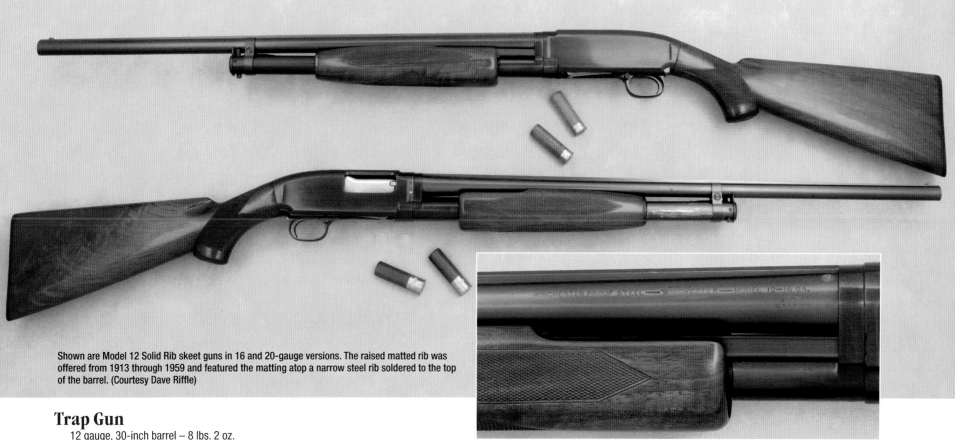

Shown are Model 12 Solid Rib skeet guns in 16 and 20-gauge versions. The raised matted rib was offered from 1913 through 1959 and featured the matting atop a narrow steel rib soldered to the top of the barrel. (Courtesy Dave Riffle)

Trap Gun

12 gauge, 30-inch barrel – 8 lbs. 2 oz.

Heavy Duck Gun

12 gauge, 30-inch barrel – 8 lbs. 9 oz.

SERIAL NUMBERS

M/12 shotguns are serially numbered from 1 up, on underside of receiver, forward end, and underside of receiver extension.

The historic success of the Model 12 is rivaled only by that of Winchester's Model 1894 rifle. From 1912 to 1980, more than two million Model 12s were produced. The 20-gauge gun was proclaimed in Winchester advertising as "The Lightest, Strongest, and Handsomest Repeating Shotgun Made." Few will argue that judgment. The Model 12 is the only Winchester shotgun that has been the subject of not one but two books, *The Winchester Model 12*, by George Madis, Arts and Reference House, Brownsboro, Texas, 1982, and what is certainly the definitive book on the Model 12, *The Greatest Hammerless Repeating Shotgun Ever Built –*

The Model 12 – 1912-1964, by Winchester collector and historian Dave Riffle. This book was published by Riffle in 1995 and has since become the bible of Model 12 reference history, mandatory reading for any serious Model 12 collector.

When looking at the history of the Model 1912 one has to take into account the times in which these remarkably advanced shotguns arrived. The majority of Americans still lived in rural areas. Most people rarely ventured outside their local townships and even fewer out of state or across the country. The automobile was just becoming an accepted means of personal transportation, displacing the horse and buggy, and the nation had finally emerged from settling the American frontier with Arizona and New Mexico being granted statehood in 1912, some 62 years after California! Thus for most people, the ownership of a shotgun, and its principal use for self defense and hunting, had changed little since the 1880s. It was into this piece of Americana that Winchester brought forth the finest shotgun of the new 20th century in 1912.

Model 12 Solid Rib Black Diamond Pigeon Grade presentation gun in the No. 5 engraving pattern by George Ulrich. The inscription reads, 1st Place New York Athletic Club Shoot July 2, 1939. (Courtesy Dave Riffle)

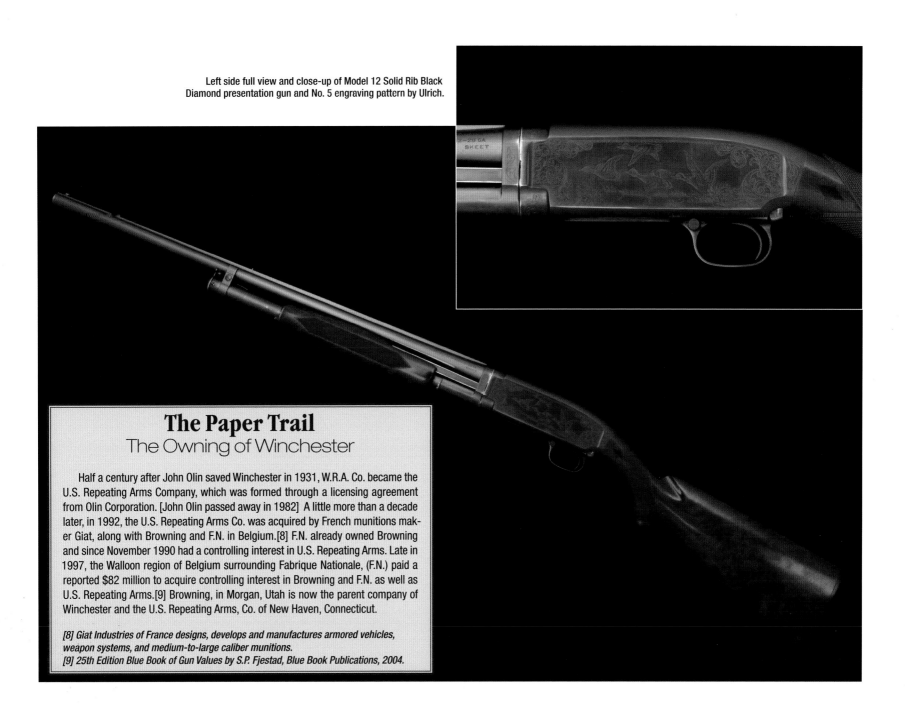

Left side full view and close-up of Model 12 Solid Rib Black Diamond presentation gun and No. 5 engraving pattern by Ulrich.

The Paper Trail
The Owning of Winchester

Half a century after John Olin saved Winchester in 1931, W.R.A. Co. became the U.S. Repeating Arms Company, which was formed through a licensing agreement from Olin Corporation. [John Olin passed away in 1982] A little more than a decade later, in 1992, the U.S. Repeating Arms Co. was acquired by French munitions maker Giat, along with Browning and F.N. in Belgium.[8] F.N. already owned Browning and since November 1990 had a controlling interest in U.S. Repeating Arms. Late in 1997, the Walloon region of Belgium surrounding Fabrique Nationale, (F.N.) paid a reported $82 million to acquire controlling interest in Browning and F.N. as well as U.S. Repeating Arms.[9] Browning, in Morgan, Utah is now the parent company of Winchester and the U.S. Repeating Arms, Co. of New Haven, Connecticut.

[8] Giat Industries of France designs, develops and manufactures armored vehicles, weapon systems, and medium-to-large caliber munitions.
[9] 25th Edition Blue Book of Gun Values by S.P. Fjestad, Blue Book Publications, 2004.

WINCHESTER PROOF STEEL — *WINCHESTER* — MODEL 12—28 GA.
MADE IN U.S.A.
TRADE MARK
SKEET

2⁷⁄₈ CHAM.

Close-up shows first Winchester Proof Steel barrel marking. Note the chamber and choke markings, 2-7/8 CHAM. and SKEET.

This view exhibits the beautiful diamond pattern and checkering on Pigeon Grade forearms.

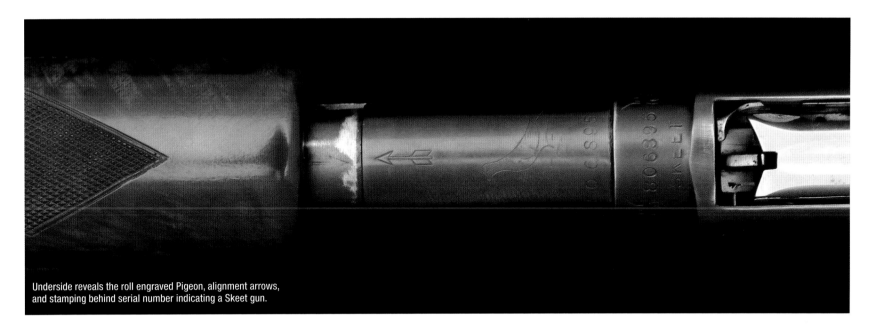
Underside reveals the roll engraved Pigeon, alignment arrows, and stamping behind serial number indicating a Skeet gun.

"In the early 1900s," writes Dave Riffle, "the pastime of sport shooting was booming. Men, women, and children were learning to enjoy trap shooting, as well as varied types of hunting. With the availability of several different manufacturers' shotguns – single barrels, doubles, lever action, pumps, etc. – the demand for a new small-gauge repeating shotgun was at its peak. Winchester answered the call, with its development of a first-class, correctly proportioned piece with a sleek, modern design: The Winchester Model 1912, 20-gauge Hammerless Repeating Shotgun." Indeed, for many collectors this is where Winchester shotgun history truly begins, in 1912.

With its $30 suggested retail price, the Model 1912 was affordable. Chambered for 2-$1/2$ inch shells, the standard gun had a plain walnut pistol grip stock and grooved action slide handle. The length of the stock was 13-5/8 inches; the drop at the comb was 1-$7/16$ inches; drop at the heel, 2-7/16 inches. The Model 1912 came with a diagonally checkered, hard rubber buttplate containing the Winchester Repeating Arms Co. logo within a circle. The standard gun weighed approximately 5-$3/4$ pounds.

Winchester immediately offered a list of options, which included a fancy walnut stock and action slide handle, not checkered for $13.00; checkering for the fancy stock and action slide handle was an additional $5.00. Changes in length or drop of stock to order were $10.00. A matted rib added another $5.00 and a second interchangeable barrel, complete with magazine and action slide handle, was priced at $16.50. If one went all out for a deluxe model with an extra barrel, the price would have been $69.50. There were a total of 12 different configurations in which one could purchase the first Model 1912.[6]

1. Standard Grade, full choke
2. Standard Grade, matted rib, full choke [a]
3. Standard Grade, modified choke
4. Standard Grade, matted rib, modified choke
5. Standard Grade, cylinder choke
6. Standard Grade, matted rib, cylinder choke
7. Fancy Finished, full choke [b]
8. Fancy Finished, matted rib, full choke [c]
9. Fancy Finished, modified choke
10. Fancy Finished, matted rib, modified choke
11. Fancy Finished, cylinder choke
12. Fancy Finished, matted rib, cylinder choke
[a] Items 2, 4 and 6 were available at an extra cost of $5.00
[b] Items 7, 9 and 11 were available at an extra cost of $18.00
[c] Items 8, 10 and 12 were available at an extra cost of $23.00

[6] The Greatest Hammerless Repeating Shotgun Ever Built – The Model 12 1912-1964 by Dave Riffle, Dave Riffle, 1995.

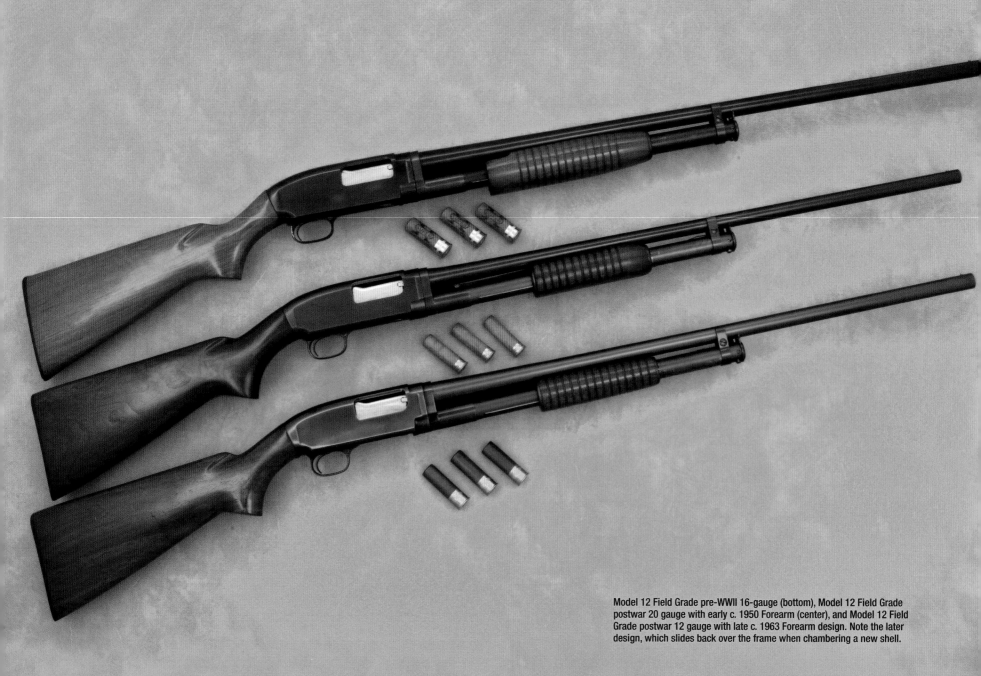

Model 12 Field Grade pre-WWII 16-gauge (bottom), Model 12 Field Grade postwar 20 gauge with early c. 1950 Forearm (center), and Model 12 Field Grade postwar 12 gauge with late c. 1963 Forearm design. Note the later design, which slides back over the frame when chambering a new shell.

The roll engraved barrel marking on the first Model 1912 shotguns had the manufacturer's address and patent dates on the right side of the barrel. The first stamping read:

MANUFACTURED BY THE WINCHESTER REPEATING ARMS CO. NEW HAVEN, CONNECTICUT. U.S.A. PAT. JULY 21. 1896. FEB. 22. JUNE 12. 1898. SEPT. 7. 1909. MAY 17. 24. 31. JUNE 7. 14. 28. JULY 5. 12. 1910.

The left side of the barrel was stamped:

TRADE MARK
NICKEL STEEL —- WINCHESTER —- MOD. 1912 – 20 GA. FULL
REG. IN U.S. PAT. OFF. & FGN.

Early examples have 13 grooves in the forearm wood and after around serial number 23500, 14 grooves. The length of the forearm also increased from 5-inches in length to 5-3/4 inches. At serial No. 23500 another notable change was made with the addition of an alignment arrow on the receiver extension and magazine tube. The arrow on the magazine tube points toward the receiver and must line up with the arrow on the receiver.

Beginning in 1914, W.R.A. Co. added 12-gauge and 16-gauge models to the Model 1912 line thus increasing the number of choices and features across the board. The new 16-gauge field guns were available with 26-inch, full choke barrels only and chambered for 2-9/16 inch shells. The new 12-gauge models came with 30-inch, full choke barrels with optional modified or cylinder choke barrels. Chambered for 2-3/4 inch shells, the heftier 12-gauge models weighed 7-1/4 pounds. Part of the added weight was a larger receiver, which T.C. Johnson regarded as a safety feature due to the greater pressures and recoil developed by 12-gauge shells.

Adding to the expanding list of options offered by Winchester was a greater selection of barrels for 12-gauge models, which were available in 26, 28, 30, or 32-inch lengths in full, modified, or cylinder choke.

One of the most distinguishing features of the Model 1912 (Model 12) is the design of the barrel. There were standard barrels, matted barrels, and raised matted barrels, and after November 1919, ventilated ribbed barrels. The most common is the matted barrel, which was designed to match the matting on the top of the receiver. This represents itself as finely scribed lines in narrow rows along the length of the barrel from the breech end to the top of the muzzle. Although attractive, its purpose was more than just styling, the matting greatly reduced glare from the top of the barrel and thus improved sighting for the shooter. The raised matted rib was of-

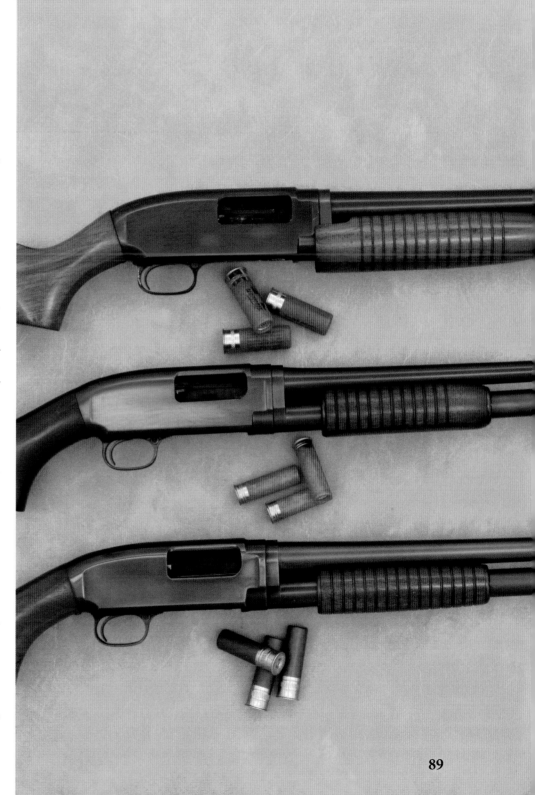

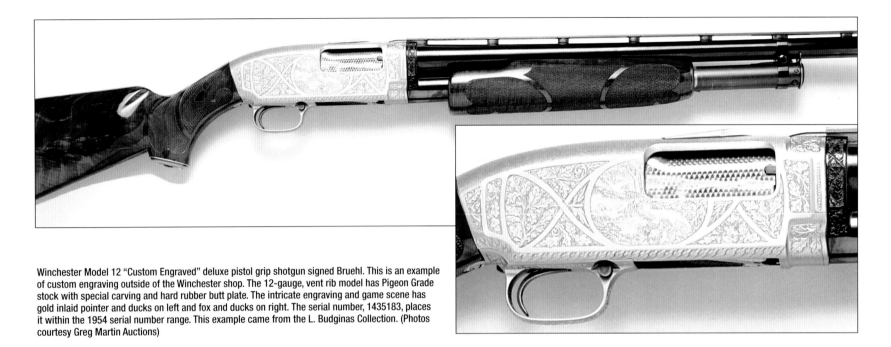

Winchester Model 12 "Custom Engraved" deluxe pistol grip shotgun signed Bruehl. This is an example of custom engraving outside of the Winchester shop. The 12-gauge, vent rib model has Pigeon Grade stock with special carving and hard rubber butt plate. The intricate engraving and game scene has gold inlaid pointer and ducks on left and fox and ducks on right. The serial number, 1435183, places it within the 1954 serial number range. This example came from the L. Budginas Collection. (Photos courtesy Greg Martin Auctions)

fered from 1913 through 1959 and featured the matting atop a narrow steel rib soldered to the top of the barrel. Winchesters with this feature are referred to as "solid rib" models. Winchester applied for the patent on its ventilated rib barrel design on November 25, 1919. Today, vent rib barrels are a standard feature on the majority of Winchester shotguns offered.

The offering of different grades of shotguns dated back to Winchester's first imported models in the 1880s. The practice had been refined with the Model 1897 and continued with the new Model 1912. The three principle types were Tournament Grade, Trap Grade, and Pigeon Grade, the latter being the first Model 1912 to provide factory engraving.

While stocks and forearms on all three grades featured select fancy walnut and intricate hand checkering, the Pigeon Grade guns were beautifully and highly embellished. In his book, Riffle paints a literary picture of Pigeon Grade engraving:

"The typical pigeon engraving, on the right side of the receiver, incorporated an English pointer and an English setter standing on a grassy hill. The two dogs are looking down at two quail, feeding, in the cover of some bushes and trees. This handsome scene is accented with mountains along the horizon. The left side of the receiver shows five mallard ducks in flight over a grassy marsh, highlighted with mountains along the horizon. Flawless and ornate, the vacant parts of the receiver were detailed in scroll: The remaining sides of the receiver, the bottom of the receiver near the serial number, the trigger guard, the top of the receiver, and the top of the receiver extension. The most significant aspect of the engraving pattern was an elaborately engraved pigeon on the top back portion of the receiver." The price of a Pigeon Grade Model 1912 was $105 in 1914. Today, these same examples trade among collectors for thousands of dollars, and deluxe, custom engraved models can easily command well over $10,000.

Of that latter category, the custom engraved Winchester has always been among the most coveted of American shotguns, regardless of model. Much of the artistry that was seen on early examples evolved from 19th century engraving styles created by Louis D. Nimschke, Gustave Young, Cuno A. Helfricht, and the very talented Ulrichs, who like Young and Nimschke, established themselves with engraving work for the Colt's Firearms Manufacturing Company in the mid to late 1800s.

Few engravers signed their work, thus their "style" often became their signature. Riffle notes that "Winchester engravers, such as Angelo Stokes, John Gough and the Ulrichs, were the premier masters of their time. Examples of these Winchester factory engravers' work are rare and considered the ultimate by collectors. John Gough was employed by Winchester from 1905 to 1918 and Anglo Stokes was employed from 1905 to 1917." Fortunately, the Ulrich family of engravers lent their talents to Winchester the longest, beginning in the late 1860s with Conrad F., John, and Herman Leslie Ulrich and continuing until the last Ulrich actively engraving, Alden George, the son of Conrad F. Ulrich, passed away in 1949 at age 62. Better known as George, he joined Winchester in 1919 just as his father and uncle were going into full retirement from general engraving. R.L. Wilson notes in his book *Winchester Engraving*, "Family history also states that George engraved a gun for every United States President from 1913 on, with the exception of Herbert Hoover for whom he engraved a fishing rod." Adds Wilson, "George was the first of the Ulrich engravers to receive published, identified recognition of his work. Unfortunately the publicity, a detailed, thoroughly illustrated article in Outdoor Life, December 1950, appeared a year after his death."

Angelo J. Stokes and William H. Gough were also prominent engravers for Winchester, however, Gough's work was limited. Stokes went to work for Winchester in 1905 and he remained in New Haven until around 1917. His later work was commissioned by a number of different manufacturers, including Winchester. Angelo Stokes died July 10, 1951 at age 83. [7]

Fortunately for Winchester, George Ulrich had taken on an apprentice, John Kusmit, and under Ulrich's guidance he began a long and illustrious career in New Haven. After George's death, John succeeded his long-time mentor in 1949, and along with brother Nick, the Kusmits became Winchester's only in-house engravers throughout the 1950s.

In 1918 Winchester officially renamed the Model 1912, the Model 12. Two new versions were also added, the Model 12 Riot gun and Model 12 Trench gun. The following year another change was initiated; the forearm was increased in length to 7-inches and had 18 grooves. The aforementioned ventilated ribbed barrel was also introduced in 1919. With the beginning of a new decade, in 1920 Winchester introduced a deluxe forearm as a special order for 12 gauge models. They were a hefty 11-3/8 inches in length with checkered side panels and a triple-checkered diamond pattern on the bottom. In 1922 Winchester answered the requests of shooters for a heavy rubber recoil pad of Winchester design. This was made available on the Model 12 in all three gauges. The first examples were marked:

MADE IN U.S.A.
Winchester
TRADE MARK
PAT. JUNE 6, 1922

[7] *Winchester Engraving by R.L. Wilson, 1975 Beinfeld Publishing, Inc.*

Choke Tubes
Getting Your Shot Together

Choke is a word that has been associated with shotguns for over 150 years and it is matter-of-factly spoken with a certain degree of assumed knowledge on the part of the gun owner. But what exactly is a choke and why are there so many variations? The answer is two fold. A choke is measured in percentages of shot within a 30-inch circle at 40 yards, and this is achieved by the constriction of the shot as it leaves the muzzle.

There are four basic chokes: Cylinder bore, Improved Cylinder, Modified, and Full. There are also variations such as Improved Modified and Skeet Choke. What it all boils down to is the amount of shot concentrated at the center of the target.

Cylinder bore is just as the name implies, the full diameter of the bore measured at the muzzle. Using a 12-gauge as our example, the bore and muzzle diameter are the same, .725 inches. This allows the widest spread of the shot, which at 40-yards in a 30-inch circle is 40-percent. That means 60 percent of the shot is going to hit outside of that circle. This was the choke usually found on Riot guns used by lawmen, thus the term "scattergun approach." The down side is that less than half of the shot is going to hit the center of the target, but you're probably going to hit something. Just pick an area and shoot.

Improved is the first choke and this is a constriction of .006, thus narrowing the muzzle from .725 to .719 inches. The net result is that the shot pattern now changes to 50-percent within a 30-inch circle. You need to be a bit more precise on where you aim but one half of all shot will be in the center of the target. This is one of the most popular of all chokes, second only to Modified.

A Modified choke increases the muzzle constriction by .015 to a diameter of .710 and now 60-percent of the shot will hit center. A combination Modified and Improved Cylinder is the most common in side-by-side and superposed shotguns, allowing the shooter to select from two chokes depending upon the size and distance of the target, thus the use of double triggers or a single selective trigger.

Last is Full choke, the most constriction, .030 with a muzzle diameter reduced to .695. The net result is a pattern with 70-percent of the shot striking within the 30-inch circle. If you're taking aim at high-flying Canadian Geese, this is the choke you want.

While the bore diameter, muzzle diameter, and constriction changes with each shotgun gauge, the percentage of shot at 40-yards within a 30-inch circle is a constant.

The use of adjustable chokes (Poly Choke, Cutts Compensator) and interchangeable chokes (such as WinChoke) in even greater varying degrees and half steps, allows a shooter to dial in the degree of choke required or simply unscrew one choke and replace it with another. This is a great advantage with today's single, double barrel, and superposed shotguns, allowing a shooter to have at his or her disposal all of the various chokes in one gun.

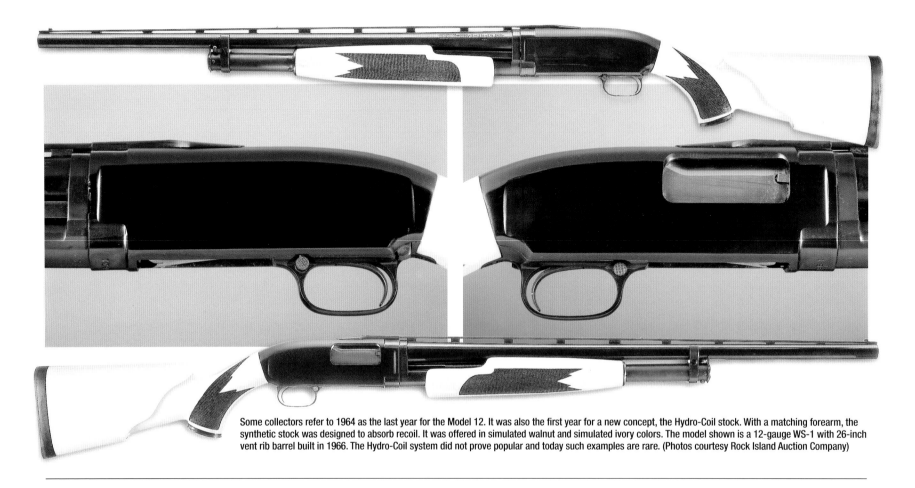

Some collectors refer to 1964 as the last year for the Model 12. It was also the first year for a new concept, the Hydro-Coil stock. With a matching forearm, the synthetic stock was designed to absorb recoil. It was offered in simulated walnut and simulated ivory colors. The model shown is a 12-gauge WS-1 with 26-inch vent rib barrel built in 1966. The Hydro-Coil system did not prove popular and today such examples are rare. (Photos courtesy Rock Island Auction Company)

By the mid 1920s George Ulrich had created standardized engraving patterns for the Model 12, which were cataloged and numbered 12-1 through 12-5. There were, however, more variations because Ulrich had additional 12-1A, 12-1B, and 12-1C versions, all of which offered detailed hunting scenes. The basic pattern, 12-1, featured only scrollwork on the receiver, while style 12-5 was the most elaborate. Custom-engraved examples could also be made to order featuring elaborate scrollwork on the barrel and frame, and highly embellished hunting scenes on the receiver. Today, these very rare examples are highly prized among collectors, especially if signed by one of the Ulrichs.

From the mid- to late-1920s the United States had experienced unprecedented financial growth, but on October 28, 1929 America's seemingly endless eco-nomic boom went bust. In one day U.S. securities lost $26 billion in value. The stock market crash delivered a staggering blow to the nation's economy, and though it would take nearly a year before the deeper ramifications were realized, the world had embarked on a treacherous financial path.

Today, we tend to think of the Great Depression's impact in very general terms – unemployment, bread lines, soup kitchens, and economic strife. All true. America was shaken to its very roots and it would take the better part of the 1930s for the nation to recover. Among U.S. industries, automakers suffered greater losses than almost any component of the American economy, and the attrition rate among long established manufacturers was nearly overwhelming. Gone by the end of the decade

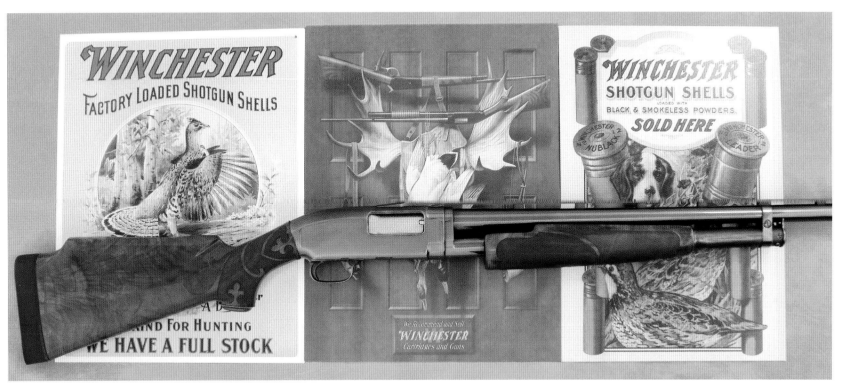

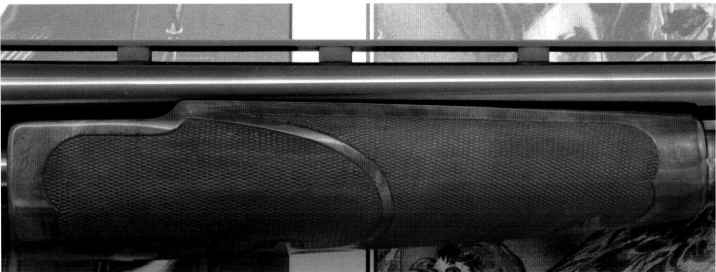

In the early postwar era, this was the most deluxe version one could buy in a Model 12, a Pigeon Grade gun. This example built in 1949 has all of the deluxe features except for an engraved receiver. A skeet gun with ventilated rib and engine turned breech bolt; the base price in 1949 was $230. The deluxe wood and style 12-B carving was an additional $40.00. Had the original purchaser added style 12-5 engraving, the cost would have been an additional $112. (Author's Collection)

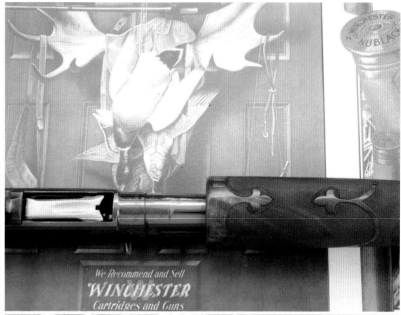

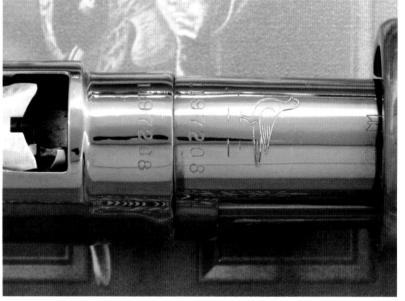

Pistol grip and underside of forearm displays the beautiful style 12-B checkering and carving with profuse fleur-de-lis patterns.

The gold Pigeon on the receiver extension was the mark of the finest Model 12 Winchester. In 1940 the Pigeon on the bottom of the receiver extension became a permanent insignia for all Pigeon Grade guns. Also note the engine-turned carrier.

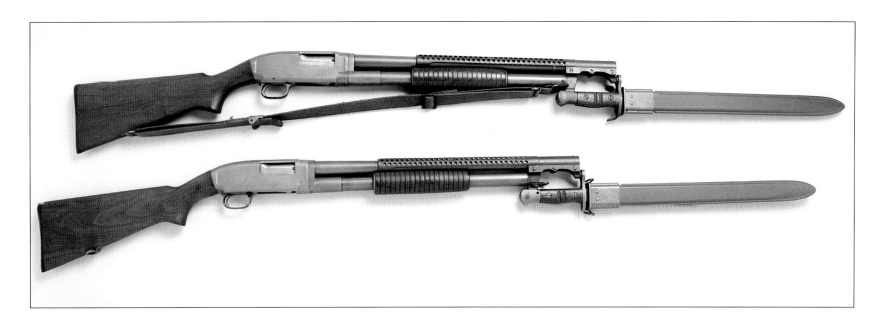

were Marmon, Franklin, Pierce-Arrow, Auburn, Cord, and Duesenberg, among others.

The American firearms industry was not immune to the effects of a struggling economy either. In 1930, Winchester lowered the advertised price for the standard grade Model 12 from $48.95 to $39.50. This was the first time in the company's history that prices had been reduced. Further compounding Winchester's problems were its stainless steel barrels introduced in 1926. They had been a dismal failure on the market and were withdrawn in 1931. The timing, however, worked in Winchester's favor, as this was also the year New Haven introduced its new Winchester Proof Steel barrel technology. The new steel alloy was hailed as the finest development in metal known to gun making and won Winchester recognition as a leader in the treatment of alloy steels.

Beginning in 1931, Model 12 barrels were proudly stamped:

MADE IN U.S.A.

WINCHESTER PROOF STEEL —- WINCHESTER —- MOD. 12 – 12 GA.

TRADE MARK

The same legend was applied to 16 and 20 gauge models, and the chamber size and choke stamped beneath the gauge stamping.

Despite this success, there were serious financial problems brewing in New Haven, problems that were rooted to the past. Beginning in 1917 Winchester had expanded its production facilities to meet U.S. and Allied military demands during World War I. However, following the Armistice, Winchester found itself with surplus workspace, and this did not set well with the board of directors. Management decided that the facilities would be utilized to manufacture a line of non-firearms related products bearing the trademarked Winchester name. In theory, this was a very good idea. Winchester was one of the most recognized brand names in America, and trading on its reputation should have worked in the company's favor. New products included fishing tackle, pocketknives, sporting goods, gardening and work tools, and clay targets, among others. Winchester had also been manufacturing its own ammunition for rifles and shotguns since the late 19th century. Winchester was almost a household name, but most of the new secondary products, including a line of Winchester refrigerators, were just marginally successful, or in

Winchester went to war in 1941 and by the time U.S. troops were in battle many were armed with the U.S. Model 12 Trench gun. The combat ready shotguns were 12-gauge 2-3/4 inch, with 21-inch barrel and cylinder choke. The beautiful blue Winchester finish, however, was not for combat and the Trench guns were given a dull Parkerized finish with oil finished walnut stock. U.S. Model 12s are marked with U.S. and Ordnance bomb motif on the right side of the frame. Like the Model 97 Trench guns of WWI, the Model 12s were fitted with perforated steel cooling sleeves and bayonet lugs. (Photo courtesy Greg Martin Auctions)

the case of the latter, unsuccessful. The heavy financial losses from these investments were to prove Winchester's undoing as the Great Depression swept prosperity from every corner of the nation. After 74 years in business the Winchester Repeating Arms Company went into receivership in 1931.

This was not a time of Federal bailouts or easy money. Had it not been for the Depression, Winchester's competitors might have flocked to the kill like turkey buzzards, but they did not. Saunders Norvell, the President of Remington in Ilion, New York, investigated the purchase of Winchester, but due to anti-trust laws and low cash reserves, Remington's board of directors decided against it. It would have been an ironic turn of events had Remington purchased Winchester. Back in 1887, E. Remington & Sons had itself gone into receivership and was purchased by Marcellus Hartley and the New York sporting good firm of Hartley & Graham for $200,000. Winchester then paid Hartley $100,000 for one-half interest, with W.R.A. Co. President T.G. Bennett appointed Vice President of Remington! No doubt it was a novel situation for the Ilion, New York, arms maker, having the head of its principal competitor privy to every design. The novelty, however, wore off and eight years later Winchester sold its interests back to Marcellus Hartley. In 1912 he merged Remington with Hartley & Graham and the Union Metallic Cartridge Company (founded by Hartley after the Civil War) to form Remington-UMC.

The point of this dissertation is to underscore the financial wealth of munitions manufacturers, for it was one of Remington-UMC's largest competitors who finally stepped in to save Winchester in 1931 – John Olin and the Western Cartridge Company.

With the Olin family money and Western Cartridge behind it, Winchester weathered the 1930s like Cadillac under the protective wing of General Motors, and production of the Model 12 continued at a brisk pace throughout the decade and into the 1940s.

During the 1930s a number of additional improvements were made to the Model 12's design and on February 15, 1935, Winchester announced a new longer range fowling gun, the Model 12 Heavy Duck gun. Offered only in 12 gauge with either 30-inch or 32-inch full choke barrel, it was shipped with the new two-shot wooden plug already inserted into the magazine, in keeping with the Presidential Proclamation of February 2, 1935, regarding migratory bird hunting.

In 1937 a new 28 gauge small-bore shotgun was added to the Model 12 line. This was the first new chambering since 1914, and notes Riffle, "This new model was light and fast handling, with little recoil, and all of the advantages for which the Model 12 was renowned."

Winchester Model 12 No. 1 20-gauge with an original Winchester canvas and leather gun case. (Courtesy Dave Riffle)

Built on the 20-gauge frame but designed to use 28-gauge shells, the first examples in 1937 were Standard/Field Grades only, chambered for 2-7/8 inch shells, with 2-1/2 inch chambering available as an option. In a supplemental flyer in November 1937, Winchester announced the additional availability of the 28-gauge model in Standard Trap, Skeet Grade, Special Trap and Pigeon Grade with either 26-inch or 28-inch barrel lengths. Chokes offered were full, modified, Winchester skeet choke (WS1) and cylinder bore. The lower-priced Field Grade guns could be ordered only with solid matted rib barrels in full or modified choke.

The introduction of the 28-gauge model also saw the first use of a cartridge guide attached to the side of the carrier to prevent the smaller shells from dropping out of the ejector port. The following year this feature was adopted on all Model 12 shotguns.

When America entered World War II following the attack on Pearl Harbor, Winchester too, went to war as it had in 1917 producing ammunition and Trench guns for the U.S. military and its Allies. On December 15, 1942, the 1,000,000th Model 12 was presented to General Henry A. "Hap" Arnold, Chief of the Army Air Forces. The presentation had a somewhat surprising benefit for Winchester. General Arnold used the Model 12 in a demonstration before a group of student gunners, showing them how to shoot ahead of a fast-moving target to bring it down. "Instead of airplanes, clay pigeons and shotguns were the ideal weapon to teach the technique of knocking Axis ducks out of the sky," said Arnold. The ceremonial Winchester Model 12 given to the General was of the type adopted for use in gunnery training. Winchester Model 12s were ordered and sent to the various military training centers for gunnery school.[8]

During the war Winchester continued to produce shotguns for both the military and civilian use. The only changes were in price, which increased significantly in the years between 1942 and 1944. The Standard Field Grade guns went from $56.70 to $78.50, while the most expensive production model (Pigeon Grade was a special order), the Model 12 Trap Gun went from $117.00 to $161.30. [9]

In 1947 one significant styling change was introduced, a new style flat bottom forearm with 11 grooves for Field Grade guns. The new design gave shooters better purchase of the forearm, improving both accuracy and balance. It was also the best looking standard forearm offered for the Model 12. It was changed once again in 1955 for a new style known as a Beavertail forearm variation. This last style is distinguished by a tapered rear, which slides under the frame, and 14 grooves along its length.

Winchester entered the postwar market with strong finances, a product line of Model 12s offered in 90 different variations and a booming demand from consumers willing to pay higher prices. For Winchester, the 1950s held nothing but promise.

Production continued throughout the '50s with "running changes" in design and manufacturing. The Model 12 remained the most popular shotgun sold in America, despite significant increases in pricing, especially for Pigeon Grade guns, special orders and engraving. By 1955 a Pigeon Grade gun was averaging $250 (a low of $209.90 to high of $295.50 for a Trap Gun with ventilated rib), a Monte Carlo stock with cheek piece or offset added another $30.00, and engraving ranged from $65.00 for style 12-1 to $210.00 for style 12-5. One could easily spend over $530.00 for a top-of-the-line Pigeon Grade Model 12. In 1955, that was a very expensive shotgun. A Series Sixty-Two Cadillac coupe sold for only $3,568.00. And that's a fair comparison, because the Winchester Pigeon Grade was the Cadillac of shotguns.

The first new postwar addition to the Model 12 line came in 1959 with the introduction of the 12-gauge Featherweight. Available in Field Grade only, four different combinations of barrel lengths and chokes were offered. The Featherweight was not only distinguished by its lighter construction (approximately six pounds, 10 ounces) and economic $94.95 retail price, but by the absence of a cartridge guide. This year also marked the end of production for the Model 12 Super Grade field guns.

As another new decade approached Winchester was slowly beginning a transformation in its manufacturing process to reduce costs. It began in 1959 with an almost insignificant change. The magazine band and carriers for the Model 12 were investment cast, rather than machined. It didn't seem like much at the time but the future of the Model 12, and that of nearly all Winchesters, was about to take a new direction.

In 1960 Winchester discontinued the 28-gauge Model 12. This was also the first year the factory offered cataloged "Special Ornamentation" for all Model 12s. There were eight engraving styles for the receiver and two carving styles for the stock (there had been special carving styles for stocks and forearms since the 1940s), either a 10kt. gold or silver oval nameplate inlet into the stock, a Gold Plated Trigger, Gold Inlaid Initials on the trigger guard, and leather covering on Winchester recoil pads. Special order engraving and carving were still offered and noted as, "Price on application."

In 1963 Winchester was on the verge of a manufacturing epiphany, or as author Dave Riffle described it, "The end was near." This was to be the last year for Field Grade guns. The final price was $109.95. Magnum Duck guns were

[8] *The Greatest Hammerless Repeating Shotgun Ever Built – The Model 12 1912-1964 by Dave Riffle, Dave Riffle, 1995.*
[9] *Ibid.*

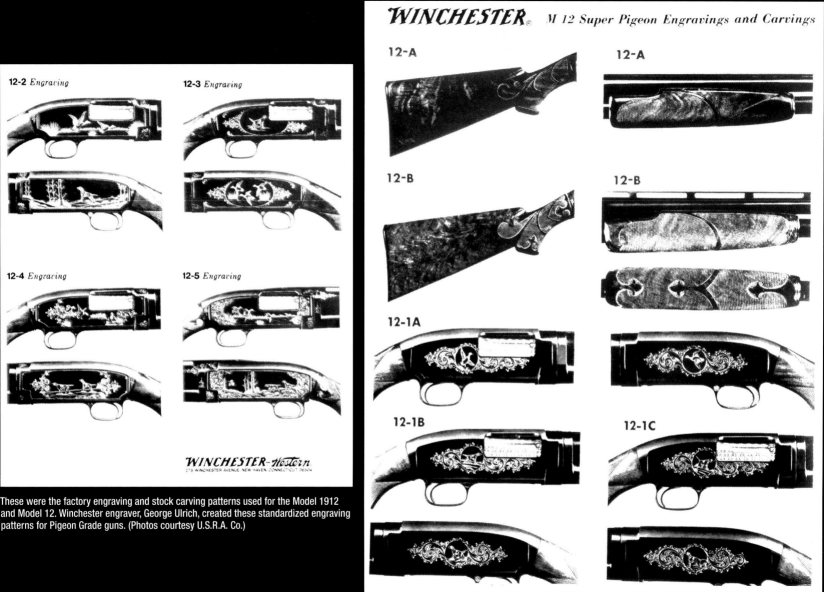

12-2 *Engraving*

12-3 *Engraving*

12-4 *Engraving*

12-5 *Engraving*

WINCHESTER-Western
275 WINCHESTER AVENUE, NEW HAVEN, CONNECTICUT 06504

These were the factory engraving and stock carving patterns used for the Model 1912 and Model 12. Winchester engraver, George Ulrich, created these standardized engraving patterns for Pigeon Grade guns. (Photos courtesy U.S.R.A. Co.)

WINCHESTER® *M 12 Super Pigeon Engravings and Carvings*

12-A

12-A

12-B

12-B

12-1A

12-1B

12-1C

also discontinued and offered for $122. The base price of Pigeon Grade models was increased to $297.50 and for good reason. This would be one of the only models left in production beginning in 1964. All Winchester Model 12s were discontinued except the Pigeon, Trap and Skeet guns, and the new Hydro-Coil systems were advertised on the Model 12s.

According to Winchester, "The kick in the world-famous Winchester Model 12 skeet and trap shotguns has been reduced to a gentle shove." Hydro-Coil was claimed to reduce felt recoil by 85 percent. "Whether you are an occasional shooter, hunter, or competitive shooter who fires steadily for hours, Winchester shotguns equipped with Hydro-Coil have plenty to offer," claimed promotional literature in 1964. At the heart of the Hydro-Coil system was a design that took Winchester five years to perfect, a three part unit, something like an automobile shock absorber, built into a special plastic butt stock. Most of the recoil was taken up by the system before it could reach the shooter's shoulder, with the rest of the "kick" spread over a longer period of time so that felt recoil was more of a gentle shove. It was, if nothing else, an unusual looking stock with a larger rear portion shrouding a primary stock attached to the receiver. It was offered in both standard and Monte Carlo styles. The pistol grip and forearm were accented with simulated checkering. In all other respects the gun was a Model 12. Despite the support of John Olin, who thought the Hydro-Coil system showed promise, it was not a sales success. Hydro-Coil remained an option through the late 1960s.

We often hear the term "Pre-'64" applied to the Winchester Model 12, as well as Model 70 bolt-action rifles, and Model 88 lever-action rifles. This is historically a line of demarcation for Winchester collectors. These models all continued in production after 1964 but they were no longer built the same way.

After 1964 Model 12s have a Y prefix within the serial number. This indicates a model produced through an investment casting process, the technique first used in 1959. With investment casting nothing is hand machined or hand made. The frames and all exterior parts are cast, even the vent rib, which is pinned to the barrel rather than being milled.

Model 12s built from 1965 through 1980, although superb, are often regarded as lacking the handcraftsmanship, fit and finish typical of Model 1912 and Model 12 shotguns built from 1912 to 1964. Author and Winchester collector Dave Riffle summed it up best: "The finesse of the old craftsmen was gone. They simply cast the parts, assembled and blued them, and out the door they went."

This doesn't mean that today's Winchesters and all those built since 1965 are not as good, or even better mechanically, but guns, like cars assembled by robots with parts turned out by CNC machines, lack something that only a craftsmen's touch can provide. You could say that these inanimate objects of our desires have lost their humanity.

Post '64 Model 12 shotguns were offered in a variety of models beginning with the Super Pigeon Grade, available with 26, 28, or 30-inch vent rib barrel and any choke. As custom as post '64 examples can be, the action was hand honed, and the breech block and loading flap were engine turned. The guns featured "B" checkering and No. 5 engraving and were also available with custom order grade walnut stocks. The Super Pigeon Grade was built through 1972.

The Model 12 Field Grade offered the same barrel and choke selections, had a jeweled bolt and hand checkering. This model was discontinued in 1975.

Model 12 Skeet guns were produced with a 26-inch vent rib barrel, skeet style stock and recoil pad. They were offered from 1972 through 1975.

A Model 12 Trap Grade was built from 1972 until Model 12 production ended in 1980. The Trap featured a 30-inch vent rib barrel, full choke, trap-style stock, straight or Monte Carlo, and recoil pad.

There were three Limited Edition Model 12s produced beginning with a special Model 12 DU exclusively for Ducks Unlimited chapters. Miroku built 4,000 Model 12 Grade I shotguns in 20-gauge with 2-3/4 inch chambers and 26-inch vent rib barrels bored modified. These were available from 1993 to 1995. As with other models built for Winchester by Miroku, the barrels were stamped Made in Japan. The last Limited Edition Model 12 was a Grade IV 20-gauge similar to the Grade I but with select walnut, 22 lines per inch checkering and high gloss finish. The Grade IV was embellished with extensive game scenes and multiple gold inlays. Production was limited to 1,000 examples built from 1993 to 1995.

The entire Model 12 line was "technically" discontinued after 1980, ending a remarkable 68 years of continuous production. However, in 1984 Y series Model 12s were offered one last time through a private contract with U.S.R.A. Co. They were offered with Grades 1A through 1C and Grade 2 through 5 engraving and available in Field, Trap, or Skeet configurations. Suggested retail prices ranged from $1,375 to $2,450. There was also a 3-barrel set with Grade 5 engraving and gold inlays which sold for $6,000.[10]

Throughout all its changes, and even after 1964, the Model 12 was just as Winchester had claimed in its very first advertisement – "The Lightest, Strongest, and Handsomest Repeating Shotgun Made."[11]

[10] 25th Edition Blue Book of Gun Values by S.P. Fjestad, Blue Book Publications, 2004.
[11] This was a claim Winchester proudly made, however, Winchester's Model 1912 hammerless was not the first. The John Browning-designed Stevens Model 520 preceded it in 1904, the first modern "hammerless" pump shotgun. In 1907 Remington introduced its Model 10 hammerless pump. The Marlin Model 28 hammerless pump shotgun was introduced in 1913, a year after the Winchester Model 1912. Early Pump Guns by John Malloy.

Three of the cased Eight of Eight Grand American three barrel sets chambered in 20, 28, and .410-gauge. Built by U.S Repeating Arms Company in the early 1980s, the sets featured 26-inch ventilated rib barrels. Each barrel, as shown, had its own forearm. Only four of the proposed eight sets were produced, each engraved by the legendary Howard Dove. These are among the most valuable of all Custom Shop Model 21 Winchesters. (Courtesy Dave Riffle)

Chapter Four
The Greatest American Side-by-Side of the 20th Century
Winchester Model 21 and the Master Engravers

In the world of shotguns, progress may march on, but it does not necessarily march over previous designs. As a point of fact, the Winchester Model 1897 remained in production until 1957 despite the superior design and greater popularity of the Model 12. European and British gunmakers still, to this day, manufacture high-quality, handcrafted, breech-loading double hammer guns, even though that design dates back to the 1870s. Double guns by Holland and Holland, J. Purdey & Sons, Ltd. and Boss & Co. Ltd. are still regarded as the best in the world. Gun collectors' seek out the finest examples of vintage Parker, L.C. Smith, A.H. Fox, Lefever, Winchester Model 21, and Ithaca doubles, and reproductions of the Winchester Model 1901 lever-action shotgun and Model 1897 slide-action shotgun are presently being made in China. This would be akin to Ford running an assembly line of Model T Touring cars alongside the latest Mustang GT. Obsolescence, it seems, is not in the gun maker's lexicon. And this was just as true in the 1920s, when Winchester was the world leader in every field of shotgun design and manufacturing…except one.

It was no surprise then, that Winchester introduced a double gun in 1930. Well, considering the financial state of W.R.A. Co. in 1930, maybe it was a surprise. The financial plight of the company, discussed in the previous chapter, truly underscores Winchester's commitment to design and produce what head gun designer T.C. Johnson considered an American side-by-side equal to the best European doubles. However, without the support of John M. Olin, who was a great enthusiast of the double gun, the Model 21 would never have succeeded in the financially turbulent era of the 1930s.

T.G. Bennett had long considered the idea of a Winchester-built double. The company had experienced considerable success with its imported British-built side-by-sides in the 1880s, but that had come to a stop when P.G. Sanford, manager of Winchester's New York store, expressed doubt that the company should continue to sell imported shotguns while Winchester was manufacturing American ammunition and firearms.[1] Bennett agreed, and the practice stopped on May 12, 1884.

While the Browning-design for the Model 1887 lever-action shotgun was being refined at Winchester from 1884 to 1886, W.R.A. Co. was without a shotgun and the subject of building a double gun no doubt came up, but nothing was done for almost a quarter of a century until T.C. Johnson pursued the idea in 1911. While finalizing the design for the Model 1912, Johnson applied for a patent on April 10, 1911 covering his design for a superior safety mechanism for double barrel shotguns. United States Patent No. 995,790 was given to Johnson on June 20, 1911, and subsequently assigned to W.R.A. Co. Winchester, however, was focused on the launch of the Model 1912 slide-action, 20-gauge repeater, and a double barrel shotgun seemed, at the moment, obsolete. This, however, was not the case, as pointed out just as few years later by one of Winchester's own managers, Edwin Pugsly, who was to become instrumental in the creation of the Model 21.

While on a hunting trip in 1919, Pugsly wrote a letter to J.E. Otterson, the new President of Winchester, (T.G. Bennett having become Chairman of the Board)[2], "It seems to me now that the double barrel gun is going to play an increasingly important part as a game gun in this country and I would suggest that we consider carefully the possibility of developing a double barrel hammers… gun…"[3] However convincing Pugsly's letter might have been, it was not until 1924 that any further consideration was given to building a double gun.

---

[1] Winchester's Finest The Model 21 by Ned Schwing, Krause Publications, 1990. [2] In 1919 control of W.R.A. Co. passed from the Winchester-Bennett Family to Kidder, Peabody & Co. in a financial restructuring that aborted bankruptcy and gave the New Haven company much need operating cash. Bennett was made Chairman of the Board, J.E. Otterson, President, and Louis K. Liggett (founder of Rexall Drug Stores and United Drug Co.) who served as Director of W.R.A. Co. Winchester An American Legend by R.L. Wilson, Random House, 1991. [3] Winchester's Finest The Model 21 by Ned Schwing, Krause Publications, 1990.

Introduced in 1930 and produced though 1959 the vast majority of Model 21s were Field Grade. Pictured are a Field Grade12-gauge, Field Grade 16-gauge, and Field Grade 20-gauge. The 12-gauge has 26-inch barrels choked WS1 WS2, the 16-gauge (manufactured in 1948) has 26-inch barrels choked Improved/Modified, and the 20-gauge, 26-inch barrels choked WS1 WS2. (Courtesy Dave Riffle)

The real inspiration behind the first Winchester double, as always, was competition. The list of high-quality, American-made side-by-side shotguns was growing, and Winchester's name was absent. By the mid 1920s, Johnson and his staff were at work on a new design but soon realized that building a high-quality double gun wasn't easy. The complexity of the double was more problematic for Johnson than that of the Model 1911 semi-automatic shotgun or Model 1912 slide-action. Edwin Pugsley, who was Winchester's factory manager, brought in George Lewis, an inventor who had spent the better part of his career specializing in the design and improvement of double guns. Working alongside Johnson and his staff, which included factory designers Louis Stiennon and Frank Burton, the blueprint for what was to become the Winchester Model 21 emerged. The first patents were filed by Burton in December 1929.

Thomas Johnson had told his long-time friend and boss, T.G. Bennett, that the Model 21 would be "equal in design and quality to any double model anywhere, and of superior design and craftsmanship. This will be a lifetime gun for the most particular shooter," he assured Bennett.[4] Sadly, Thomas Gray Bennett, who had guided Winchester since assuming the President's chair from his father-in-law in 1880, passed away in 1930.

The American economy was on shaky ground, much the same as Winchester, which had already been facing hard financial decisions before the stock market crash. Though hampered financially, the New Haven gunmaker somehow managed to get the Model 21 into production by 1930, but less than a year later, on January 22, 1931, Winchester went into receivership. In an otherwise disastrous year, the strikingly handsome Model 21 side-by-side shotgun was the company's only triumph. And that was fortunate, because the new double gun had an immediate champion in John M. Olin, the son of Winchester Repeating Arms Company's new owner, Franklin W. Olin.

John Olin was already a Model 21 owner before the Western Cartridge Company and Olin family stepped in and purchased Winchester in December 1931. A 39 year-old chemical engineer who had begun his career at Western Cartridge, John Olin

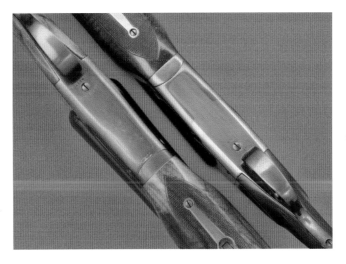

Underside shows the TRAP SKEET markings forward of the trigger guard distinguishing this 20-gauge model built in 1938. The other example is a Tournament Grade Model 21 stamped SKEET. The Tournament Grade was discontinued in 1934.

was appointed first vice president of Winchester. In 1944 he became president of Olin Industries, the parent company of both Western Cartridge Company and W.R.A. Co.

The Model 21 was an innovative design that broke with the traditional canons of 19th and early 20th century double gun construction. First was the frame. The finest examples being built at the time made use of color-casehardened steel. Winchester eschewed this custom and built the frame using its patented Winchester Proof Steel, a chrome molybdenum alloy having a tensile strength of over 90 tons per square inch.[5] Structurally, the Model 21 was unrivaled. The design of the action and locking mechanism alone encompassed nine new patents by Louis Stiennon, and Frank Burton, then head of the Design Section in Winchester's Research and Development Department. Burton's new barrel stop and locking device revolutionized the double gun. He was assigned U.S. Patent No. 1,785,764 on December 23, 1930, for his barrel stop design and Patent No. 1,797,320 on March 24, 1931, for the gun's adjustable locking mechanism. The Model 21's design also reduced the angle of the barrels and their travel in relation to the frame, thereby shortening the time required to open the action, eject spent shells, reload and close the action.

[4] *The Winchester Era, by George Madis.*
[5] *Winchester's Finest The Model 21 by Ned Schwing, Krause Publications, 1990.*

This Field Grade Model 21 in 12-gauge is shown with the breech open. The smaller angle necessary for the barrels to clear the frame allowed faster loading and unloading.

Winchester also changed the way side-by-side barrels were constructed. The usual method was to braze two barrels together. The Model 21 instead used a vertical, interlocking dovetail (covered by a raised matted rib), thus the barrels were never exposed to the heat of brazing which had the potential to distort the temper or strength of the steel. Each Model 21 barrel was forged from a single billet of Winchester Proof Steel. The half lugs were part of the original barrel forging and thus when united, formed the locking lug of the barrel unit. It might be a bit of a cliché, but the design was truly bulletproof.

Following are the general specifications for the Model 21:

TYPE

Double barrel, concealed hammer shotgun, tang-mounted safety, single or double triggers (1931).

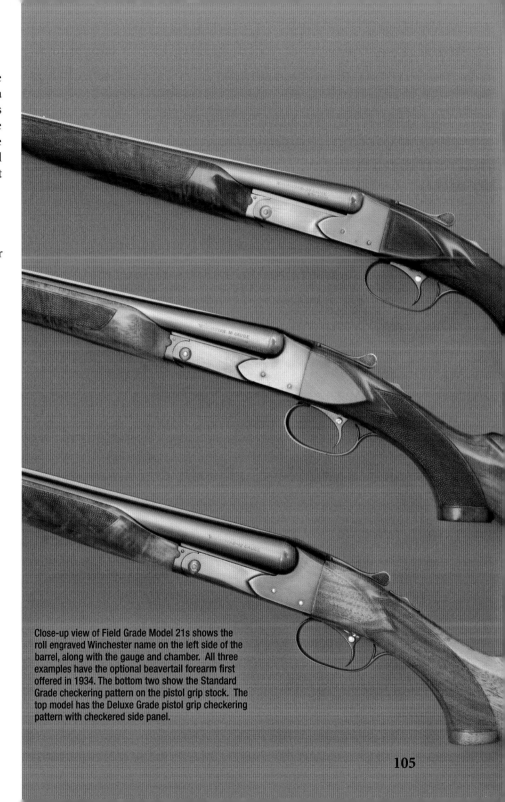

Close-up view of Field Grade Model 21s shows the roll engraved Winchester name on the left side of the barrel, along with the gauge and chamber. All three examples have the optional beavertail forearm first offered in 1934. The bottom two show the Standard Grade checkering pattern on the pistol grip stock. The top model has the Deluxe Grade pistol grip checkering pattern with checkered side panel.

STYLE	YEARS PRODUCED
Field Grade	1930 - 1959
Custom Built	1933 - 1941
Custom Built-Field	1936 - 1941
Custom Built-Trap	1936 - 1941
Custom Built-Skeet	1936 - 1941
Deluxe	1942 - 1950
Deluxe-Field	1942 - 1950
Deluxe-Trap	1942 - 1950
Deluxe-Skeet	1942 - 1950
Deluxe-Duck	1942 - 1950
Custom Deluxe	1951 - 1952
Custom Deluxe-Field	1951 - 1952
Custom Deluxe-Trap	1951 - 1952
Custom Deluxe-Skeet	1951 - 1952
Custom Built	1953 - 1959
Custom Built-Field	1953 - 1959
Custom Built-Trap	1953 - 1959
Custom Built-Skeet	1953 - 1959
Custom Built-Magnum	1953 - 1959
Custom Built-20magnum	1955 - 1959
Trap	1932 - 1959
Trap-Skeet	1933 - 1940
Trap-Field	1937 - 1938
Tournament	1932 - 1935
Tournament-Skeet	1933 - 1935
Duck	1940 - 1952
Skeet	1936 - 1959
Magnum	1953 - 1959

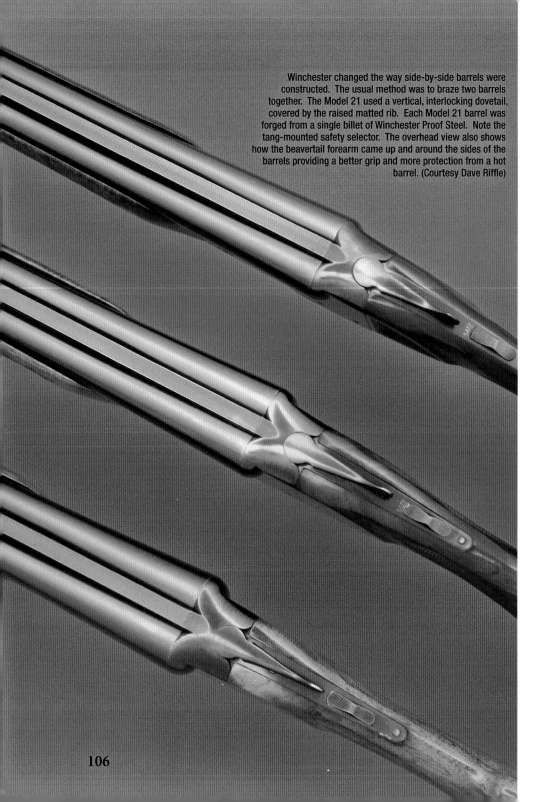

Winchester changed the way side-by-side barrels were constructed. The usual method was to braze two barrels together. The Model 21 used a vertical, interlocking dovetail, covered by the raised matted rib. Each Model 21 barrel was forged from a single billet of Winchester Proof Steel. Note the tang-mounted safety selector. The overhead view also shows how the beavertail forearm came up and around the sides of the barrels providing a better grip and more protection from a hot barrel. (Courtesy Dave Riffle)

BARRELS

12 gauge: 26-inch, 28-inch, 30-inch, 32-inch. Barrel lengths based on Grade and year of production, i.e. Skeet Grade 12-gauge would have a 26-inch barrel in 1938-39, a 28-inch barrel 1947-1959, etc.

16 gauge:	**26-inch, 28-inch.**
20 gauge:	**26-inch, 28-inch.**
28 gauge:	**26-inch.**
.410 gauge:	**26-inch. (Introduced 1955)**

RIB STYLES

There were two different rib styles during Model 21 production; the original standard raised matted rib, and a ventilated rib patented by Louis Stiennon, that was introduced in 1931. The latter was initially offered only on 12-gauge models with 32-inch barrels. Later made available for other gauges and barrel lengths through 1990.

CHOKES

Full choke, modified choke, improved modified, cylinder choke (discontinued in 1947), improved cylinder, Winchester skeet WS 1 & 2, (introduced 1933).

CHAMBERS

Gauges 12, 20, 16 all with 2-3/4-inch chambers, 3-inch at slight additional cost (1932-1949). From 1950 to 1955 the 3-inch was available only for 12-gauge models, in 1956 available again for both 12 and 20-gauge. The 28-gauge model was offered with 2-7/8-inch chambers through 1945, thereafter with 2-3/4-inch chambers. The .410-gauge was offered with 3-inch chambers.

STOCKS AND FOREARMS

Standard Grade: Checkered half Pistol grip stock without grip cap. Regular forearm (splinter type), optional beavertail (beginning 1934). Full checkered pistol grip stock standard (beginning in 1934).

Trap Grade: Pistol grip or straight stock with finely figured select walnut. Forearm, finely figured select walnut, beavertail style optional, (standard after 1940). Monte Carlo stock or cheek piece, optional. Beginning 1933 optional pistol grip cap, hard rubber grip cap standard after 1945. Winchester recoil pad standard.

Skeet Grade: Pistol grip or straight stock with checkered walnut butt and beavertail forearm.

Duck and Magnum Grade: Select walnut pistol grip stock with Win-

chester recoil pad, beavertail forearm. Straight grip stock available after 1945.

CARVING

Style 21, 21-A and 21-B carving for stocks and forearms were available on order.

ENGRAVING

Beginning in 1934 custom factory engraving was cataloged in six standard patterns numbered 1 through 6, pattern 6 being the most elaborate. Principal engravers were George Ulrich (until his death in 1949), John Kusmit, Rudolph J. Kornbrath (an outside engraver contracted for special engraving commissions 1931 to 1937), and in the 1950s Nick Kusmit, who joined his brother John in the Winchester Custom Shop. From 1935 to 1949 there was also a pattern 5A, which was comprised solely of scrollwork. Beginning in 1948, the patterns were re-designated 21-1 through 21-6. Special order custom engraving was offered beginning in 1931 and continued to be available until 1990.

BUTT PLATES AND PADS

Hard rubber butt plate standard, checkered diagonally with round WINCHESTER REPEATING ARMS CO. logo in the center. The Model 21 was also offered without a butt plate. When there was no butt plate, the butt stock was checkered. This was standard on the Skeet gun in Trap Grade, Tournament Grade and Skeet Grade. A new design for 12-gauge models only was introduced in the mid-1950s, which featured WINCHESTER and TRADE MARK embossed vertically through the middle. Winchester trade mark recoil pads were offered along with Noshoc, Hawkins, D-W No. b, Goodrich Air Cushion, Jostam Hy-Gun, Jostam Sponge Rubber 1 ply, 2 ply, or 3 ply, Jostam Anti-Flinch, and Jostam Air Cushion recoil pads. Leather covered pads in three styles were also available on special order beginning in 1955.

GRIP CAPS

Hard rubber grip caps were used in two styles from 1930 to the mid-1950s, and then changed to all steel. Early styles were embossed WINCHESTER REPEATING ARMS CO. Steel caps were not embossed. These caps were often engraved on custom models. Steel caps were also available in mid 1930s as an option on deluxe guns for the purpose of engraving.

Factory cutaway section of Model 21 action shows the solid construction of the frame that gives exceptional strength to this vital part; cocking lever acts directly on cocking rod, which gives exceptional ease and smoothness in breaking down the gun; hammer and firing pin made integral from one piece of steel; sturdy coiled hammer spring; specially long extractor movement, which gives increased ease in removing shells; each barrel and its half lug is a single integral mass forged from one billet of steel. (U.S. Repeating Arms Co. Collection)

This factory cutaway shows the single selective trigger mechanism patented by L. Stiennon on December 6, 1932. Note the brass barrel selector at the top of the trigger. In this view the hammers are cocked. (U.S. Repeating Arms Co. Collection)

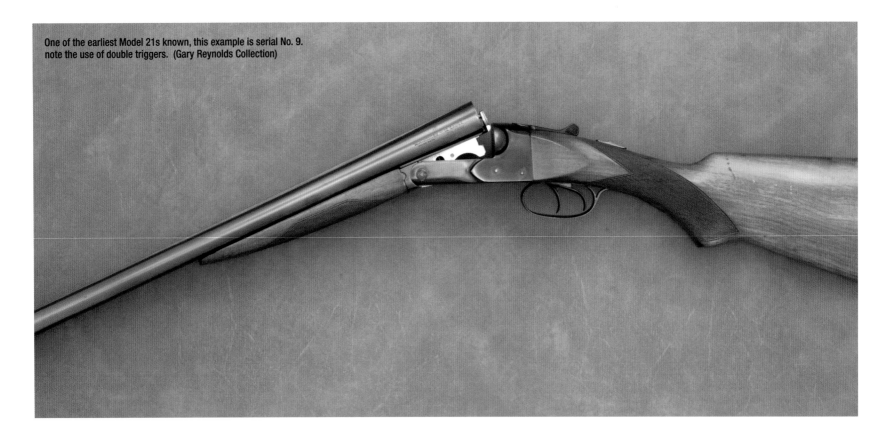

One of the earliest Model 21s known, this example is serial No. 9. note the use of double triggers. (Gary Reynolds Collection)

Though originally introduced with double triggers and extractors, beginning in 1931 the Model 21 was also available with a single selective trigger designed and patented by Louis Stiennon. One could choose either the right or left barrel by simply pressing the selector, located at the top of the trigger. The mechanism was engineered to eliminate the possibility of doubling. Authors Ned Schwing and Don Criswell noted in *Winchester's Finest – The Model 21*, "This rugged single trigger used recoil forces to actuate an inertia weight that postponed the firing of the second barrel until the recoil and counter-recoil forces had expended their energy. The sear could not move forward until the trigger had returned to normal." Stiennon summed up the design in his patent application, "[the invention] is characterized by fewness of parts, compactness of organization, certainty of operation, durability in use, and convenience of operation." The new design gave Winchester yet another advantage over competitive double guns.

The Model 21 was given the highest degree of attention to fit and finish, especially finish, which was essential since the Winchester was entirely blued. Rather than brilliant case colors on the frame to dazzle the eye, a lustrous, deep blue finish had to supply all the necessary aesthetics of appearance. To that end, only the master bluer was allowed to work on the Model 21. Over the life of the model, which was discontinued from regular production in 1959, the blueing process was changed to keep pace with both technology and economies of scale. By the post-World War II era, the Model 21 was finished using a more cost efficient dip blueing process, but even then, the Winchester doubles were given extra attention commensurate with their price.

When the double gun was introduced, Winchester regarded it as another production model, a companion to its slide-action shotguns. Even with an introductory price of $59.50, by 1931 the Model 21 was already becoming more than "another production gun" and a year later when the Trap Grade was in-

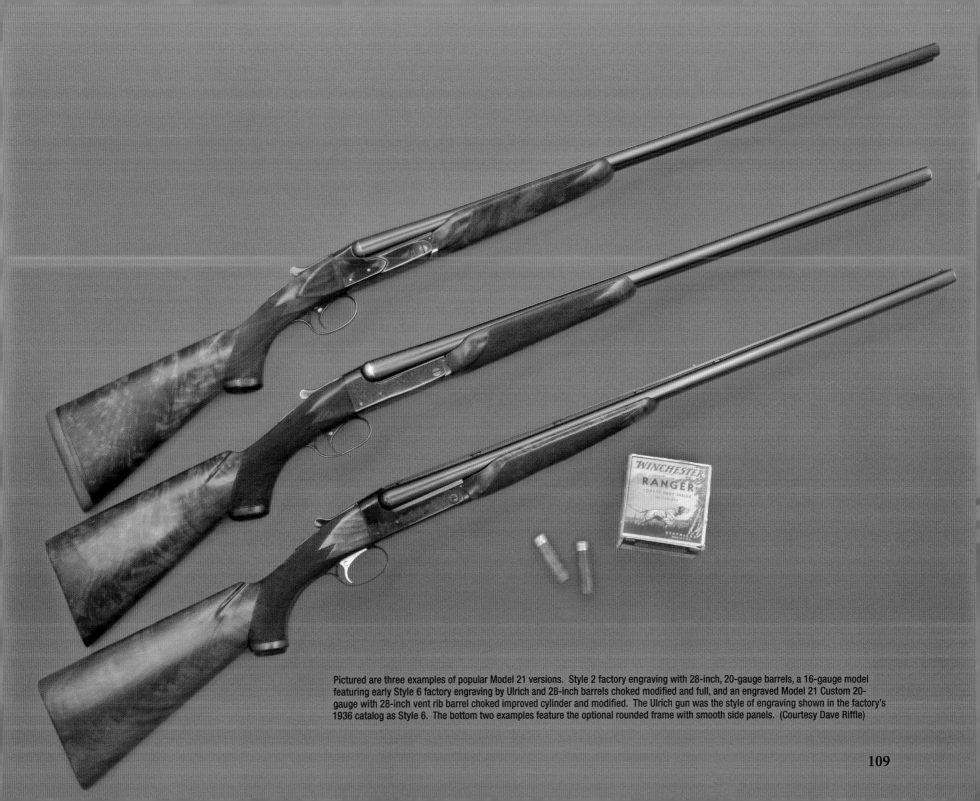

Pictured are three examples of popular Model 21 versions. Style 2 factory engraving with 28-inch, 20-gauge barrels, a 16-gauge model featuring early Style 6 factory engraving by Ulrich and 28-inch barrels choked modified and full, and an engraved Model 21 Custom 20-gauge with 28-inch vent rib barrel choked improved cylinder and modified. The Ulrich gun was the style of engraving shown in the factory's 1936 catalog as Style 6. The bottom two examples feature the optional rounded frame with smooth side panels. (Courtesy Dave Riffle)

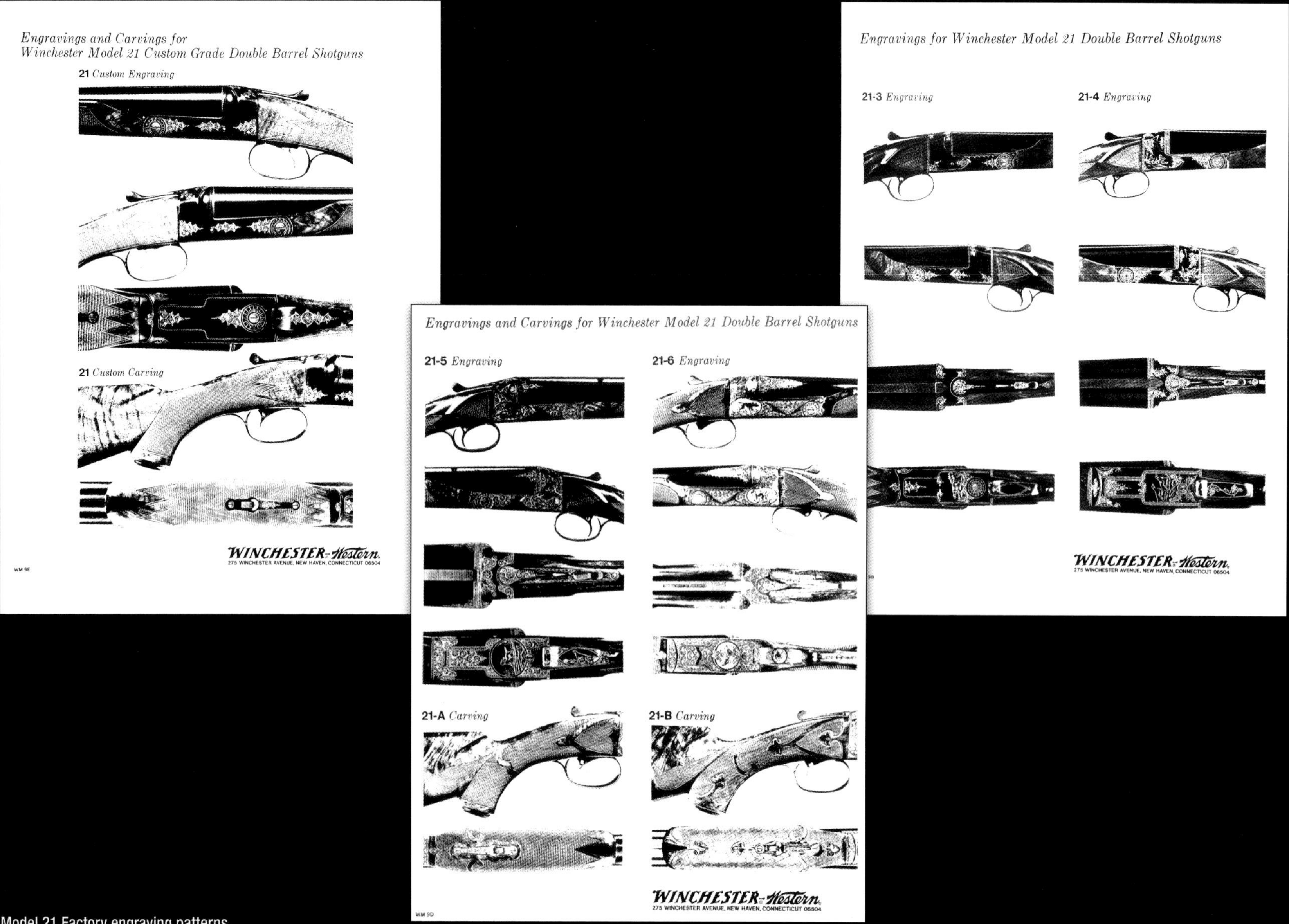
Engravings and Carvings for
Winchester Model 21 Custom Grade Double Barrel Shotguns
21 Custom Engraving
21 Custom Carving
WINCHESTER-Western
275 WINCHESTER AVENUE, NEW HAVEN, CONNECTICUT 06504
WM 9E
Engravings for Winchester Model 21 Double Barrel Shotguns
21-3 Engraving
21-4 Engraving
WINCHESTER-Western
275 WINCHESTER AVENUE, NEW HAVEN, CONNECTICUT 06504
Engravings and Carvings for Winchester Model 21 Double Barrel Shotguns
21-5 Engraving
21-6 Engraving
21-A Carving
21-B Carving
WINCHESTER-Western
275 WINCHESTER AVENUE, NEW HAVEN, CONNECTICUT 06504
WM 9D

Model 21 Factory engraving patterns.
(Photos courtesy R.L. Wilson)

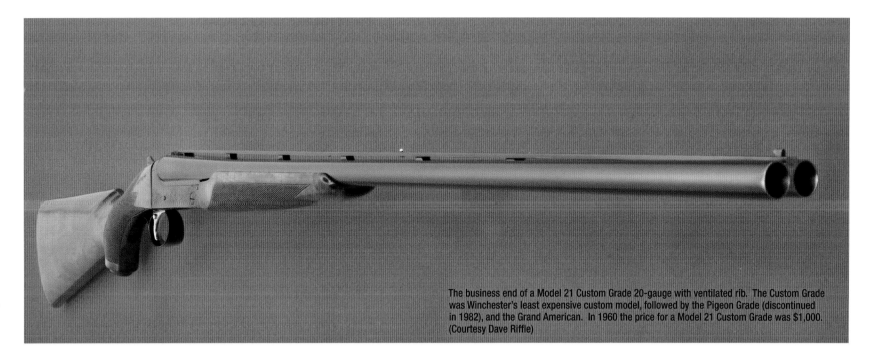

The business end of a Model 21 Custom Grade 20-gauge with ventilated rib. The Custom Grade was Winchester's least expensive custom model, followed by the Pigeon Grade (discontinued in 1982), and the Grand American. In 1960 the price for a Model 21 Custom Grade was $1,000. (Courtesy Dave Riffle)

troduced, the Winchester side-by-side was on the road to becoming America's greatest double gun.

In 1930 the Model 12 was priced at $48.95, only $10.55 less than the Model 21, but a year later Winchester reduced the Model 12 Field Gun to just $39.50. Thus by the time Winchester came under the ownership of Western Cartridge Co. and the Olin family in December 1931, the price disparity between the Model 12 and Model 21 had greatly widened. It was clear to John Olin by 1932 that the future of the Winchester double gun would not be built on Field Grade guns but on Trap, Skeet and custom built models.

Between 1933 and 1959 Winchester created 27 different grades for the Model 21. As a custom built gun, the Model 21 could be ordered in any configuration the purchaser desired, the only limits were the size of one's pocketbook.

It is estimated that between 1930 and 1959 Winchester produced a total of 28,850 Model 21 shotguns, the majority of which were Field Grade. After standard production of the Model 21 ended in 1959, the double guns were available only by special order. As noted by numerous authors over the years, it was John M. Olin, by then Chairman of the Board, who kept the Model 21 alive. The last frames had been built in 1955 and the Model 21 should simply have faded into history after 1959, but Olin had a vision for the Model 21 that had not yet

been fulfilled. He wanted to make the Model 21 into the finest double gun in the world. All Model 21 Winchesters thereafter were completely hand built in the Custom Shop, with the exception of the Dulite blueing and polishing of the frame, which was carried out in the main plant.

Model 21 double guns built in the Custom Shop are recognizable by their distinctive frame contours. Frames for the Model 21 built from 1930 to 1959 have bold, inset side panels and a sharp edge to the shoulders of the frame behind the barrel, whereas all Custom Shop guns have smooth sides and contoured shoulders. This was done to slightly lighten the frame by removing surface metal not critical to its integrity or strength, and to provide a smoother surface for engraving. While this is generally the fastest way to distinguish a Custom Shop gun, this same design was also an option from the 1930s through 1959, known as a "rounded frame" special order. This was usually seen on highly embellished examples.

Approximately 1,030 Model 21 double guns were produced in the Custom Shop between 1960 and 1990. And as John Olin had wished, they were the finest double guns in the world. And while that may be subject to debate among collectors of other American and British-built side-by-side shotguns, the values placed on Custom Shop Model 21 doubles today speak for themselves.

111

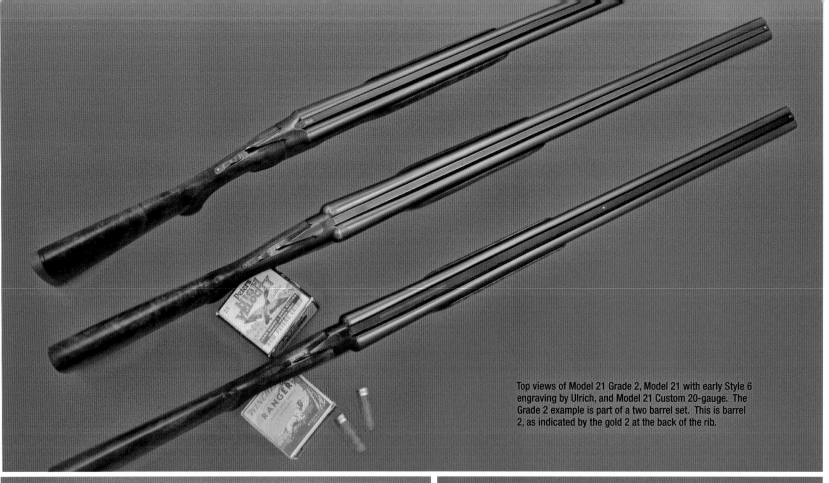

Top views of Model 21 Grade 2, Model 21 with early Style 6 engraving by Ulrich, and Model 21 Custom 20-gauge. The Grade 2 example is part of a two barrel set. This is barrel 2, as indicated by the gold 2 at the back of the rib.

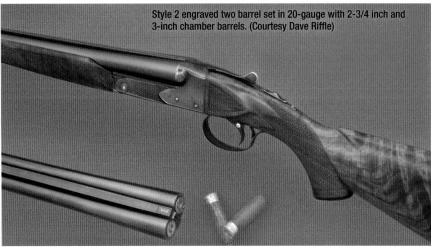

Style 2 engraved two barrel set in 20-gauge with 2-3/4 inch and 3-inch chamber barrels. (Courtesy Dave Riffle)

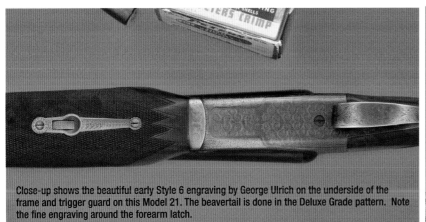

Close-up shows the beautiful early Style 6 engraving by George Ulrich on the underside of the frame and trigger guard on this Model 21. The beavertail is done in the Deluxe Grade pattern. Note the fine engraving around the forearm latch.

Early Style 6 engraving. Later Style 6 had a panel with a hunting dog on the sides of the frame and a game bird in a panel on the bottom of the frame, forward of the trigger guard. This example features the optional rounded frame with smooth side panels. An example with just scrollwork is very rare. (Courtesy Dave Riffle)

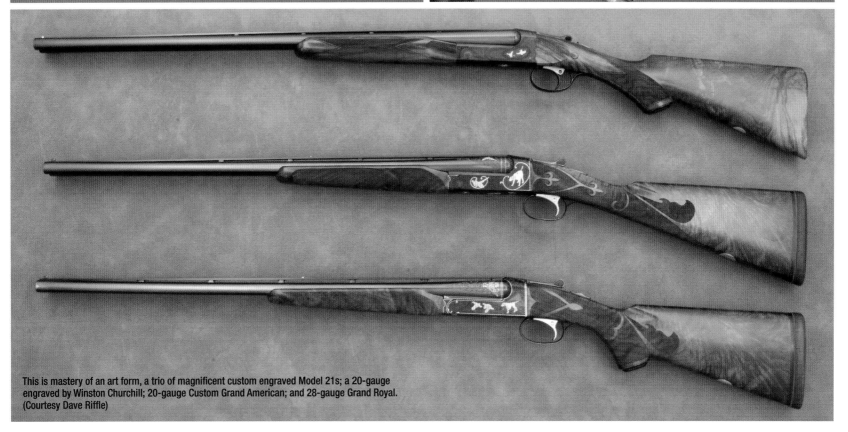

This is mastery of an art form, a trio of magnificent custom engraved Model 21s; a 20-gauge engraved by Winston Churchill; 20-gauge Custom Grand American; and 28-gauge Grand Royal. (Courtesy Dave Riffle)

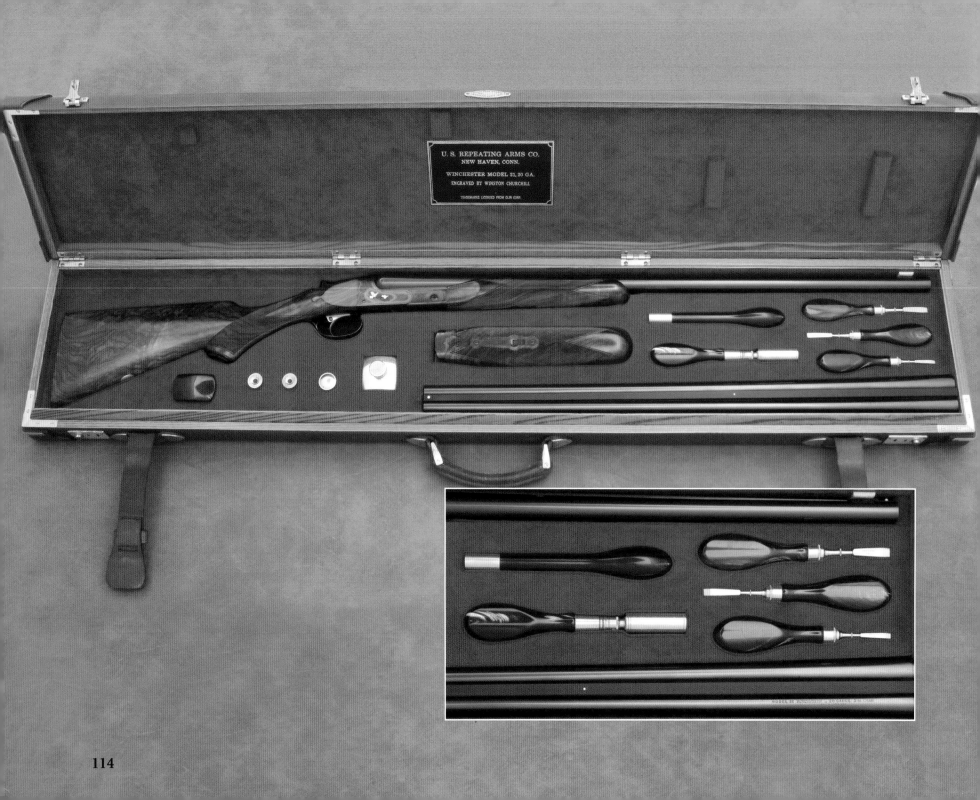

114

The Winston Churchill Engraved
Model 21 Grand American

This 20-gauge Exhibition Grand American is the only Model 21 Winchester ever factory engraved by American Master, Winston Churchill. This special gun was a joint project of Thomas Koessl and Bill Jaqua with the cooperation of the Winchester Custom Shop. It began in the fall of 1983 and was finished and displayed at the February 1987 Las Vegas Gun Show. The purpose of this project was to create a one-of-a-kind Exhibition Grade Model 21 combining the talents of Churchill with America's premier stock maker, Jerry Fisher.

Fisher selected the finest exhibition grade English walnut for the pistol grip, stock, and both beavertail forearms. He also did extensive metal work by scalloping the rear portion of the action and reshaping the sides of the action body and forearms. A special handmade trigger guard, similar to the classic Purdey shotgun, elegantly flows into the handmade engraved grip cap. Even the special single trigger was handcrafted by Jerry Fisher. The execution of the woodwork, classic point pattern checkering, checkered butt with engraved heel and toe plates, and non-engraved gold oval, all attest to the quality and experience of Fisher.

The engraving by Winston Churchill is exquisite and beyond comparison. Two gold inlaid Ruffed Grouse flushing from the deep forest adorn the right side of the receiver. Two gold inlaid Woodcock, again in flight, grace the right side. On the underside, two gold inlaid Cock Pheasant are vividly exiting a cornfield. All game scenes, as well as trigger guard, grip cap, heel and toe plates, and forearm iron, are framed in the finest English scroll imaginable. Winston Churchill created another masterpiece on this Winchester Model 21. The finished product is a testimonial to American craftsmanship at its finest. This Model 21 is a 20-gauge, 3-inch magnum with two vent rib sets of barrels, one 28-inch M/F and one 26-inch IC/M.

The entire creation is elegantly displayed in a custom Marvin Huey French fitted oak and leather case. Handmade accessories by T.F. Wood of London, England include buffalo horned screwdrivers, chamber brush, cleaning rod, and action block. Also included are gold plated oil bottle, snap caps, and striker bottle with all items carrying the "Winchester USA" markings. As quoted in the factory letter, "These are the finest artisans in their field and certainly make this one of the finest collectible M21's ever produced in conjunction with the Custom Shop."

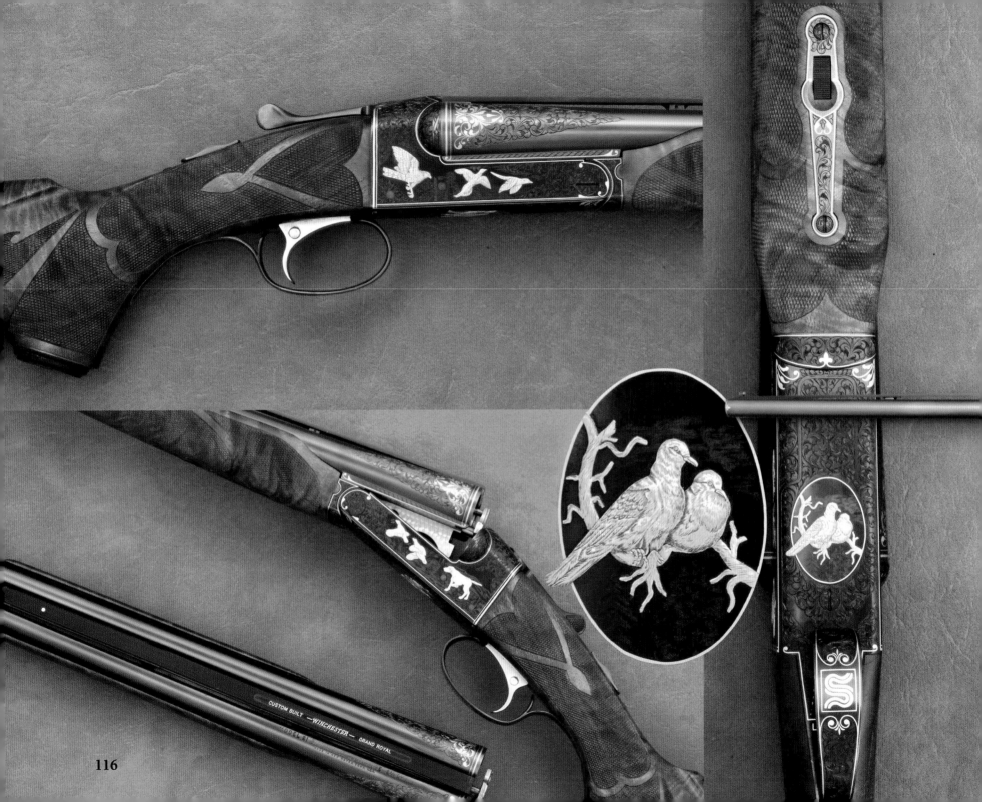

CUSTOM BUILT — WINCHESTER — GRAND ROYAL

This is a beautifully engraved and gold inlaid Grand Royal two-barrel set. Built in 1981, this was the only example that ever left the factory with two sets of vent rib 28-gauge barrels. Howard Dove engraved this example for U.S. Repeating Arms Co. A total of seven Grand Royals were planned. The first was for John Olin and engraved by Alvin A. White, but it was not finished before Mr. Olin's death. The second gun, pictured, was by Howard Dove. Only three others were completed. (Courtesy Dave Riffle)

This rare example is a 20-gauge and 28-gauge two-barrel Grand American. John Kusmit engraved the gun in 1967. Showing Style 21-B carving, Kusmit's engraving on this example is some of his finest work on the Model 21. Notice the exceptionally fine scrolls around the gold inlaid hunting dog and game birds, contrasted by the bold leaf design on the barrel balls. Kusmit used multiple shading of the gold to add character detail to both the hunting dogs on the side panels and game birds on the bottom of the frame. Only 171 Grand Americans were built. In 1960 the price was $3,500. (Courtesy Dave Riffle)

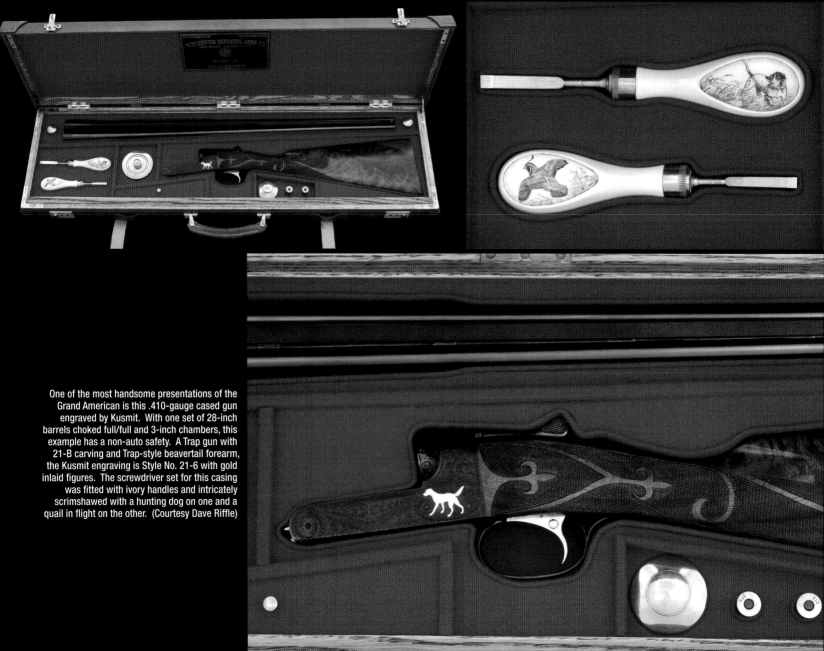

One of the most handsome presentations of the Grand American is this .410-gauge cased gun engraved by Kusmit. With one set of 28-inch barrels choked full/full and 3-inch chambers, this example has a non-auto safety. A Trap gun with 21-B carving and Trap-style beavertail forearm, the Kusmit engraving is Style No. 21-6 with gold inlaid figures. The screwdriver set for this casing was fitted with ivory handles and intricately scrimshawed with a hunting dog on one and a quail in flight on the other. (Courtesy Dave Riffle)

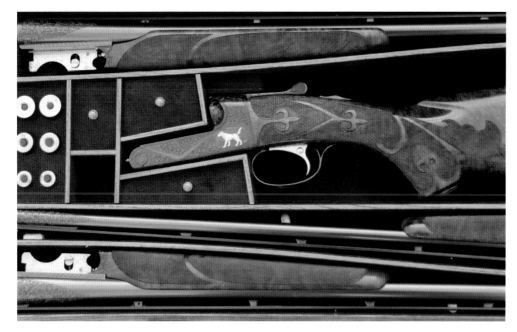

Rare in terms of Winchester Grand Americans can be easily defined by the Eight of Eight examples. This is gun No. 2, one of only four three-barrel sets produced by U.S. Repeating Arms Co. The selling price back in 1986 was $55,000! Could explain why they only sold four. (Courtesy Dave Riffle)

Model 21 Grade Designations 1960-1990

Grade	Years Produced	Standard Features
Custom	1960 – 1990	21 Custom Carving
Pigeon Grade	1960 – 1982	21-A Carving
Standard Custom Built (no engraving)	1983 – 1990	
Special Custom Built (made to order)	1983 – 1990	Carving to order
Grand American	1960 – 1990	21-B Carving

The average time from order until delivery of a Custom Grade Model 21 was 12 to 14 months. The highly engraved and gold inlaid Grand American and Special Custom Built models required up to 18 months to complete. Principal engravers for the Model 21 during this period were John and Nick Kusmit. In 1965 Jasper Salerno joined the Kusmit brothers and in 1970 Joe Crowley became the fourth Custom Shop engraver.

After a long career with Winchester that began working alongside George Ulrich in 1937, John Kusmit retired in 1977. Brother Nick and engraver Joe Crowley both retired in 1980, the same year Winchester hired Pauline Muerrle, the last Custom Shop engraver. She left U.S. Repeating Arms in 1984. Jasper Salerno, who retired from Winchester in 1978, continued to engrave for Winchester and U.S.R.A. Co. as an independent contractor until 1983. Between 1984 and 1990 all engraving for

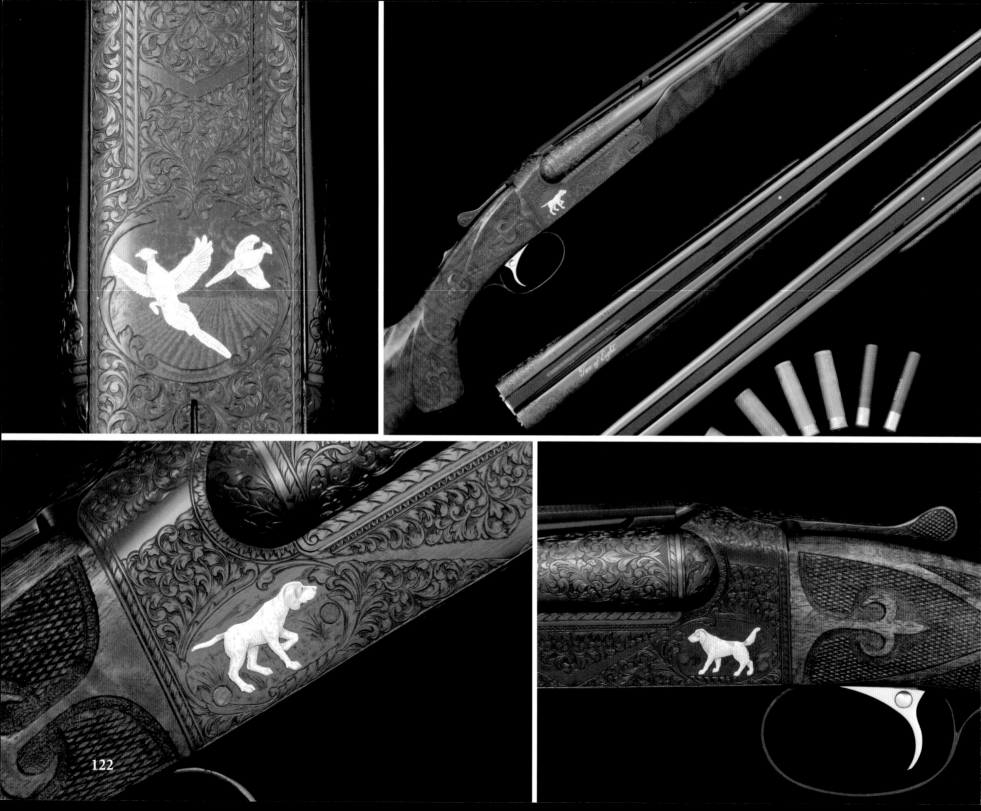

Each of the four Eight of Eight Grand Americans built has its own numbering on the barrels. This example, Two of Eight, was built for Carl E. Press.

Preceding page: The Eight of Eight Grand American three-barrel sets were chambered in 20, 28, and .410-gauge. Built by U.S Repeating Arms Company in the early 1980s, the sets featured 26-inch ventilated rib barrels with a choice of any available choke combinations. Each barrel had its own beavertail forearm. The stock and forearm were select AA full fancy American walnut. The guns were engraved in Style 21-6 with all figures gold inlaid. Special features included a gold oval nameplate, Style 21-B carving, optional non-automatic safety, gold-plated trigger, and custom leather gun case. Only four of the proposed eight sets were ever produced, each elaborately engraved by Howard Dove. These are by far the most beautiful Model 21s ever built. (Courtesy Dave Riffle)

the Model 21 was contracted. Winchester sent work to Alvin A. White Engraving, Inc., (later American Master Engravers), Winston Churchill, Siegfried Rentzschke, Howard Dove, and Angelo Bee. Custom work on the Model 21 was also commissioned from Alvin White's associate Andrew Bourbon. At the time, from 1966 to the early 1970s, renowned author and historian R.L. Wilson was the Managing Director of A.A. White Engraving, Inc., (later American Master Engravers). Producing a stunning catalog of work for Colt's, among other leading arms makers, American Master Engravers continued to operate until the late 1990s, when Alvin A. White suffered a stroke. White, who began his career in 1947, was one of the greatest firearms engravers of the 20th century. Today, Andrew Bourbon continues the tradition of handcrafted styling pioneered by White and American Master Engravers.

After 1990, the Model 21 did not go quietly into the pages of firearms history. A handful of custom orders were still being built, and in 1996 the U.S. Repeating Arms Co. contracted with Tony Galazan and Connecticut Shotgun Manufacturing in New Britain, to continue producing the Model 21 on a special order basis. In fact, if you want a brand new Model 21 today, it can be ordered through the U.S. Repeating Arms Co. Just one catch, Galazan produces only one grade: The Grand Royal, a beautifully engraved, 20, 28, and .410 gauge three barrel combination gun that retails for an incredible $75,000. (Think of it as a continuation of the highly desirable Eight of Eight Model 21s).

If you want a Model 21 without the blessings of U.S.R.A. Co. and sans the Winchester name on the barrel, Galazan builds the Connecticut Shotgun Model 21 with Grade 21-1, 21-5, 21-6, Grand American, or Royal Exhibition engraving. A used original Field Grade Model 21 sells for around $5,000 to $8,000 today. Galazan's engraved CSM Model 21s range in price from $9,995 to $30,000.[6]

{6] *American Rifleman, September 2004, On Again, Off Again – The American Double Struggles to Return by Terry Weiland.*

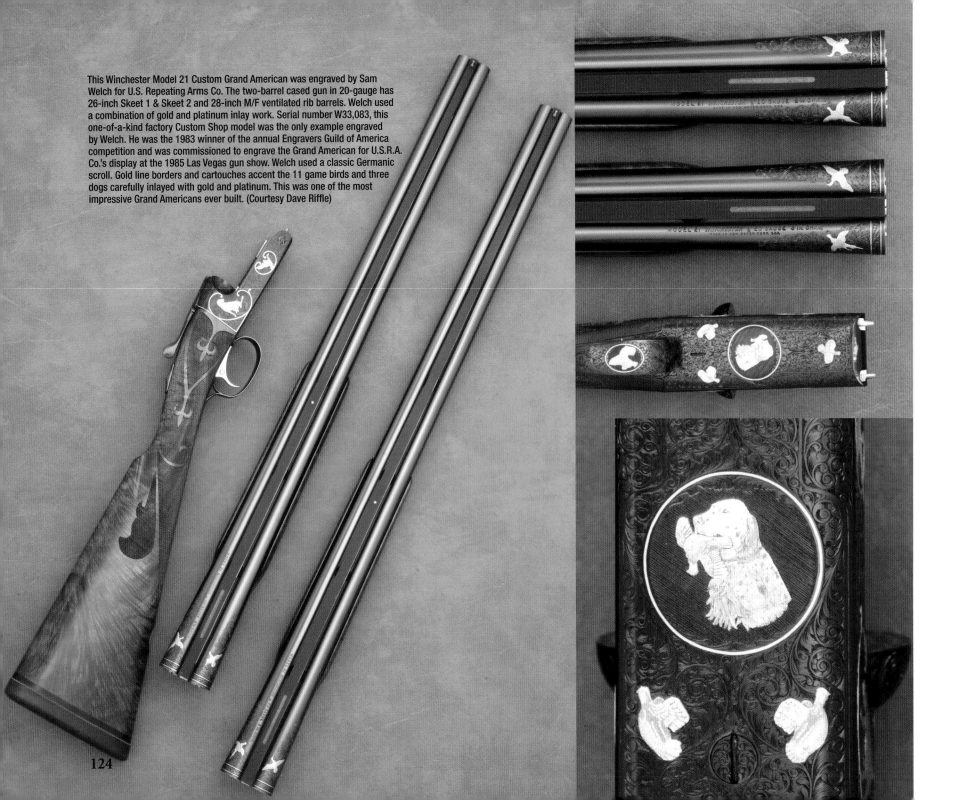

This Winchester Model 21 Custom Grand American was engraved by Sam Welch for U.S. Repeating Arms Co. The two-barrel cased gun in 20-gauge has 26-inch Skeet 1 & Skeet 2 and 28-inch M/F ventilated rib barrels. Welch used a combination of gold and platinum inlay work. Serial number W33,083, this one-of-a-kind factory Custom Shop model was the only example engraved by Welch. He was the 1983 winner of the annual Engravers Guild of America competition and was commissioned to engrave the Grand American for U.S.R.A. Co.'s display at the 1985 Las Vegas gun show. Welch used a classic Germanic scroll. Gold line borders and cartouches accent the 11 game birds and three dogs carefully inlayed with gold and platinum. This was one of the most impressive Grand Americans ever built. (Courtesy Dave Riffle)

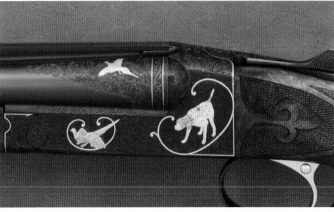

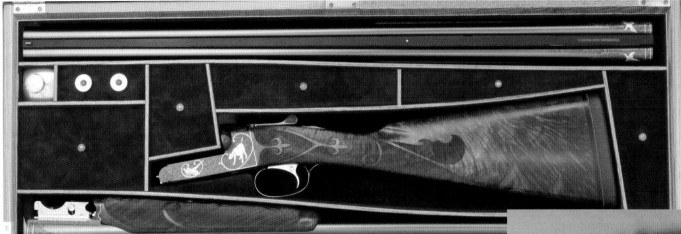

Below: The Galazan Model 21 opens up entirely new possibilities in engraving, such as this custom example with a vivid and colorful southwestern game bird theme. Galazan also duplicates the original factory engraving for the Model 21s sold under the CSM label and of course, the Grand Royal Winchester Model 21. (Photo courtesy Tony Galazan)

Complementing Galazan's Model 21s, Peter Werner, the son of R.L. Wilson and grandson of Arno Werner, whose work on firearms cases dates back to the early 1960s, produces original style Model 21 cases. During his career, Arno Werner built custom cases for Colt's and other American and European arms makers, private collectors, dealers, and for presentations to several American Presidents. Peter Werner learned the art of custom case making at his grandfather's side and today carries on a proud family tradition.

Tradition, and an appreciation for handcraftsmanship seem to be the driving force behind the renewed enthusiasm for side-by-side doubles, a design rooted in the 19th century that continues to find favor among collectors and gunmakers in the 21st. For Winchester, maker of the world's most popular shotguns for more than 100 years, the past and present seem much closer.

With the introduction of the Model 23 XTR Pigeon Grade in 1978 Winchester had finally created an exclusive 12-gauge and 20-gauge double gun in the tradition of the Model 21. In 1986 when the model was discontinued the selling price was $1,460. Values today average $2,500 for the 20-gauge models.

Chapter Five
Winchester Side-by-Side Shotguns
Model 22, Model 23, Model 24, and Winchester
Parker Reproductions

By the end of the 1930s Winchester-Western was offering a total of 11 different Grades for the Model 21. Customers could choose from four gauges, a selection of barrel lengths with or without ventilated ribs, a variety of chokes, single or double triggers, straight or pistol grip stocks, fancy wood, stock and forearm carving, and six standard engraving patterns, plus custom factory engraving. What was more telling, however, was that from 1931 to 1941 the retail price of a Standard Grade (Field Grade) Model 21 with a single selective trigger and automatic ejectors had gone from $79.50 to $105.69, an increase of 33 percent. The retail price for Custom/Deluxe Grades during the mid to late 1930s averaged a little over $200.[1] Despite The Depression, which had humbled American industry, Winchester had succeeded in building the finest American double gun of the 20th century, and had done it in the midst of our nation's worst economic crisis. The Model 21 was, however, fast becoming a wealthy man's shotgun. By the late 1930s there was an entire segment of the American firearms market that Winchester could no longer address with the Model 21. But that changed in 1939 with the introduction of New Haven's second side-by-side shotgun, the Model 24.

Interestingly, rather than evolve the Model 21 into a less expensive double gun, Winchester chose instead to build an entirely new model based on its popular single barrel Model 37 introduced in 1936. The Model 24 made use of many Model 37 design and manufacturing features. Like the single barrel Winchester, the double gun had a very trim, streamlined shape; a solid wrist with a wide taper into the pistol grip stock, and a nicely contoured semi-beavertail forearm. In profile, the Model 24 almost looked like a Model 37 with double triggers. It even had the same long hinge pin. The boxlock, hammerless double went into production in late April 1939, and was first announced in the January 2, 1940 catalog.

The following description of the new Winchester double gun was published in 1939.

"With new modern streamline styling, Model 24 is the latest in standard double-barrel hammerless shotgun design. Built to sell at a very moderate price, a distinct new contribution to the long era of double-barrel hammerless shotgun popularity, it is a remarkable value. A surprisingly nice handling, finely balanced, hard shooting gun, for the shooter who has his heart set on a finely styled double gun yet must buy in the moderate-priced bracket. Receiver, barrels and all important parts are made of high-grade steel. There are no castings anywhere. Frame is machined from a solid steel forging, and extra strong. Extra strength is carried out in the action design, combining locking bolt, barrel lug, hinge pin, forearm shoe, and forearm lug. Barrels fit down deep and snugly in the receiver, giving the whole gun breech an especially attractive rounded contour. Locking bolt, barrel lug and hinge pin are wide and sturdy, with large bearing surfaces. Lug fits snugly in a deep recess in the receiver. Bolting is exceptionally strong, simple, dependable. Firing action is exceedingly fast. Barrels are of Winchester selected steel, with matted rib: 12 ga., 30", 28" or 26"; 16 ga. and 20 ga., 28" or 26". Extractors, cam operated, with supplemental spring action. Stock is genuine American walnut, with full-rounded low, streamlined comb and full pistol grip; streamlined to receiver. Dimensions: 14-$\frac{1}{2}$" x 1-$\frac{1}{2}$" x 2-$\frac{1}{2}$",

[1] Winchester's Finest The Model 21 by Ned Schwing, Krause Publications, 1990.

Introduced late in 1939, the Model 24 was the second New Haven-built double gun of the decade. To produce a much lower-priced side-by-side than the Model 21, Winchester made use of many Model 37 design and manufacturing features. Like the single barrel Model 37, the new double gun had a very trim, streamlined shape; a solid wrist with a wide taper into the pistol grip stock, and a nicely contoured semi-beavertail forearm. More than 116,000 were sold over a period of 18 years. (U.S. Repeating Arms Co. Collection)

with 2" down pitch. Streamlined semi-beavertail forearm of matching walnut, shaped to the barrels, coming up high at the sides, and accurately fitted. Automatic safety. Take down. Weight approximately 7-$\frac{1}{2}$ lbs."

Selling for around $50, the Model 24 offered a lot of shotgun for not a lot of money. Initially offered in 12-gauge, both 16-gauge and 20-gauge versions were added in 1940. Following are Model 24 specifications.

TYPE

Double barrel, hammerless shotgun, automatic safety, double triggers.

STYLE	YEARS PRODUCED	TOTAL PRODUCTION
Field Grade	1939 – 1957	116,280

BARRELS AND CHOKES

Gauge	Barrel	Right	Left
12 gauge	30-inch	Mod.	Full
12 gauge	28-inch	Mod	Full
12 gauge	28-inch	*Cyl.	Mod.
12 gauge	26-inch	*Cyl.	Mod.
16 gauge	28-inch	Mod.	Full
16 gauge	26-inch	*Cyl.	Mod.
20 gauge	28-inch	Mod.	Full
20 gauge	26-inch	*Cyl.	Mod.

*Changed to Improved Cylinder and Modified in 1947

Sold in a Winchester fitted case, the Model 23 Light Duck was only produced in 20-gauge. Introduced in 1985 this is one of the more desirable models for collectors due to its limited production.

RIBS:
Raised, matted rib only.

CHAMBERS
Gauges 12, 20, 16 all with 2-³/₄-inch chambers.

STOCKS AND FOREARMS
Plain walnut stock with pistol grip, semi-beavertail forearm, not checkered. Straight grip stocks available at no extra charge. Fancy walnut, checkered stock and forearm on special order only.

BUTT PLATES
Checkered composition butt plate.

WEIGHTS (approximate)

12 gauge:	7 lbs. 7 oz.
16 gauge:	6 lbs. 9 oz.
20 gauge:	6 lbs. 8 oz.

The Model 24 was a solid, American made shotgun that unfortunately arrived at the wrong time in history. Less than two years after its introduction America was at war. The Model 24 languished, and in the postwar years the greater emphasis was on semi-auto

The Light Duck barrel featured a raised matted rib, blued receiver and barrels and hand checkered select walnut stock and beavertail forearm.

and slide-action shotguns. The Model 24 faded quietly from the scene in 1957, though they were still being sold from inventory as late as 1958. The last suggested retail price was $86.95. Today, excellent examples bring from $650 in 12-gauge up to $1,000 in 20-gauge.

With only the Model 21 remaining after 1958, and that fading from the scene as a regular production model beginning in 1960, Winchester was without a mainstream double gun for the first time since 1939. For the American market there would not be another until the introduction of the Model 22 in 1975. A lot would happen in New Haven between 1957 and 1975, and the costs of building a new double gun in Connecticut would be considered prohibitive by the 1970s. Thus for the first time since the late 1870s, the house of Winchester would venture abroad to find a maker for a new double gun bearing the famous American name.

Laurona Armas, located in Eibar, Spain, was chosen in 1974 to build the new Winchester side-by-side. Founded in 1941 by four craftsmen, Laurona, which in Basque means "of the four," had specialized in side-by-side shotguns since 1941. (They continued to build only SXS models through 1978, after which they began building superposed shotguns and express rifle/combination guns.)[2]

In general appearance the Model 22 was almost the spitting image of the earlier Model 21 Field Guns. The stocks were oil-finished walnut, with a choice of straight or pistol grip styles featuring a deeply fluted comb, hand checkering through the wrist (and pistol grip) and a handsome, hand-checkered beavertail forearm. Intended for the international market,

[2] 25th Edition Blue Book of Gun Values by S.P. Fjestad, Blue Book Publications, Inc.

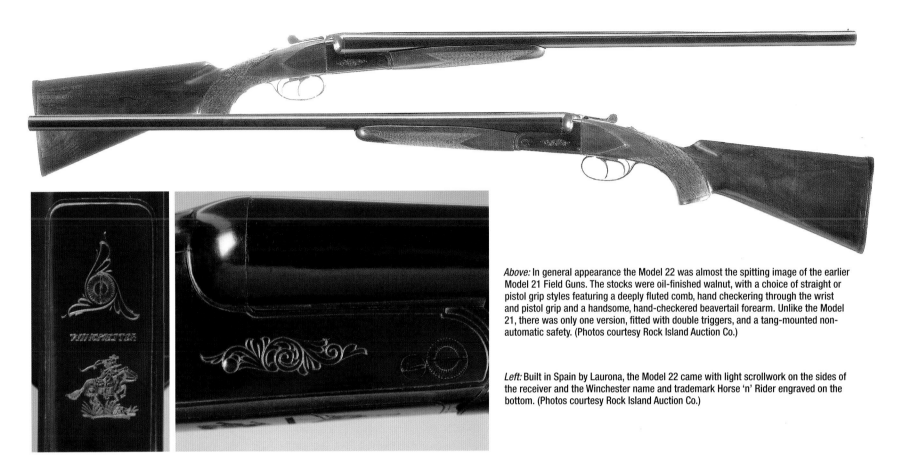

Above: In general appearance the Model 22 was almost the spitting image of the earlier Model 21 Field Guns. The stocks were oil-finished walnut, with a choice of straight or pistol grip styles featuring a deeply fluted comb, hand checkering through the wrist and pistol grip and a handsome, hand-checkered beavertail forearm. Unlike the Model 21, there was only one version, fitted with double triggers, and a tang-mounted non-automatic safety. (Photos courtesy Rock Island Auction Co.)

Left: Built in Spain by Laurona, the Model 22 came with light scrollwork on the sides of the receiver and the Winchester name and trademark Horse 'n' Rider engraved on the bottom. (Photos courtesy Rock Island Auction Co.)

the Model 22 Field Gun was only available in 12-gauge and with a choice of 28-inch, bored improved cylinder and modified, or modified and full choke barrels. The double guns came standard with light scroll engraving on the sides of the receiver, and the Winchester name and trademark Horse 'n' Rider engraved on the bottom. Unlike the Model 21, there was only one version, fitted with double triggers, and a tang-mounted non-automatic safety.

Laurona built the Model 22 using Winchester Proof Steel, and that meant that it was rugged and all but unbreakable. While well assembled, the quality just wasn't that of Winchester, nor was the finish; a dark black chrome that was deep, but lacking the refinement of New Haven's finely honed blueing techniques. The black chrome finish did, however, offer one advantage; it was highly resistant to oxidation.

Though classic in its appearance, the Model 22 differed greatly from Ameri-

can-made Winchesters in overall fit and finish. It was, in the end, a Winchester built to a price, rather than one built to a standard. With a limited production run the guns have become modestly collectible today with prices averaging around $1,000 to $1,500 for examples in excellent condition.

Following are Model 22 specifications.

TYPE

Double barrel, hammerless shotgun, double triggers, matted top rib, non-automatic safety on top of tang.

STYLE

Field Gun

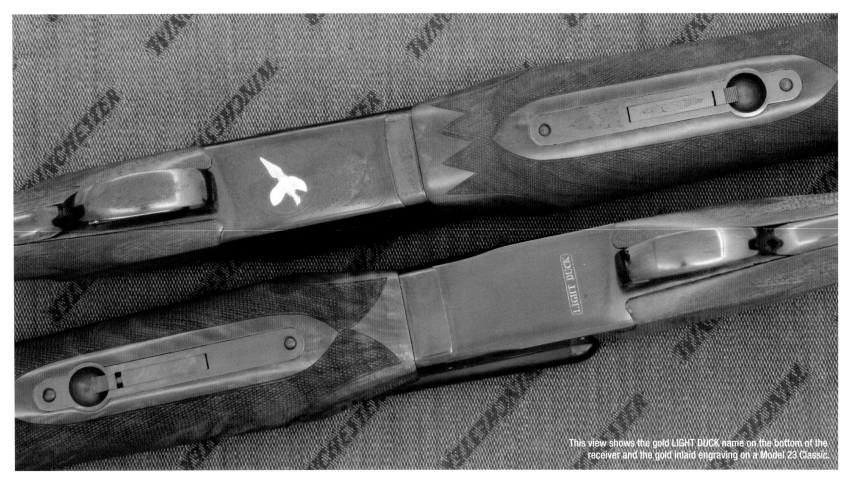

This view shows the gold LIGHT DUCK name on the bottom of the receiver and the gold inlaid engraving on a Model 23 Classic.

BARRELS AND CHOKES

Gauge	Barrel
12 gauge	28-inch, Improved Cylinder and Mod.
12 gauge	28-inch, Mod. and Full.

RIBS:

Raised, matted rib only.

SIGHTS

Brass front bead.

STOCKS AND FOREARMS

Hand-checkered walnut pistol grip stock and beavertail forearm. Available with straight stock at no additional charge.

WEIGHT (approximate)

12 gauge: 6-³/₄ lbs.

Part of the problem with the Model 22's success might have been the introduction of the beautifully built Model 23 XTR in 1978. This was the first Winchester side-by-side to be manufactured by Olin Industries' Japanese subsidiary.

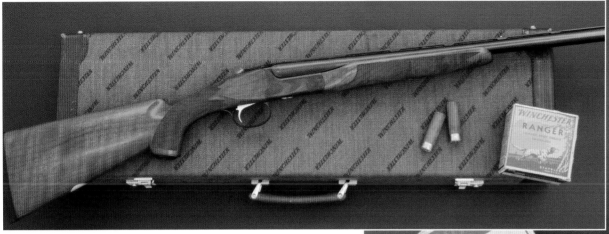

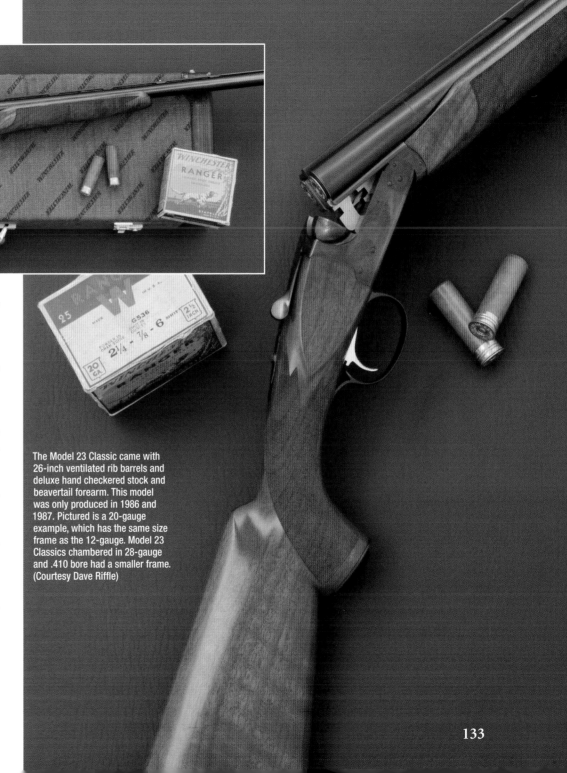

In 1954 Olin Industries had merged with the Mathieson Chemical Corporation to form Olin-Mathieson Corporation. The new firearms, munitions, and chemical conglomerate headed by John Olin was now global in its scope with 46 domestic and 17 foreign plants.[3] In the 1960s Olin established a new manufacturing facility in Japan, Olin-Kodensha Company, created to build quality guns at a more affordable price. The most famous of the Japanese-built Winchesters was the Model 101 superposed first seen in 1963. While the Winchester O/U models were playing to rave reviews throughout the 1960s and 1970s, Winchester and its Japanese manufacturing partners were developing the next great double gun, the Model 23 XTR, which was introduced in 1978. This was to be the first gun of its type to be marketed in the United States, following the classification of the Model 21 as strictly a custom order.

Writing about the Model 23 XTR Pigeon Grade, R.L. Wilson noted that "…an eye-catching feature was the gray finish to the frame, triggerguard, and top lever. Contributing to the 23's appeal were its auto ejectors, single selective trigger, automatic safety, and reasonable price." Wilson's observations regarding the new double gun's features could well have described a Model 21, with the exception of "reasonable price." Winchester had achieved something with the Model 23 that it had not been able to accomplish with the Model 24 or Model 22. Here at last was a suitable, affordable substitute for the Model 21.

[3] Winchester An American Legend by R.L. Wilson, Random House, 1991.

The Model 23 Classic came with 26-inch ventilated rib barrels and deluxe hand checkered stock and beavertail forearm. This model was only produced in 1986 and 1987. Pictured is a 20-gauge example, which has the same size frame as the 12-gauge. Model 23 Classics chambered in 28-gauge and .410 bore had a smaller frame. (Courtesy Dave Riffle)

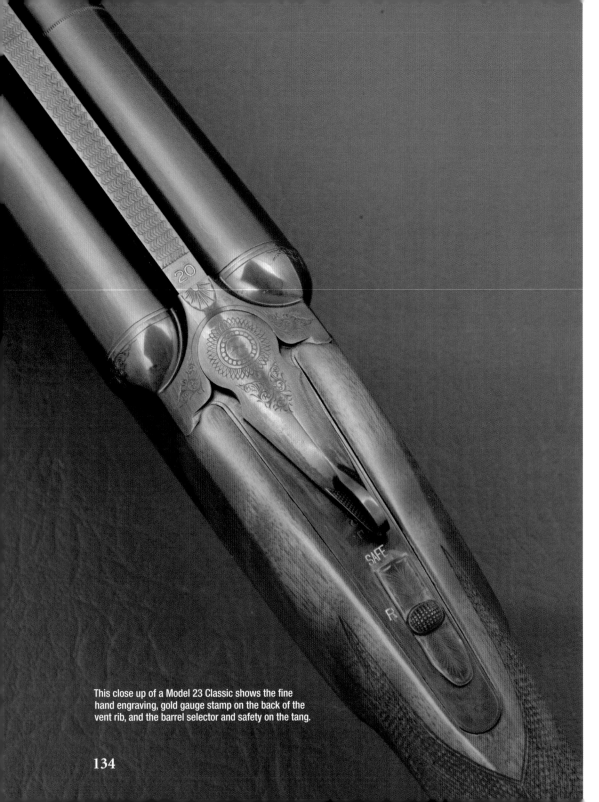

This close up of a Model 23 Classic shows the fine hand engraving, gold gauge stamp on the back of the vent rib, and the barrel selector and safety on the tang.

Initially the Model 23 XTR was offered only in 12-gauge, with 20-gauge added in 1979. The new Winchester double featured 3-inch chambers, 25-$\frac{1}{2}$ inch, 26-inch, 28-inch, or 30-inch vent rib barrels in a variety of chokes, a single selective trigger, and checkered walnut stock and forearm. The Model 23 was also the first commercial gun to employ the interchangeable Winchester chokes.

The Pigeon Grade Model 23 XTR displayed a bright coin finished receiver with fine line Pigeon Grade scrollwork, and an engraved pigeon on the bottom of the receiver flat. The fluted comb stock and beavertail forearm were manufactured from fancy grade American walnut that literally shined thanks to the new high-luster XTR finish introduced on Winchester guns in 1978. Both the forearm and European-style rounded pistol grip had fine line hand-cut checkering, and a white spacer was used to accent and separate the buttstock from the horizontal line Winchester butt plate.

The Model 23's design used a mechanical trigger system that did not depend upon the gun's recoil to discharge the second barrel, thus allowing a very quick follow-up shot for trap and skeet shooting. A single selective trigger, selective automatic ejectors, automatic safety, tapered ventilated rib, and chrome bores, to help resist corrosion and barrel fouling, were all standard features.

Following are Model 23 specifications.

TYPE

Double barrel, hammerless shotgun, automatic safety, single selective trigger, automatic ejectors.

STYLES

Field Gun, Pigeon Grade, Pigeon Grade Lightweight, Pigeon Grade Ducks Unlimited (only 500 manufactured in 1981), Golden Quail Model Series, Model 23 Light Duck, Model 23 Heavy Duck, Model 23 Grande Canadian, Model 23 Custom, and Model 23 Classic.

The bottom of the Model 23 Classic receiver was beautifully hand engraved and gold inlaid with a quail in flight.

BARRELS AND CHOKES

Model	Gauge	Barrel
23 XTR	12-gauge and 20-gauge	25-1/2 inch*, 26 inch, 28 inch, or 30 inch VR.
Light Duck	20-gauge	30-inch barrels F/F
Heavy Duck	12-gauge	30-inch barrels F/F
Heavy Duck	20-gauge and 28-gauge two-barrel set	26-inch barrels F/F
Grand Canadian	12-gauge or 20 gauge	25-1/2 inch barrels
23 Custom	12-gauge only	27-inch barrels with Winchoke
23 Classic	12-gauge, 20-gauge, 28-gauge, .410-gauge	26-inch VR barrels

*Pigeon Grade Lightweight only with 25-1/2 inch barrels bored IM/IC in 12-gauge, and IM/CM in 20-gauge, or with Winchokes.

RIBS

Solid rib and ventilated rib barrels.

CHAMBERS

All gauges 3-inch chambers.

STOCKS AND FOREARMS

Deluxe hand-checkered walnut round grip stocks and beavertail forearms. Straight English stock on Golden Quail, English AAA select walnut stock and forearm on Grande Canadian, English straight stock on Pigeon Grade Lightweight.

LIGHT DUCK was stamped on top of the barrel rib and the left barrel marked WINCHESTER MODEL 23DU – 20 GAUGE – 2" & 3".

BUTT PLATES

Horizontal line composition butt plate.

WEIGHTS (approximate)

12 gauge and 20 Gauge XTR	6-$\frac{1}{4}$ to 6-$\frac{3}{4}$ lbs.
Light Duck and Heavy Duck	8-$\frac{1}{2}$ lbs.
Model 23 Custom and Classic	7 lbs.

For many Winchester double gun enthusiasts the Model 23 was as close to the style, fit and finish of a Model 21 as they would ever get. The series was discontinued in 1987[4], and since that time, the values of Model 23 XTR Pigeon Grades, Golden Quail Series, Light and Heavy Duck models, Grand Canadian, and Custom and Classic Model 23s have continued to increase.

For Winchester, the Model 23 was the last great double gun. Or was it?

[4] The Model 23 Pigeon Grade and Pigeon Grade Lightweight were discontinued in 1986.

Winchester Parker Reproductions
The Other Winchester Double Gun

Parker was one of the great American double guns that Winchester had sought to challenge in the 1930s with its Model 21. Parker Brothers was one of America's premier double gun makers, founded in 1866 in the city of Meridian, Connecticut, where the company had flourished for more than four decades before the dark days of the 1930s. For Parker, the high-quality shotguns they had built since the 1880s were a hard sell during the early years of The Great Depression. Unlike Winchester or Remington, they did not have other lines to offer. Parker Brothers built shotguns and that was all they built. Even the Trojan, Parker's lowest priced model, wasn't inexpensive, and there were 10 grades above that ranging from VH through PH, GH, DH, CH, BH, AHE, AAHE, A-1 Special Grade, and Invincible Grade, of which only three were ever documented as having been built. In 1930 the Invincible Grade Parker

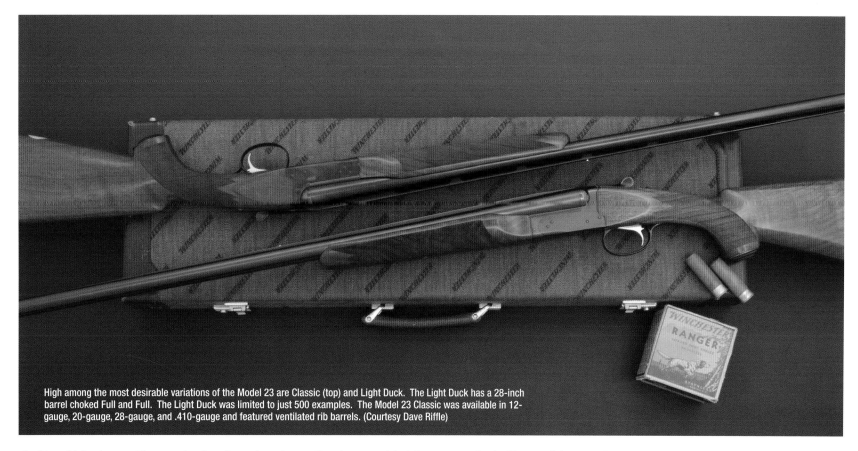
High among the most desirable variations of the Model 23 are Classic (top) and Light Duck. The Light Duck has a 28-inch barrel choked Full and Full. The Light Duck was limited to just 500 examples. The Model 23 Classic was available in 12-gauge, 20-gauge, 28-gauge, and .410-gauge and featured ventilated rib barrels. (Courtesy Dave Riffle)

double sold for $1,250. That was $25 less than a brand new Chrysler Imperial Eight Coupe with rumble seat!

In 1934 Parker Brothers sold out to Remington, and four years later production was moved from Meridian to Ilion, New York. Parker shotguns continued to be produced by Remington until the early part of World War II and the last examples were built c.1942. [5]

In the early 1980s the value of vintage Parker doubles was rising quickly among collectors trading a handful of exceptional examples and a fair quantity of guns in "good" condition. They were and remain to this day, one of the most desirable American shotguns ever built. This robust enthusiasm for the originals brought about the creation of Parker Reproductions in 1984. A division of Reagent Chemical & Research, Inc. in Middlesex, New Jersey, Parker Reproductions was created with the intent of bringing the legendary Parker double guns back to the American market. It was a bold venture into

waters that had been still for more than 40 years.

Reagent contracted with Winchester (U.S. Repeating Arms Co.) to build 20-gauge and 28-gauge DHE models (a DH with ejectors, thus DHE) at the Olin-Kodensha factory in Japan. These were not intended to be Winchesters, and the specifications for the double guns were to be as close to the original Parker Brothers model as possible. Winchester did such a good job, in fact, that most of the parts are interchangeable with the original guns.

When the Parker Reproduction was finally introduced it was cataloged as a Parker Reproduction by Winchester, and was so marked on the inside gun case lid, and in the sales literature. The barrels were also roll engraved Parker Reproductions by Winchester.

The Parker Reproduction made its debut in 1985 in both 20-gauge and 28-gauge versions, many in two barrel and multi gauge sets with prices beginning at $3,500. It was a

[5] 25th Edition Blue Book of Gun Values by S.P. Fjestad, Blue Book Publications, Inc.

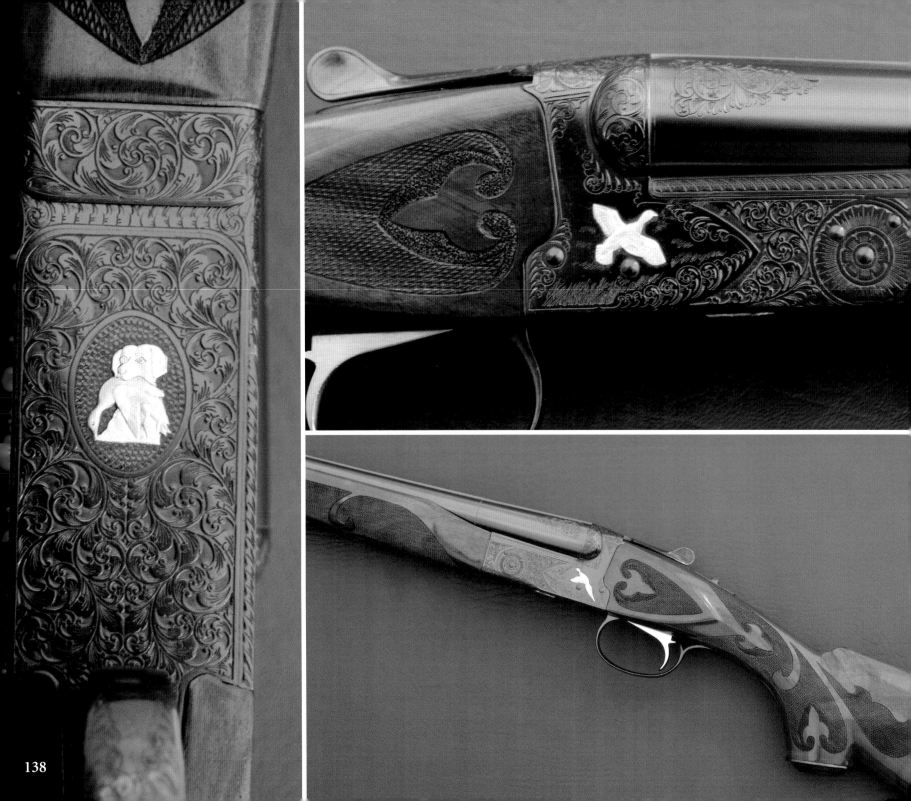

This is as ornate as the Model 23 could get, a Custom Pigeon Grade. This example in 28-gauge, is part of a two-barrel cased set. The deluxe stock has style 23-B carving and engraved pistol grip cap. The entire receiver is deeply engraved and inlaid in gold with game birds on both sides and a retriever with game bird on the bottom. Only 500 sets were made. (Courtesy Dave Riffle)

139

The Model 23 XTR Pigeon Grade was the premier model in the line. Introduced in 1978 and produced through 1986 it provided Winchester enthusiasts with a high-quality and distinctive double gun at a reasonable price. Built in 12-gauge and 20-gauge, as shown, the Pigeon Grade Model 23 XTR sold for $1,460. (Author's Collection)

U.S. Repeating Arms Co. and Olin-Kodensha in Japan were turning out high-quality products bearing the Winchester name. The Pigeon Grade Model 23 XTR offered a very fine level of engraving, fit and finish at an affordable price. The left side of the barrel was marked with the Winchester name, model, gauge, and chamber, the latter in both inches and millimeters. Pigeon Grade was stamped both on the right side of the barrel and on top of the vent rib.

The detailed engraving on the coin finished receiver was more extensive on the bottom than the sides, which were elegant but not overly ornate. The traditional pigeon was engraved on the bottom of the receiver as well.

142

Top: The Model 23 XTR came in a Winchester box, however, they were also sold with a vinyl covered hard case. (Photo courtesy Rock Island Auction Co.)

Above: There were two other variations of the Pigeon Grade Model, Lightweight, which had 25-1/2 inch barrels bored IM/IC in 12-gauge and IC/M in 20-gauge, and the Limited Edition Pigeon Grade Ducks Unlimited model built only in 1981. The DU was limited to 500 guns and came cased. (Photos courtesy Rock Island Auction Co.)

Left: The Pigeon Grade Ducks Unlimited Model 23 XTR featured a unique engraving pattern, special gold DUCKS UNLIMITED legend on top of the barrel rib, and a gold inlaid mallard's head in place of the usual pigeon. (Photos courtesy Rock Island Auction Co.)

143

Reagent Chemical & Research, Inc. teamed up with U.S. Repeating Arms and Olin-Kodensha to breathe new life into the legendary Parker Brothers double guns in the beginning in 1984. The author's Parker Reproduction DHE 28-gauge, with 26-inch and 28-inch barrels and single selective trigger sold for $4,200.

lot to ask, but in comparison to an original Parker Brothers DHE Grade, less than half the price then being paid for quality 20-gauge examples. Even today, 20 years later, a DHE grade Parker in 98 percent condition, according to the 26th Edition Blue Book of Gun Values, commands upwards of $10,000 for a 20-gauge and over $16,000 for a 28-gauge model. A DHE 28-gauge, two-barrel set, (26-inch and 28-inch) Parker Reproduction is valued today at $4,725.

The Parker Reproductions, with their fine hand engraving, striking color-casehardened frames, superb, extra fancy walnut stocks and forearms, and brilliant rust blued barrels, should have been a rousing success, and for a while they were. By 1989 there was a full line of Parker Reproductions that included the DHE Grade in 20-gauge, 28-gauge, and 12-gauge (added in 1986), a DHE Steel Shot Special in 12-gauge, DHE Small gauge combo, with 28-gauge and .410 gauge barrels or 16-gauge and 20-gauge barrels (added in 1993), and a three-barrel set with two 28-gauge barrels and one .410-gauge

barrel. In addition, between 1987 and 1989 Parker Reproductions offered a BHE Grade (two grades higher) in 12-gauge, 20-gauge, 28-gauge, or .410-gauge, and an A-1 Special (originally one grade below the Invincible) in a choice of 12-gauge, 20-gauge or 28-gauge. They were produced only in 1988 and 1989. The price for an A-1 Special cased with accessories was $11,200 in 1989 (That same year an original 20-gauge A-1 Special in 100 percent condition listed in the Blue Book of Gun Values for $92,000). There was also a limited edition Federal Duck Stamp Collector's Series authorized by the U.S. Department of Interior and built in either 12-gauge or 20-gauge to A-1 Special specifications. This was a cased set with two barrels limited to only 10 examples in 1988 and 10 in 1989. When new, they sold for $14,000.[6] The last Parker Reproductions model was the DHE Small Gauge Combo sold from 1993 to 1997. The author has a 1993 color brochure and Retail Price List, which shows the availability of the DHE D-Grade in 12-gauge, 20-

[6] Ibid

144

The author's two-barrel 28-gauge set is comprised of 26-inch and 28-inch barrels. The guns could also be ordered with different gauge barrel sets. Each Parker Reproduction came with a leather trunk case, canvas and leather protective cover, and Parker Reproductions stamped snap caps.

Inside lid of the leather case bore the ornate Parker Reproductions emblem, which also stated by Winchester.

gauge, and 28-gauge, listing for $3,370 with one barrel, and $4,200 with two barrels. An extra $172 was charged for a beavertail forearm. Additionally a 20-gauge and 16-gauge two-barrel set was listed for $4,870 and a three-barrel 20/20/16-gauge set offered for $5,630. The A-1 Special was also still available in 1993 and priced in either 12-gauge or 20-gauge at $11,200. The Parker Reproductions brochure made special note of the new Limited Edition 16/20 Combo, which featured a 16-gauge barrel manufactured in Germany by Krieghoff. Only 500 barrels were produced and this offering was discontinued in 1994. Examples in excellent condition now bring upwards of $6,250.[7]

The Parker Reproductions, like the original Parker Brothers double guns were a success, but on a far smaller scale and for a much shorter period. Most production had been completed by 1989 when Olin-Kodensha closed, and by the mid 1990s, interest in the Parker Reproductions had begun to fade. In the September 2004 issue of *American Rifleman*, author Terry Wieland offered several explanations for Parker Reproduction's failure in an article titled *On Again, Off Again, The American Double Struggles to Return*. Noted Wieland, "[A Parker Reproduction] lacked the virtues of a fully custom-made gun, with every measurement matched to the individual. At the same time, it had neither the appeal of an antique, nor a low price to put it within reach of those who could not afford an original Parker. The Parker Reproduction was too expensive for the average guy, and not good enough for the wealthy aficionado. One approach to bringing back the American double had been tried and failed."

A decade later the Parker Reproductions are at last becoming what they could not be in the 1980s and early 1990s – collectible. On the average, a Parker Reproduction is worth more today than it was when new. Whether or not the roll engraved Winchester name on the barrels has had anything to do with that is hard to say, but what is certain, without Winchester and U.S. Repeating Arms Co., there would never have been a Parker Reproduction.

[7] Ibid

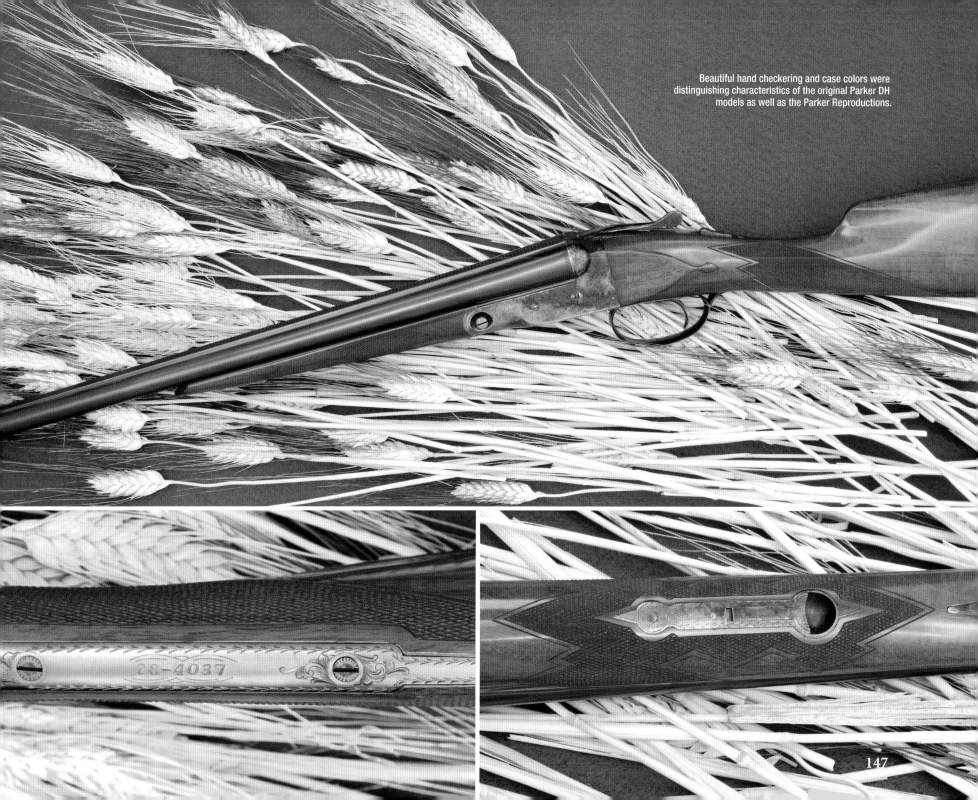

Beautiful hand checkering and case colors were distinguishing characteristics of the original Parker DH models as well as the Parker Reproductions.

28-4037

147

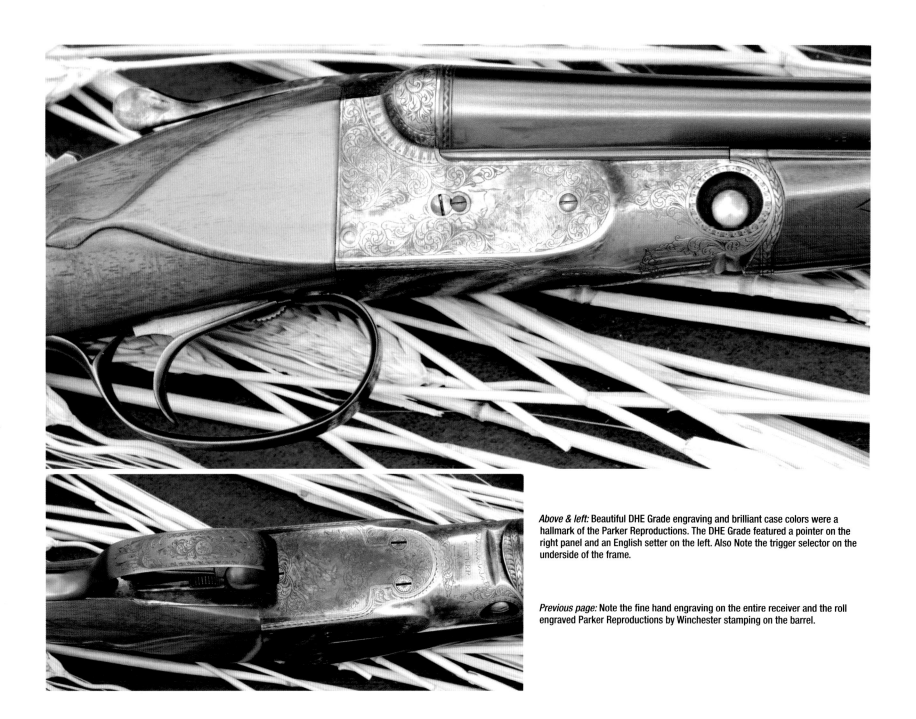

Above & left: Beautiful DHE Grade engraving and brilliant case colors were a hallmark of the Parker Reproductions. The DHE Grade featured a pointer on the right panel and an English setter on the left. Also Note the trigger selector on the underside of the frame.

Previous page: Note the fine hand engraving on the entire receiver and the roll engraved Parker Reproductions by Winchester stamping on the barrel.

Shown are three prime examples of the great little Winchester .410 Model 42 slide-action repeater. At top, a No. 42-5 engraved model built in 1954. This example has a 28-inch barrel choked Skeet, fitted with the round post-donut base ventilated rib barrel. In the middle, a Skeet Grade .410 choked Skeet with 26-inch barrel. Bottom, a superb example of the Field Grade gun with a 28-inch barrel choked Full. This example was manufactured in 1951. (Courtesy Dave Riffle)

Chapter Six
The Great Little .410
Model 42 Slide-action Shotguns

With the introduction of the Model 1912, Winchester had created the most successful shotgun of the 20th century. Available at the time in 12-gauge, 16-gauge, and 20-gauge, by 1932 Winchester-Western had developed a new 3-inch .410-gauge shell. Since the Model 12's design did not readily lend itself to anything smaller than 20-gauge (although in 1937 a new 28-gauge model would be introduced), John Olin decided that New Haven should design an entirely new slide-action shotgun chambered exclusively for Winchester-Western's new 3-inch .410-gauge. In the world of shotguns, the Model 42 could be described in one word. Innovative.

Announced in August 1933 the new slide-action repeater looked like a scaled down Model 12, but was in fact a totally new design, as noted in the 1934 Winchester sales catalog.

The first description appeared in Catalog No. 89:

"The new Model 42 Winchester Slide-action Hammerless .410 Repeater is of completely new design and construction. It has a general similarity in appearance to the famous Model 12 Winchester, but in each and every part, it is a .410 shotgun. Model 42 is the first American made .410 repeater to handle a 3 inch shell and the first pump action gun designed for such a shell. This chambering for 3 inch shells makes the Model 42 a unique achievement in American gun making.

"Model 42 is made in two styles, the Standard Grade gun and the Model 42 Skeet Gun. Both styles are chambered expressly for 3" shells, but in addition will also handle the regular 2-$\frac{1}{2}$ inch .410 gauge shell.

"The Standard Grade is furnished with either 26" or 28" full choke, modified choke or cylinder bore barrel of Winchester Proof Steel, pistol grip walnut stock, hard rubber butt plate and round slide handle with circular grooves. The Skeet Gun is furnished with 26 inch Skeet Choke Barrel of Winchester Proof Steel, straight grip walnut stock, checkered, hard rubber butt plate, and extension action slide handle, checkered. The magazine of each gun has a capacity of five 3 inch shells or six 2-$\frac{1}{2}$ inch shells.

"You have in this new Winchester not only a light, entirely new designed and built man-sized six-shot repeater, but a gun that with its new Winchester 3 inch Repeater Super Speed .410 gauge shell actually doubles the usual .410-gauge performance – a gun actually putting double the usual number of shot in a 20 inch circle at 30 yards – patterning more than the entire charge of other .410-gauge guns. With this 3 inch shell, the Model 42 equals the performance of a 28 gauge gun, and in fact is not far behind the performance expected from 20 gauge guns a few years ago. The 3 inch shell is conspicuously imprinted on the body, marking it for the 3 inch chamber only.

"Model 42 will prove ideal for the wide variety of sport which hand trap shooting provides, in addition to its fine service for field and skeet shooting. With the rapidly increasing popularity of Skeet and the inclusion of .410 events in all of the big Skeet Tournaments, the Model 42 now places every shooter in a position to own a hammerless, take down, six shot .410 repeater.

"This new Winchester handles exquisitely. It is excellently balanced, light in

151

Here we see three examples of Model 42 stock design. At top is carving 42-B. Center the Skeet Gauge with checkered English stock, and bottom the Standard or Field Grade walnut stock with full pistol grip.

weight, and beautiful in its line. It has a racy appearance and will appeal to every lover of fine guns as in every respect a thoroughbred. The Standard Grade gun with 26" barrel weighs 5-$^7/_8$ pounds and with 28"barrel 6 pounds. The Model 42 Skeet Gun weighs 6 pounds.

"Another distinctive feature of the Model 42 is the special Winchester Skeet Choke boring which has been developed and is standard on the Skeet Gun. Barrels with this Skeet boring can also be had, if so specified, on the Model 42 Standard Grade gun. This boring delivers remarkably effective and consistent patterns for skeet shooting which places this gun in a class by itself for small gauge skeet shooting. In addition, the Skeet Choke is admirably adapted to small gauge upland shooting."[1]

With the new 3-inch .410-gauge shell and Model 42 Slide-Action shotgun, Winchester had defined an entirely new class of sport shooting, and also opened the door for women and younger shooters to compete in trap, skeet, and wing shooting. The Model 42 also redefined the styling of the Model 12, with sleeker, sportier lines.

Following are Model 42 specifications.

TYPE

Take down, slide-action repeating shotgun, hammerless, tubular magazine, cross lock safety operated horizontally across front of trigger guard.

STYLES

Standard or Field Grade (1933-1963); Trap Grade (1934-1939); Skeet Gun (1934-1963); Skeet Gun – Trap Grade (1934-1939); DeLuxe Grade, (comparable to Pigeon Grade in Model 12, c.1950-1963. Most examples factory engraved).

RECEIVER

Straight line matting on top of receiver.

BARRELS AND CHOKES

Standard or Field Grade: 28-inch barrel with choice of Full, Modified, or Cylinder Bore choke, 26-inch barrel with Skeet Choke only. Skeet Choke available as special order for 28-inch barrels.

[1] Winchester Shotguns and Shotshells by Ronald W. Stadt, 1984, Armory Publications.

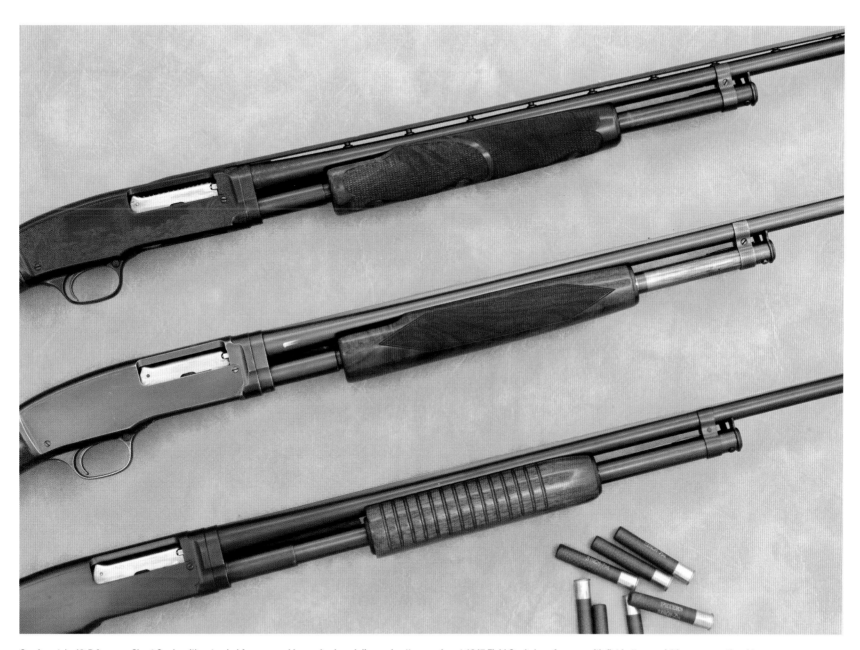

Carving style 42-B forearm, Skeet Grade with extended forearm and large checkered diamond pattern, and post 1947 Field Grade long forearm with flat bottom and 14 grooves on the sides.

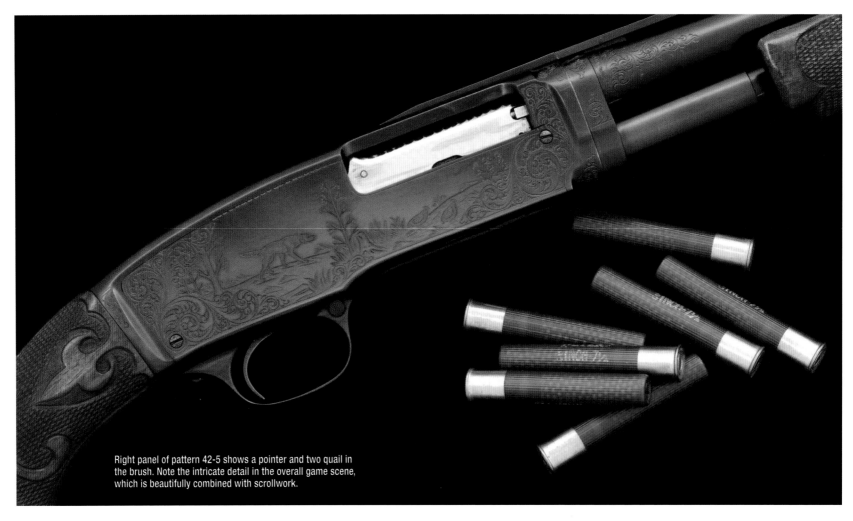

Right panel of pattern 42-5 shows a pointer and two quail in the brush. Note the intricate detail in the overall game scene, which is beautifully combined with scrollwork.

Trap Grade: 26-inch barrel usually choked Skeet, stamped TRAP at bottom of receiver. Only 231 manufactured.

Skeet Gun: 26-inch No. 1 Skeet choke barrel when introduced. Also made available beginning late in 1934 with 26-inch or 28-inch barrels choked Full, Modified, or Cylinder Bore choke. No. 1 Skeet choke changed to No. 2 skeet choke after 1935. Cylinder choke was dropped in 1953 and Improved Cylinder added. The 28-inch barrel option dropped after 1938. Reintroduced in 1948 and 26-inch barrels dropped thereafter. Winchester Special Ventilated Rib barrels (installed by Simmons for Winchester) avail-able at extra cost beginning in 1954. Cutts Compensators available on Skeet Gun beginning 1954.

Skeet Gun – Trap Grade: 26-inch barrel with Full choke or 28-inch barrel with Full, Modified, or Cylinder Bore choke. (Model discontinued after 1939)

DeLuxe Grade: Introduced c.1950. Same configuration as Trap Grade, standard with Winchester Special Ventilated Rib barrels beginning in 1954. Made on special order only. There were also a few Pigeon Grade models, which are distinguished by the engraved pigeon on the underside of the magazine tube. Most were factory engraved.

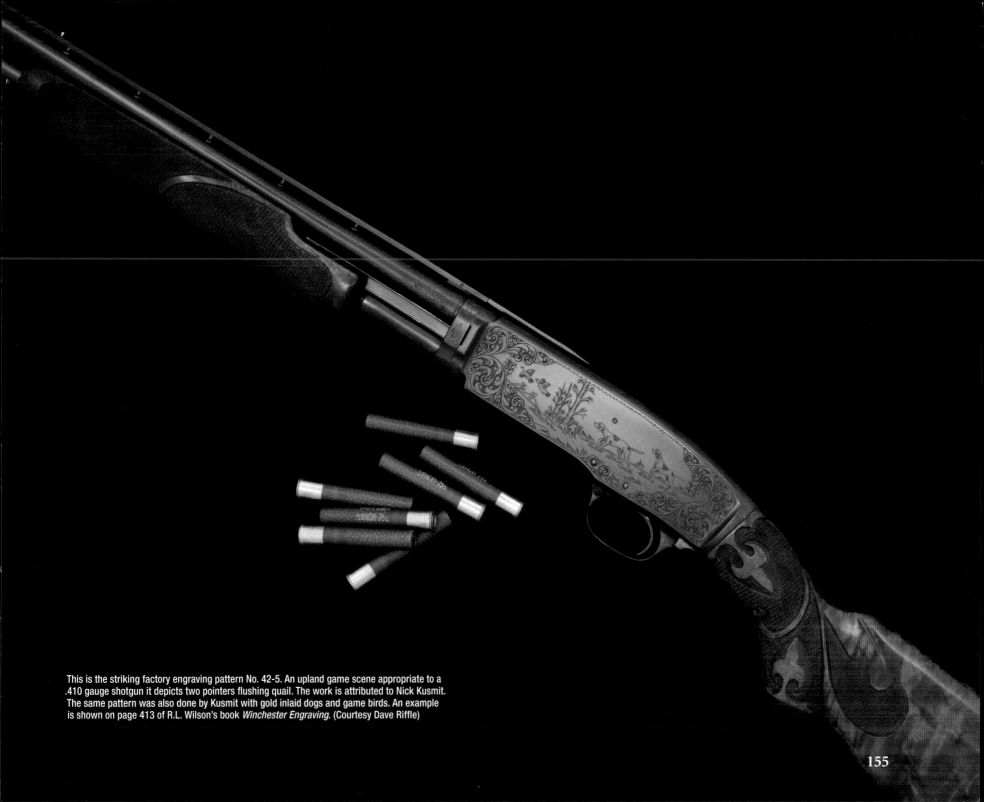

This is the striking factory engraving pattern No. 42-5. An upland game scene appropriate to a .410 gauge shotgun it depicts two pointers flushing quail. The work is attributed to Nick Kusmit. The same pattern was also done by Kusmit with gold inlaid dogs and game birds. An example is shown on page 413 of R.L. Wilson's book *Winchester Engraving*. (Courtesy Dave Riffle)

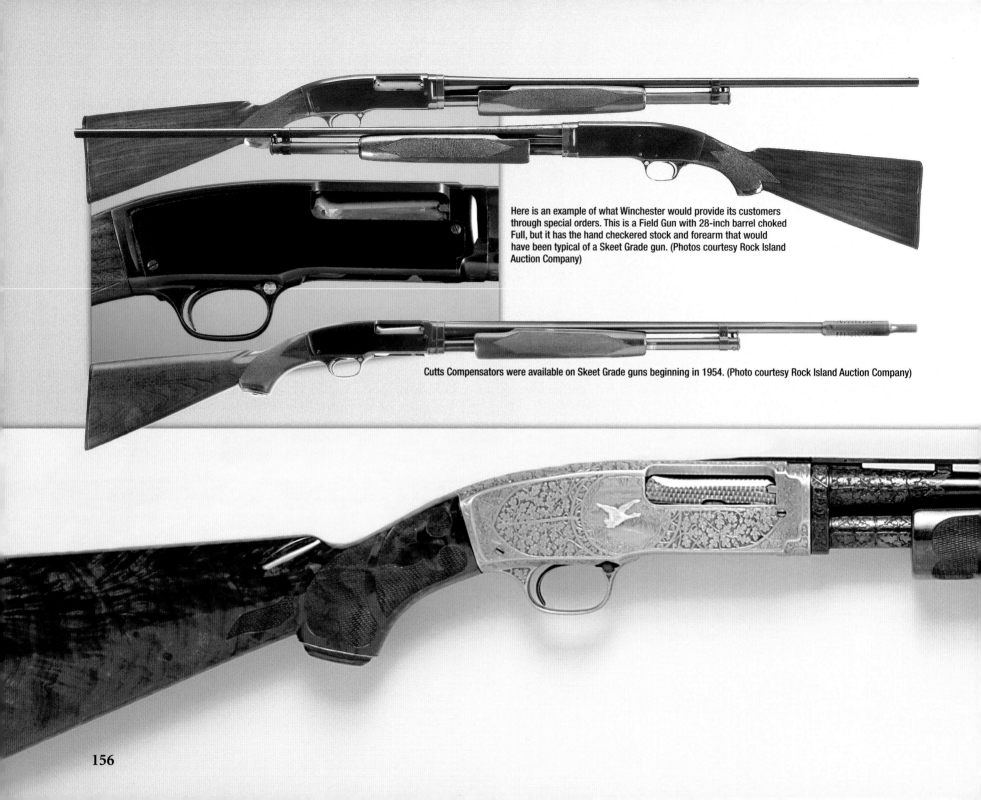

Here is an example of what Winchester would provide its customers through special orders. This is a Field Gun with 28-inch barrel choked Full, but it has the hand checkered stock and forearm that would have been typical of a Skeet Grade gun. (Photos courtesy Rock Island Auction Company)

Cutts Compensators were available on Skeet Grade guns beginning in 1954. (Photo courtesy Rock Island Auction Company)

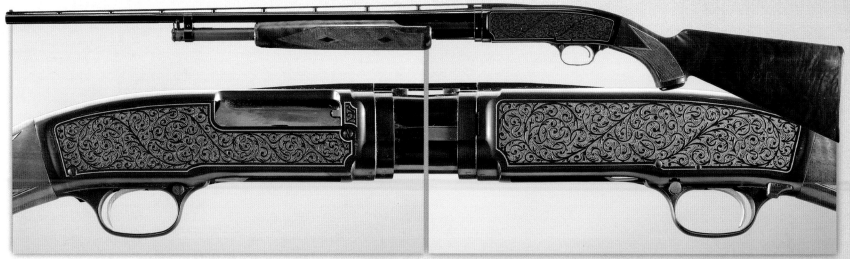

This is an exceptional example of a Model 42. This special order bears serial number 1. WFTEXP1 and has a 26-inch vent rib barrel, checkered walnut stock and forearm, beautiful scrollwork with a punch dot background on both sides of the receiver, and a gold border. It also has a gold plated trigger. This gun was made in Japan by Miroku (Winchester's manufacturing partner) and was originally owned by the President of U.S. Repeating Arms Co. It became part of the Peter and Patty Murray collection in 1997 and was sold at auction in 2004. (Photos courtesy Rock Island Auction Company)

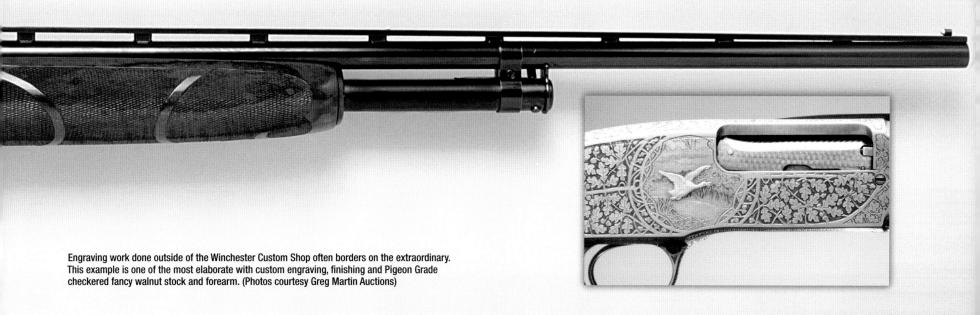

Engraving work done outside of the Winchester Custom Shop often borders on the extraordinary. This example is one of the most elaborate with custom engraving, finishing and Pigeon Grade checkered fancy walnut stock and forearm. (Photos courtesy Greg Martin Auctions)

Angelo Bee, who was one of Winchester's outside engravers, did work on Model 12s, Model 42, and Model 21s, among others. This is indicative of his style which focuses on highly embellished hunting scenes and intricate backgrounds and foregrounds. His use of gold and platinum creates shadings that highlight his figures, which most often are within a panel surrounded by high relief scrollwork. The engraver's signature is in the lower right edge of the panel. Another example of Angelo Bee's work can be seen on page 462 of *Winchester Engraving* by R.L. Wilson.

RIBS

Plain, raised matted rib, and Winchester Special Ventilated rib barrels. Field Grade guns could be special ordered with Winchester Special Ventilated Rib barrels beginning in 1954. Plain and raised matted rib barrels were available on Field Grade, plain or raised matted rib on Skeet Gun, Winchester Special Ventilated Rib barrels at extra cost for Skeet Gun beginning in 1954. The vent ribs were installed by Simmons on Model 42's which were returned to New Haven in the white.[2] Like the Model 12, there were three styles of vent ribs: round post-donut base, round post, and rectangular post.

CHAMBERS

3-inch chambers standard. Optional 2-$\frac{1}{2}$ inch chambers on special order beginning 1935.

[2] Ibid

STOCKS AND FOREARMS

Field Grade: walnut stock with half pistol grip and grooved round forearm. A longer, flat bottom forearm with 14 grooves on the sides only was introduced in 1947. Later models c.1940 also have full pistol grip stocks as standard.

Skeet Grade: select checkered walnut straight grip or pistol grip stocks and checkered extended forearm.

Trap Grade: checkered fancy walnut stocks, pistol grip or straight English style, checkered extended forearm. First variation had small checkered forearm with one un-checkered diamond in center, second variation has large checkered forearm with two un-checkered diamonds in center, and one un-checkered diamond on each side of pistol grip, or one un-checkered diamond on underside of grip on English style stocks.

Facing page: One of the most striking Model 42 Winchesters produced was this Skeet Grade gun originally built c. 1937 and engraved by Angelo Bee around 1975, at which time it was refinished. The gun has custom carving of the extra fancy walnut stock and extended forearm and is engraved and inlaid in gold and platinum. (Author's Collection)

Carving and checkering on this custom Model 42 is similar to style 42B.

Facing page: In creating an interesting game scene on this Model 42, Angel Bee chose to use a fox, rather than a hunting dog to scatter these morning doves. Note the use of gold and platinum to shade the fox.

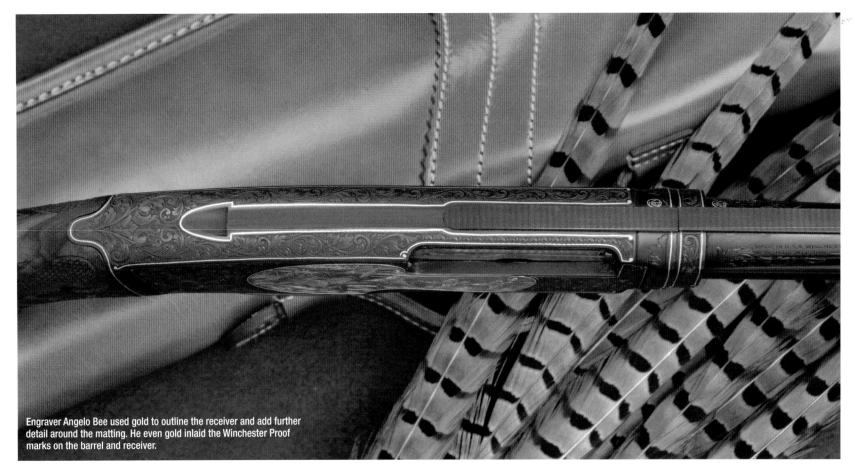

Engraver Angelo Bee used gold to outline the receiver and add further detail around the matting. He even gold inlaid the Winchester Proof marks on the barrel and receiver.

Skeet Gun – Trap Grade: fancy walnut straight grip English stock and extended forearm with two un-checkered diamond-shaped areas.

DeLuxe Grade: full fancy walnut stock with fancy checkering, one un-checkered diamond-shaped area on the side of the grip, and two on the side of the slide handle. Also offered with offset, cheek piece, or Monte Carlo stock at additional cost.

BUTT PLATES
Hard rubber.

GRIP CAPS
Skeet and DeLuxe models with pistol grip stocks had a hard rubber grip cap

(same as found on the Model 12) and later they were fitted with the first variety metal cap. These were also engraved on DeLuxe and Pigeon Grade Model 42s.

The Model 42 was an elegant shotgun. Many examples were handsomely embellished by Winchester Custom Shop engraver Nick Kusmit in standard engraving patterns 42-1, 42-1A, 42-1B, 42-1C, 42-2, 42-3, 42-4, or 42-5. Stock carving patterns, 42-A and 42-B, were similar to those of the Model 12. Engraving was also comparable to the Model 12 and patterns with hunting dogs and birds featured upland game scenes appropriate to the .410-gauge, such as the example pictured which features a Golden Retriever flushing quail. Engravers outside the factory, such as Angelo Bee, who lent his artistic touch to both the Model 12 and Model 42 in later years, added further distinctiveness to the genteel .410 repeaters.

Serial numbers and trigger are finished in gold. The trigger guard also received a great deal of engraving and gold inlay.

Beginning in 1935 a special shaped wood magazine plug was included with each Model 42 to reduce magazine capacity to two shells. This was done in compliance with the Presidential Proclamation signed February 2, 1935, regarding the use of repeating shotguns for hunting migratory birds. This limited capacity to two shells in the magazine and one in the chamber.

Of all Winchester slide-action shotguns, the Model 42 has one of the highest survival rates for guns in very good original condition. Between 1933 and 1963 a total of 159,353 were produced.[3] In 1956 a Field Grade Model 42 retailed for $93.45. A well-maintained example in 100 percent condition will bring $1,200 today. For a Skeet Grade gun you can add an additional $1,600 to the price, and due to their rarity, a Trap Grade that once sold for $180 is now worth $8,500.[4] Dollar for dollar the Model 42 has proven to be one of the best investments one could have made in a Winchester shotgun.

As author Ronald W. Stadt noted in Winchester Shotguns and Shotshells, "Probably no Winchester model was so universally loved and so little used as the Model 42. Almost no one who owned a 42 said anything bad about it."

For three decades the Model 42 Winchester was the best .410-gauge shotgun that money could buy, and among gun collectors that statement is equally true today.

[3] According to the 25th Edition Blue Book of Gun Values production is estimated at 164,800 between 1933 and 1963.
[4] 25th Edition Blue Book of Gun Values by S.P. Fjestad.

WINCHESTER
SMALL ARMS AMMUNITION
SHOT GUN CARTRIDGES
MANUFACTURED BY THE
REPEATING ARMS CO.
NEW HAVEN, CONN. U.S.A.

Chapter Seven
Single Barrel and Bolt Action Shotguns
Models 20, 36, 37, 37A, 38, 41, 370, 840, and 1370 Slagblaster

If there's one thing that makes you a better shot…it's having only one shot.

Winchester has offered more single shot, single barrel shotguns in more gauges and calibers than any other arms maker in the world. Over the years there have been Winchester single shots chambered to handle everything from .22 caliber and 9mm shot shells to .410, 28, 20, 16 and 12-gauge.

From 1936, until the early 1960s, the single barrel Model 37 Winchester was the "first" shotgun for more Americans than any other, with models chambered in .410-gauge, 28-gauge, 20-gauge, 16-gauge and 12-gauge. However, the Model 37 wasn't the first single shot to come from New Haven. Winchester had claimed that honor way back in 1913.

The very first Winchester single was based on the John Browning designed Model 1885 single shot rifle, which was built in both high wall and low wall variations up until 1920. The 1885 shotgun was the same design as the high wall rifle but chambered in 20-gauge. Offered in both solid frame and take down versions, the Model 1885 had a 26-inch full choked nickel steel barrel, straight grip stock and forearm of plain walnut. The original price was just $16.00.

The introductory literature noted that the action of the Model 1885 was "…the old reliable Sharp's breech-bolt and lever. This is a very simple and strong form of construction and one that gives light and easy action. The opening movement of the lever automatically withdraws the firing pin and draws down the bolt, leaving the breech clear. The closing movement [of the lever] leaves the hammer in a locked position at half cock. To fire the gun, the hammer must be brought to full cock by hand."

Christopher Spencer had used a similar breech-bolt design for his Model 1882 slide-action shotgun, which though never produced in great numbers was well ahead of both the Browning-designed Winchester Model 1893 and T.C. Bennett-designed Model 1912.

The best version of the Model 1885 was the take down gun, which was quickly disassembled by pushing forward the take down lock, dropping the lever, and giving the barrel a quarter twist. The take down model was an additional $5.00. A pistol grip stock was an option for $3.00, an extra barrel complete with forearm $12.00, and a matted rib or matted barrel was an extra $5.00.

Above: The first successful Winchester single was the Model 1885, which looked like the single shot high wall rifle. The Model 20 (pictured), a top break .410-gauge hammer gun with 26-inch full choked barrel, succeeded it in 1920. The Model 20 had a well-finished black walnut forearm with a stylish front lip, and a full pistol grip stock. Discontinued in 1924, a total of 23,616 were built. (Photo courtesy Rock Island Auction Company)

Facing page: It was the most successful single shot, single barrel shotgun in history. The Winchester Model 37 was introduced in 1936 and remained popular for nearly 30 years. More than 1 million were produced by the time the Model 37 was discontinued in 1963. Pictured is a 12-gauge model built in the late 1940s. (Author's Collection)

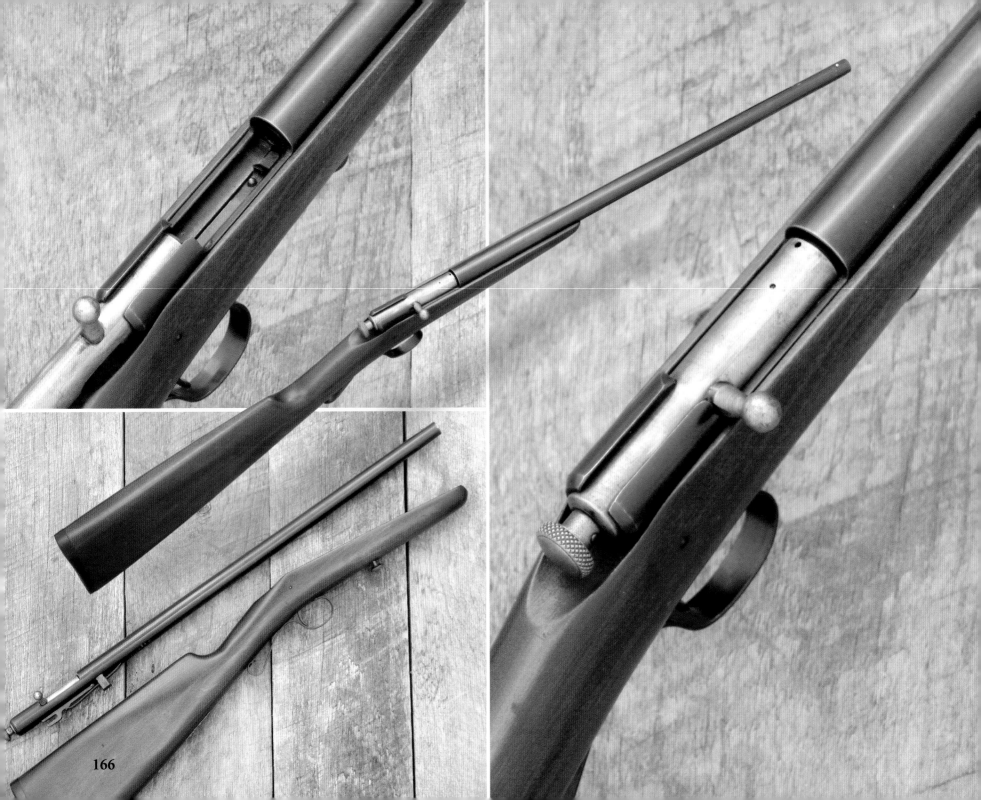

Also introduced in 1920 was the Model 41, Winchester's second bolt-action shotgun, this one chambered in .410-gauge. A high quality shotgun, the Model 41 was a take down gun, which like the Model 36, was disassembled by turning the knurled screw under the forearm and removing the barrel. (U.S. Repeating Arms Company Collection)

Facing page: In 1920 Winchester introduced its first bolt-action shotgun, the Model 36, a small take down gun chambered for the Winchester 9mm rimfire shot shell. Winchester advertised the Model 36 as ideal for vermin. More the size of a youth model the simple bolt action allowed quick loading. The action was cocked by pulling back on the knurled bolt knob. The Model 36 was easily disassembled by turning the knurled screw under the forearm and removing the barrel. (U.S. Repeating Arms Company Collection)

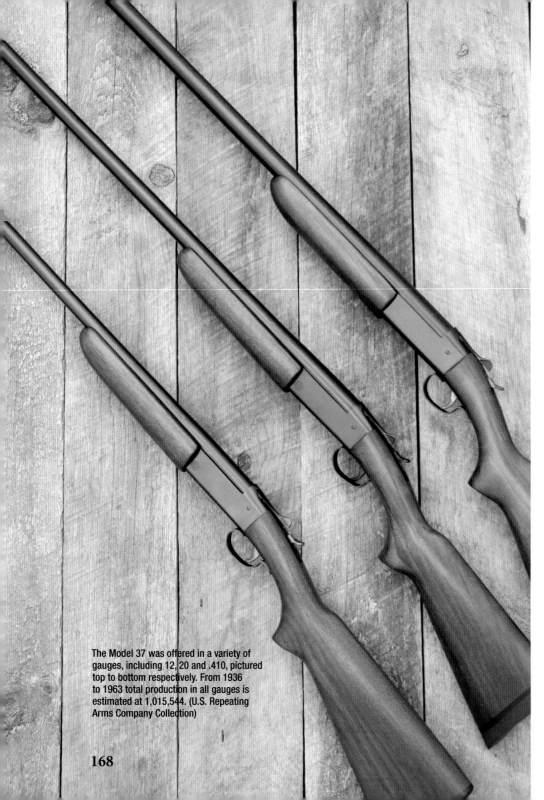

The Model 37 was offered in a variety of gauges, including 12, 20 and .410, pictured top to bottom respectively. From 1936 to 1963 total production in all gauges is estimated at 1,015,544. (U.S. Repeating Arms Company Collection)

After approximately 139,725 were made, the Model 1885 single shot shotgun was discontinued in 1920 along with the original high wall and low wall rifles.

Immediately after the Model 1885 was discontinued Winchester introduced three new post-World War I single shot shotguns, Models 20, 36, and 41. As noted in the 1920 sales catalog the Model 20 was a new .410 bore shotgun. A top break hammer gun with a 26-inch Full choked barrel, the Model 20 had a well-finished black walnut forearm with a stylish front lip, and a full pistol grip stock. Fancy walnut and hand checkering could also be special ordered.

The Model 20 was also part of what Winchester billed as a "Junior Trapshooting Outfit." The set, which was well promoted by Winchester for use by "the whole family," included a Winchester Midget Hand Trap for throwing clay pigeons, 150 Winchester .410 shells, 100 clay targets, and a cleaning kit all handsomely packaged in a rugged 30x8-$\frac{1}{2}$x6-inch case. The "Junior Trapshooting Outfit" came with a brochure entitled "A Whole New Field of Sport," which described the outfit and how to set up a field for junior trapshooting, a 16-page booklet, "How to Use and Care for the Winchester Junior Trapshooting Outfit," a miniature score pad, a 12-page instruction booklet, and instructions for cleaning.[1]

It was not overly successful and in 1924 the Model 20 was discontinued, however, they were still being sold as late as 1931. Approximately 23,616 were produced (including those in the "Junior Trapshooting Outfit" set). First priced at $30.00, Winchester lowered the retail price to $16.50 in 1922. While the single guns are not overly valuable today, a 100 percent example is worth around $750, the "Junior Trapshooting Outfit" set in excellent condition with all accessories is worth $3,500.[2] Happy hunting. Harrington & Richardson (H&R) still offer a model nearly identical to the Winchester Model 20 single shot chambered in every gauge from .410 to 10-gauge.

The Model 36, also introduced in the 1920 catalog, was an entirely different approach, and like the Model 1885 shotgun was based on a rifle design, in this instance the Model 1902.

The Model 36 was Winchester's first bolt-action shotgun, and it was also the most unusual, as it was chambered for a 9mm No. 9 shot cartridge.

[1] Winchester Shotguns and Shotshells by Ronald W. Stadt, 1984, Armory Publications and The History of Winchester Firearms 1886-1992 by Thomas Henshaw, 1993 Winchester Press.
[2] 25th Edition Blue Book of Gun Values by S.P. Fjestad.

The Model 37 was a quality built shotgun that employed a new manufacturing process utilizing deep-draw steel forming and copper brazing. No castings of any kind were used in the Model 37's construction. The action was top-lever breakdown with automatic ejection started by positive mechanical force as the gun was opened, the empty shell being ejected by spring power.

169

Cutaway of a Model 370 below a Model 37 shows the differences in the design of the New Haven built single versus its Canadian-built successor with full exposed hammer. (U.S. Repeating Arms Company Collection)

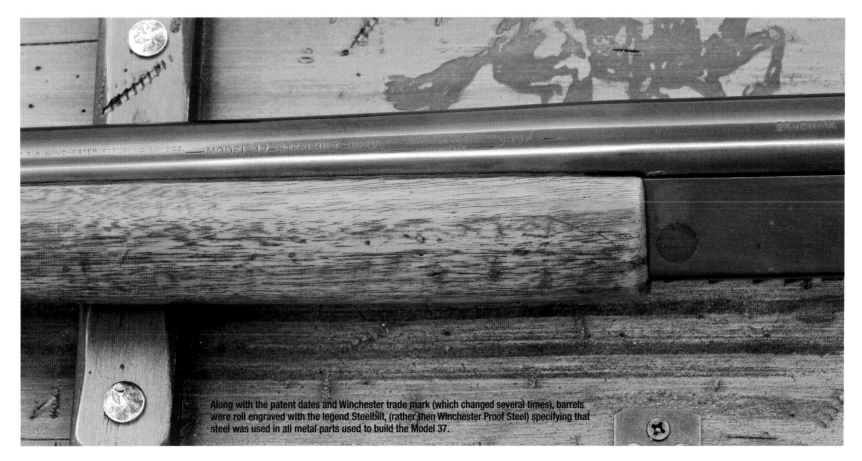

Along with the patent dates and Winchester trade mark (which changed several times), barrels were roll engraved with the legend Steelbilt, (rather then Winchester Proof Steel) specifying that steel was used in all metal parts used to build the Model 37.

Winchester advertised the small take down model as ideal for vermin. The catalog stated:

"This is a new Winchester shotgun designed for short range work with 9 m/m ammunition, much used, in some localities, for this type of work. It is a bolt action single shotgun, light in weight, and handy and economical for use."

This was the smallest shotgun Winchester had ever made and it used a gum wood stock rather than walnut, another first for New Haven. The Model 36 was easily disassembled by turning a thumbscrew under the forearm and removing the 18-inch barrel from the one-piece stock. As advertised, it was light, weighing just 2-3/4 pounds, and chambered to fire either the 9mm rimfire long or short cartridge manufactured by Winchester. The introductory price was $13.00 but it was soon reduced to $7.50. After roughly 20,000 had been built the Model 36 was discontinued in 1927. Oddly enough they

are actually rare today and specimens in very good condition are worth an average of $1,500.

The third new single shot for 1920 was the Model 41, also a bolt-action design but of a far higher grade than the Model 36, and chambered in .410-gauge. The 1920 catalog noted:

"For the lover of the small-bore shotgun the Winchester Repeating Arms Company has now developed a new shotgun of the bolt-action type, the first of this style of shotgun made in America that is of the highest grade in material, appearance, and shooting qualities. The action of this gun is of the 'upturn and pull-back' type."

Like the Model 36, this too was a take down design with the barrel again released by turning a thumbscrew under the forearm of the one-piece black walnut stock. The barrel was 24-inches long, and overall length of the Model 36

The Model 37 was a very elegant design that laid the groundwork for the double barrel Model 24, which used the same construction techniques and styling.

SMALL ARMS AMMUNITION
SHOT GUN CARTRIDGES
MANUFACTURED BY THE

WINCHESTER

REPEATING ARMS CO.
NEW HAVEN, CONN., U.S.A.

The Model 37 featured a semi-hammerless lock with low safety cocking lever located well forward on the tang, just behind the top opening lever. It is shown in both cocked (flat) and de-cocked (upright) positions. The style of the lever was changed three times from the original narrow lever (1936) to one slightly wider (1937) and finally to a concave, spade-shaped lever (as shown), approximately mid-year 1937.

173

Genuine American walnut was used in the pistol grip stock and forearm of the Model 37. The large, full, round forearm was the same diameter for its entire length providing a solid grip regardless of gauge.

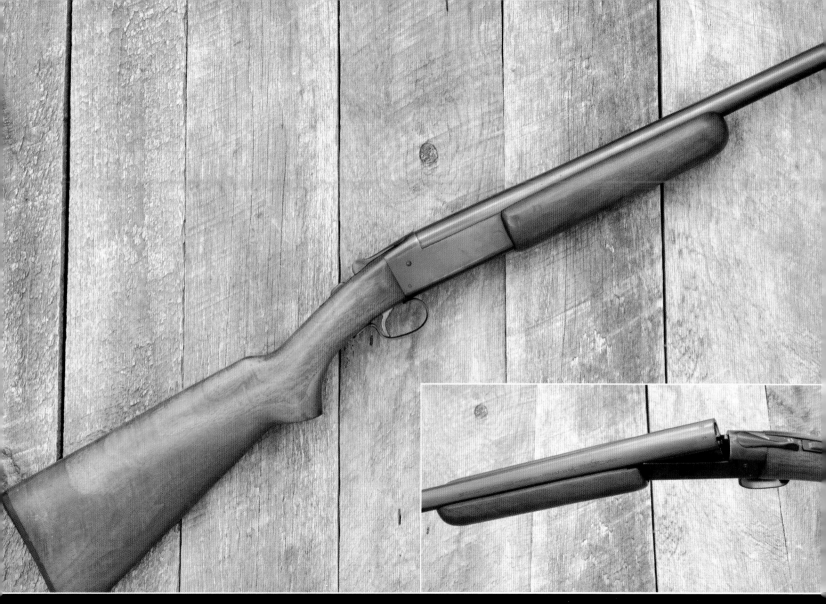

t looks like a Model 37 but there's no cocking lever, instead it's a tang safety. This is a Model 38, a design with a full internal hammer that was never put into production. It is interesting, however, that in

...fit, it looks very much like the Model 24 double barrel that was int...duced in 1940. (U.S. Repeating Arms Co...

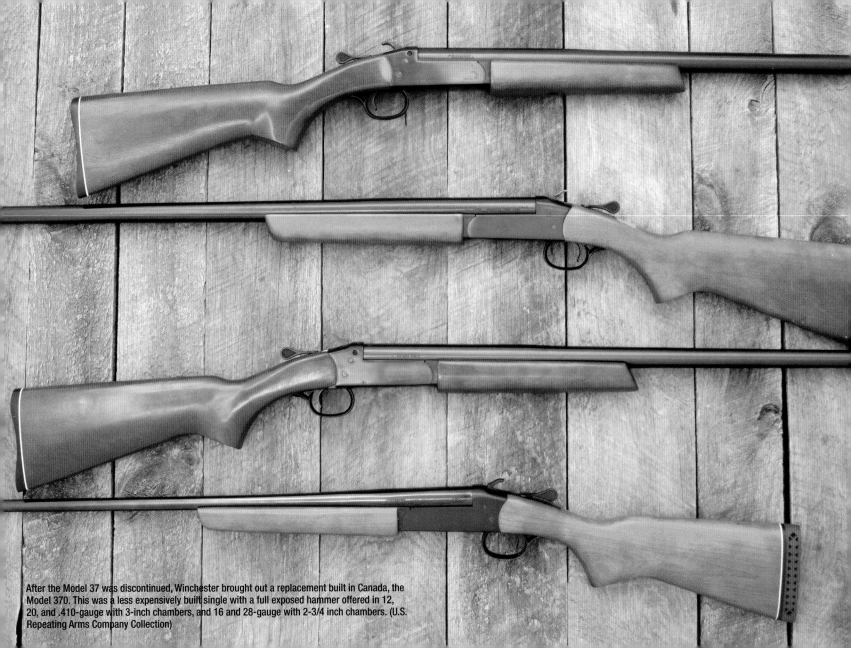

After the Model 37 was discontinued, Winchester brought out a replacement built in Canada, the Model 370. This was a less expensively built single with a full exposed hammer offered in 12, 20, and .410-gauge with 3-inch chambers, and 16 and 28-gauge with 2-3/4 inch chambers. (U.S. Repeating Arms Company Collection)

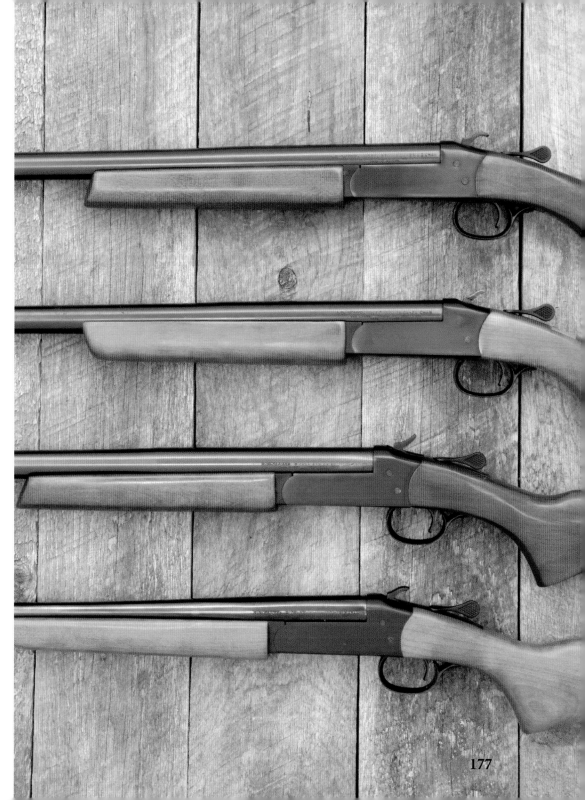

The semi-pistol grip stock and forearm were American hardwood with a walnut finish. In both appearance and quality, the Model 370 was much less of a gun than the Model 37. Roughly 221,578 were built in all gauges before production was discontinued in 1973. (U.S. Repeating Arms Company Collection)

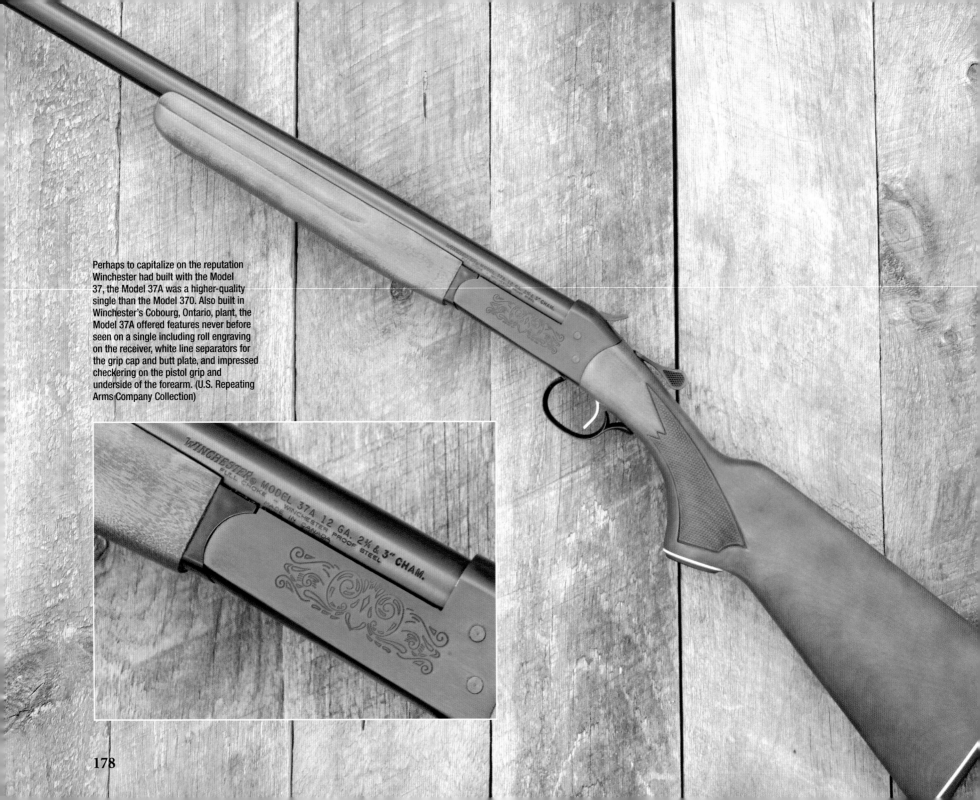

Perhaps to capitalize on the reputation Winchester had built with the Model 37, the Model 37A was a higher-quality single than the Model 370. Also built in Winchester's Cobourg, Ontario, plant, the Model 37A offered features never before seen on a single including roll engraving on the receiver, white line separators for the grip cap and butt plate, and impressed checkering on the pistol grip and underside of the forearm. (U.S. Repeating Arms Company Collection)

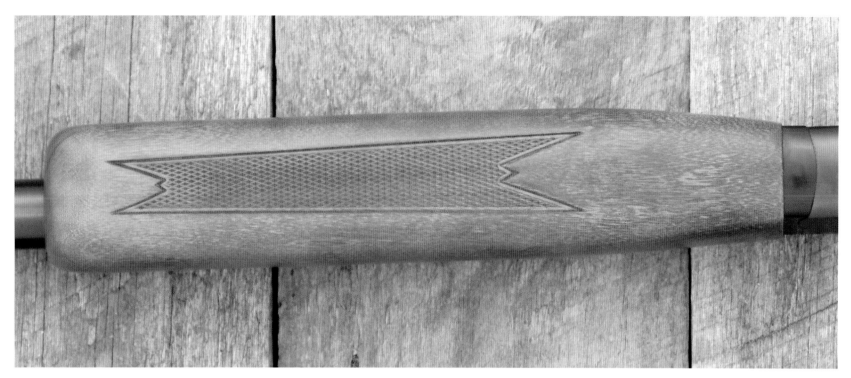

(assembled) was 44-$\frac{1}{2}$ inches. The standard version came with a full pistol grip stock but a straight stock could also be ordered at no additional cost. Originally chambered for 2-$\frac{1}{2}$ inch shells, it was changed to a 3-inch chamber in 1933. Later guns were marked "For 3 inch shells."[3]

Introduced at $14.00 the retail price was lowered to $13.25 (which in the 1920s, .75 cents actually meant something) and remained in production until 1934. It was the most successful of the three single shots introduced in 1920 but total sales were no more than 22,146 over 14 years. Another 1,189 were later assembled from leftover parts and sold from 1934 to 1941. Again, a rare gun due to attrition, a very good example will bring $500 today.

With the introduction of the Model 37 in January 1936, Winchester had built what would become the most popular single shot, single barrel shotgun of the mid-20th century. The Model 37 was a significant departure from previous manufacturing practices in its use of the deep-draw steel forming and copper brazing process. No castings of any kind were used in its construction. While unique to the firearms world, this was common practice in automobile manu-

facturing. The Model 37's rugged new design would later provide the foundation for Winchester's second double gun, the Model 24, introduced in 1940.

The 1936 World Standard Guns and Ammunition catalog described the new Winchester single shot model:

"To meet the growing demand for a strong, quick-operating single shot Winchester shotgun, shooting all standard ammunition, at a price comparable to that of an ordinary .22 rimfire rifle, Winchester has developed an altogether new gunbuilding method for the production of its new Steelbilt Model 37. This new Winchester is made with steel in all metal parts – exceedingly tough, selected steel. Its frame is of an ingenious new Winchester design – super strong – with corresponding ingenuity and strength in bolting, lock construction and assembly with the super-strong steel barrel. The all-steel bolting parts and forged barrel lug are doubly large. Action, top-lever breakdown with pivot bolting. Semi-hammerless lock with low safety cocking lever located well forward on tang. Double-action automatic ejection, starts shell extraction by positive mechanical force as gun is opened and ejects by spring power. Genuine Ameri-

[3] Winchester Shotguns and Shotshells by Ronald W. Stadt, 1984, Armory Publications.

can walnut stock with pistol grip and composition butt plate; dimensions 14"x 1-¹/₂"x 2-¹/₄". Large, full, round fore-end, same diameter entire length, fits any reach. Winchester proof-marked steel barrel is full choke, giving approximately 70% pattern. Barrel lengths: 12, 16 and 20 gauges, 32", 30" or 28"; 28 gauge, 30" or 28"; 410 gauge, 28" or 26". Chambered for 2-3/4 inch shells in 12, 16, and 20 gauges, 2-⁷/₈" in 28 gauge and 3" in 410, shooting all standard loads. Single shot. Weight in 12 gauge with 30" barrel, approximately 6-¹/₂ lbs. Take down."[4]

The list of options for the Model 37 was short. Modified choke or cylinder bore could be special ordered at no extra charge. The guns came standard with Full choked barrels. The walnut pistol grip stock and semi-beavertail forearm were not offered with checkering, nor was a straight stock available. Winchester kept it simple and for that reason the Model 37 remained popular for nearly 30 years. More than 1 million were produced by the time it was discontinued in 1963.

There were only a few minor changes throughout the production run: The shape of the cocking lever was changed three times between 1936 and the end of 1937; the first top levers, formed from sheet steel, had a teardrop opening, these were replaced by a new solid, forged lever; an export-style forearm with a more rounded front was authorized on March 22, 1936, and adopted for all Model 37's beginning December 4, 1941. One of the most distinguishing features of models built prior to c.1949 is the underside of the receiver, which is stamped

It was called "The Slagblaster" and you couldn't buy it. Built for commercial use by steel manufacturers to "blast" slag out of kilns, the Model 1370, built in Canada, featured a heavy barrel with 3-inch chamber and Full choke. Designed to break off steel residue hanging on the inside of kilns using heavy shot, the Model 1370 did not have a front bead sight. This is perhaps the least known and most obscure of all Winchester singles. (Photos courtesy Rock Island Auction Company)

[4] Ibid

Winchester with the depressed logo painted red. These are referred to as "Red Letter" Model 37s. After 1948 the receivers are unmarked.[5]

In 1958 Winchester added a Beginners Single Shot Shotgun in 20-gauge with a 26-inch barrel choked Modified. It retailed for $31.95 and had a solid red recoil pad. These were sold through 1963. In 1956 the 12-gauge model listed for just $27.80. Single barrel shotguns rarely become collectible (with the exception of unusual examples like the single barrel Model 101) and the Model 37 is no exception, with one exception, 28-gauge, which is both rare and prized by collectors. Average value for a 100 percent example today is $1,650, whereas the rest of the Model 37 line averages from $250 to $375.[6]

Shortly after the Model 37 was introduced, Winchester considered a new hammerless model (the Model 37 being semi-hammerless with a cocking lever). Designated as the Model 38, it was never put into production. Only prototypes were built, one of which is in the U.S. Repeating Arms Co. Collection. With the exception of the cocking lever and a tang-mounted safety, the general appearance of the Model 38 was otherwise identical.

After the Model 37 was discontinued the demand for a quality single still bearing the Winchester name remained, and New Haven decided to fill the void in 1968 with a Canadian-built single, the Model 370.

Produced at Winchester's Cobourg, Ontario, plant, the Model 370 was a full hammer gun featuring a large serrated hammer with rebound safety position, break open action, and an automatic ejector.

Like the Model 37, the 370 was offered in all five gauges, 12, 20, and .410 with 3-inch chambers, and 16 and 28-gauge with 2-3/4 inch chambers. The 12 gauge model was offered with a lengthy 36-inch barrel or a choice of 32 and 30-inch barrels. The 16-gauge version was available with either 32 or 30-inch barrels, 20 and 28-gauge with 28-inch tubes and the .410 with a short 26-inch barrel. There was also a Model 370 Youth in .410 or 20-gauge with 26-inch barrel, 12-1/2 inch stock and Winchester recoil pad. The number of Youth models produced is unknown.

The semi-pistol grip stock and forearm were American hardwood with a walnut finish. In both appearance and quality, the Model 370 was much less of a gun than its predecessor. Roughly 221,578 were built in all gauges before production was discontinued in 1973. This has become the least valuable of all Winchester single shots.

Immediately after the Model 370 was dropped Winchester replaced it with the Model 37A. Though trading on the heritage of the successful New Haven built Model 37, the Model 37A was also built in Canada. A higher-grade version of the Model 370, the 37A had a better quality finish and full pistol grip stock with a white spacer between the grip cap and butt plate. The most distinctive features of the Model 37A were roll engraved scrollwork on the receiver, a concave hammer spur, gold-plated trigger, and impressed checkering on the pistol grip and underside of the forearm, which was also grooved along upper two-thirds of its length.

Chambers were the same as the Model 370 and barrel lengths were again 30, 32 and 36-inches in 12-gauge, 30-inches only for 16-gauge, 28-inches for both 20 and 28-gauge, and 26-inches for the .410-gauge. A Youth model was offered once more in 20-gauge with 26-inch barrel choked Improved Modified. Full choked barrels were standard for the rest of the line.

The Model 37A was far more popular than its predecessor and between 1973 and 1980 Winchester's Canadian plant built 395,168 guns. Even so, they are still not as popular today as the original Model 37.

There were two more single shot, single barrel models produced, the Model 840, which was a cheaper version of the Model 37A, and the most unusual Winchester shotgun of all, the Model 1370, or as it was more popularly known, "The Slagblaster."

The Model 1370 was a commercial shotgun chambered in 12-gauge with a 26-inch full choke, heavy barrel. Manufactured in Canada, "The Slagblaster" was appropriately named; it was designed to blast the slag (steel residue) from the insides of kilns. Yep, you just stuck the barrel inside the kiln and let her rip. Needless to say, a very nice example would be very hard to find. Never sold to the general public, a Model 1370 in excellent condition is worth around $350. Like all of the Canadian built single shot models, the "The Slagblaster" was discontinued in 1980.

It has been a quarter of a century since Winchester last offered a production single shot, single barrel shotgun.

[5] Ibid
[6] 25th Edition Blue Book of Gun Values by S.P. Fjestad.

Chapter Eight
Semi Autos
Models 1911, 40, 50, 59, 1400, 1500 XTR, Super X1,
and Super X2

In the early 1900s, the Winchester Repeating Arms Company was lagging behind Remington, its biggest competitor, by not offering an auto-loading shotgun. Winchester had squandered the opportunity to be the world's first maker of a self-loading shotgun when John and Matthew Browning brought the design to T.G. Bennett in 1899. The Browning shotgun required neither a lever nor slide-action device to load the next shell, but fired as quickly as one could pull the trigger. It was truly innovative, especially before the dawn of the 20th century. In the late 1890s the semi-auto was a new concept, the first successful pistol, the Mauser C96 Broomhandle, had only been introduced three years before the Browning Brothers offered their design for a semi-automatic shotgun to Winchester. However, W.R.A. Co. would not offer a self-loading model of any kind until after the turn of the century, the first being a .22 caliber rifle, the Model 1903.

As R.L. Wilson relates the tale in *Winchester An American Legend*, John Browning got the idea back in the fall of 1889 when he was at the Ogden Rifle Club's weekly shoot. He noticed that when a rifle was fired, weeds located a few yards distant swayed with each muzzle blast. He recognized in those blasts a source of energy—energy that could be channeled into operating the mechanism of a repeating firearm. A decade later the Browning Brothers presented two prototype designs for a self-loading shotgun to T.G. Bennett. However, it was 1902 before any decision was reached in New Haven, and what might have been the beginning of a new era at Winchester, instead turned into an irrecon-

cilable difference of opinion between John Browning and Bennett. Browning had a new stipulation: Rather than selling the design outright to Winchester, as Browning Brothers had done since 1885, they wanted a payment against royalties for the use of the design. Bennett turned them down. It was to be one of the worst decisions in Winchester's history.

Undaunted, John Browning took the design for what would become the A5 semi-automatic shotgun to Fabrique Nationale (F.N.) in Herstal and Liege, Belgium, beginning a relationship that would last until his death in 1926 and establish Browning as one of the world's leading firearms manufacturers in direct competition with Winchester.

The Browning semi-auto shotgun, introduced in September 1903, made Winchester's slide-action Model 1897 shotguns (also designed by Browning) appear almost obsolete by comparison, although that really wasn't the case, as the two designs appealed to different buyers. Winchester was, nevertheless, conspicuously absent from this new segment of the firearms market. The notoriety of the Browning A5, compounded by the licensing of the design to Remington, which introduced a semi-auto model in 1905 (a pre-Model 11 replaced by the Model 11A in 1911), forced Winchester into developing a competitive self-loading shotgun. If only it had been that simple.

The problem W.R.A. Co. faced was not only having to catch up with its principal rival in Ilion, New York, but also developing an entirely new design. F.N. owned the rights to John Browning's patent, and to T.G. Bennett's chagrin,

Years in the making, Winchester's first semi-automatic, self-loading shotgun was designed by T.C. Johnson. The innovative 12-gauge managed to circumvent the Browning patent for an auto-loader, on which Johnson had collaborated prior to John Browning's split with W.R.A. Co. Johnson's new design made the Model 1911 one of the easiest take down shotguns ever built. (U.S. Repeating Arms Co. Collection)

Plain Finished, Model 1911.   5 Shots, $38.00.

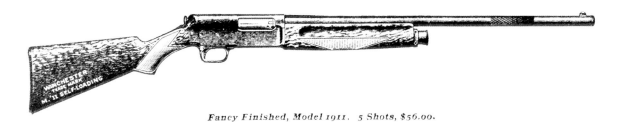

Fancy Finished, Model 1911.   5 Shots, $56.00.

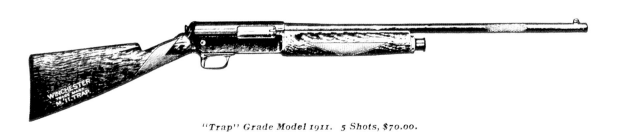

"Trap" Grade Model 1911.   5 Shots, $70.00.

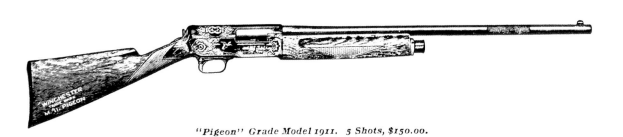

"Pigeon" Grade Model 1911.   5 Shots, $150.00.

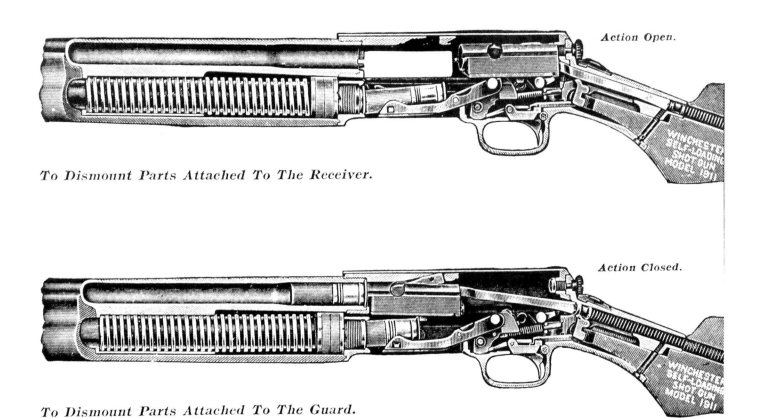

Action Open.

To Dismount Parts Attached To The Receiver.

Action Closed.

To Dismount Parts Attached To The Guard.

GUN TAKEN APART.

Winchester factory diagram shows the intricate internal workings of the Model 1911 and the two major components when taken apart. Winchester literature played up this simple take down design. The second illustration shows the four variations in which the Model 1911 was available. (Photos courtesy R.L. Wilson)

Innovative or dangerous? To chamber the first shell one had to grasp the knurling around the barrel and pull the barrel straight back toward the receiver. The intent was for the shooter to either rest the stock against one's hip, with the barrel pointing away, or grasp the stock in the off hand to perform this procedure. Done precisely in either of these methods, there was rarely a problem. Unfortunately, over time shooters took liberties with this procedure resulting in injuries and deaths.

Pictured is a Trap Grade Model 1911 which originally sold for $70.00. Trap Grade featured fancy wood with a checkered forearm and checkered wrist featuring the trademark black diamond.

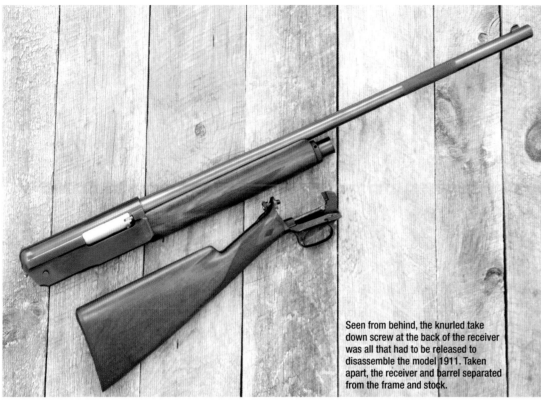

Seen from behind, the knurled take down screw at the back of the receiver was all that had to be released to disassemble the model 1911. Taken apart, the receiver and barrel separated from the frame and stock.

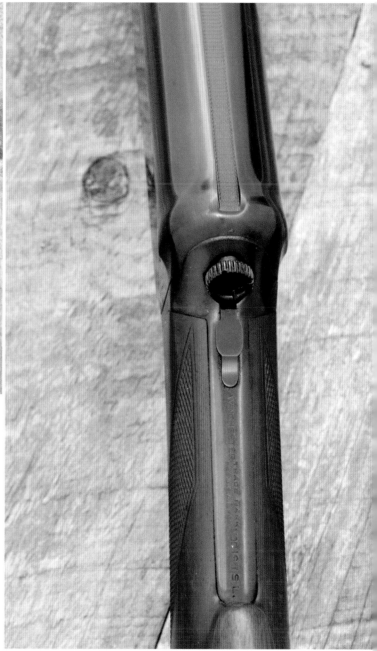

Winchester's head designer, T.C. Johnson, had helped Browning put the finishing touches on the design covering special features necessary for a self-loading action, all of which were included in the Browning patent! In order for Winchester to build a semi-auto shotgun, Johnson would have to come up with an entirely different design, a task that would take him nearly six years to complete.

In the October 1911 catalog, Winchester finally announced its new Self-Loading Shotgun Model 1911. As a new model not previously offered by W.R.A. Co., it bore a longer and more detailed description, which went to great lengths in differentiating the Model 1911 from any other semi-auto shotgun then on the market:

"The Winchester Self-Loading Shotgun is a recoil operated, hammerless, take down, five shot repeater. The recoil developed by the discharge of the gun cocks the hammer, ejects the fired shell, feeds a loaded shell from the magazine into the chamber and leaves the gun ready to be shot again. As the trigger must be pulled for each shot fired, the gun is at all times as completely under the control of the user as any double or single barreled gun. The loading and shooting of this gun being governed by the trigger finger, it has been aptly called the "Trigger Controlled Repeater." Although wonderful in operation, the Winchester Self-Loading Shotgun is neither complicated, cumbersome, nor apt to get

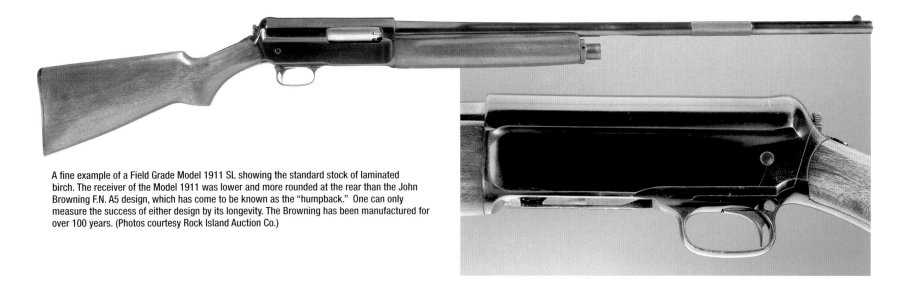

A fine example of a Field Grade Model 1911 SL showing the standard stock of laminated birch. The receiver of the Model 1911 was lower and more rounded at the rear than the John Browning F.N. A5 design, which has come to be known as the "humpback." One can only measure the success of either design by its longevity. The Browning has been manufactured for over 100 years. (Photos courtesy Rock Island Auction Co.)

out of order with any reasonable use. The design and operation of the gun are mechanically correct, and the parts, which are few and strong, are made of the very best materials, and are tested and inspected with great care before being assembled. In shooting quality, grace of outline, balance and in those many other details which go to make up a good gun, this new model keeps pace with the established high Winchester standard.

"As in all Winchester guns the element of safety has been carefully and successfully accomplished in designing the Winchester Self-Loading Shotgun. Three separate and distinct features of the construction of this gun make it impossible to discharge it before the action is completely closed and the breech-bolt locked in place. The trigger cannot come in contact with the sear until the breech-bolt is locked in place. The locking block, except when locked in place, positively prevents the firing pin from moving forward. The fall of the hammer is blocked by the locking block operating rod until the breech-bolt is locked in place.

"The Winchester Self-Loading Shotgun has all the good points of other recoil operated shotguns, but none of their faults. It also has many distinctive and exclusive features, which have led sportsmen to pronounce it the finest and latest example of progress in the art of gun making. Some of the most important of these new ideas and improvements are: The barrel, receiver, magazine and all working parts of this gun throughout are made of Nickel steel, which has a far greater tensile strength and elastic limit than the steel used by other makers. The magazine lug

and front sight are integral with the barrel, the whole piece being machined from one solid forging. This is a much stronger and more lasting construction than when these parts are made separately and brazed to the barrel.

"A gun cannot truthfully be said to boast of a "Bump of Knowledge," but the Winchester Self-Loading Shotgun has a "Bump of Strength," which greatly increases the resistance of the receiver at the point of the greatest strain. In recoil-operated shotguns, the strain of the rearward travel of the breech-bolt is greatest on the walls of the receiver where the sides and end join. Although this strain is not as great in the Winchester Self-Loading Shotgun as in other makes, because of its Divided Recoil feature, still the "Bump of Strength," by increasing the thickness of the walls of the receiver at the point of the greatest strain, and supporting it both in front and behind, adds greatly to the strength of the receiver and makes it the safest used on any similar type of gun... Instead of the accumulated force of the recoil coming upon the rear and top of the receiver, as in other recoil operated shotguns, the Winchester Self-Loader is so designed that the recoil is divided or broken. The main force of the recoil is absorbed by an elastic buffer located forward of the lower front end of the receiver and the remainder by a similar device which makes a cushion between the rear end of the bolt and the rear end of the receiver. By dividing the recoil in this way the shooter feels it much less than where any other system of absorbing it is employed. This makes the Winchester Self-Loading Shotgun much pleasanter

After a 14-year absence from the market, on January 20, 1940 Winchester introduced a new auto-loader, the Model 40. A year later it was discontinued. The design of the receiver had more graceful lines, but weaknesses quickly developed in the design such as premature firing before the action was completely closed. Many were recalled and owners who returned their guns were given new Model 12s. The example shown is a Skeet Gun with threaded on Lyman Style A compensator with Cutts Compensator body. (U.S. Repeating Arms Co. Collection)

189

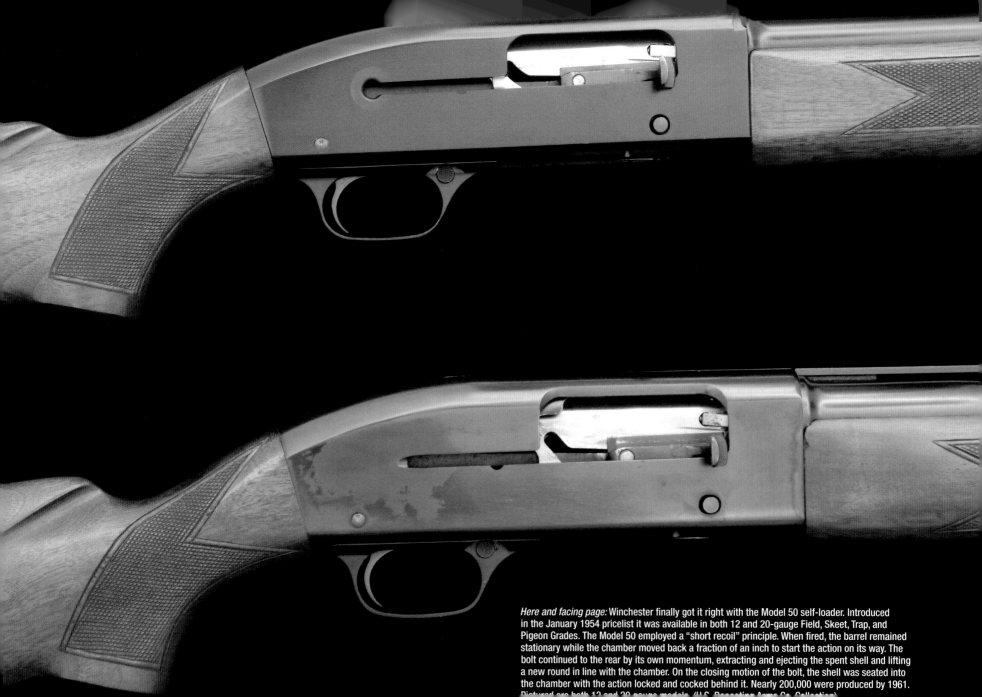

Here and facing page: Winchester finally got it right with the Model 50 self-loader. Introduced in the January 1954 pricelist it was available in both 12 and 20-gauge Field, Skeet, Trap, and Pigeon Grades. The Model 50 employed a "short recoil" principle. When fired, the barrel remained stationary while the chamber moved back a fraction of an inch to start the action on its way. The bolt continued to the rear by its own momentum, extracting and ejecting the spent shell and lifting a new round in line with the chamber. On the closing motion of the bolt, the shell was seated into the chamber with the action locked and cocked behind it. Nearly 200,000 were produced by 1961. Pictured are both 12 and 20-gauge models. (U.S. Repeating Arms Co. Collection.

to shoot than any other similar type of gun. We do not make the absurd claim that all recoil is eliminated in this gun, because it is utilized to operate the reloading mechanism, but we do say, without fear of contradiction, that the Winchester Self-Loading Shotgun "kicks" less than any other recoil operated gun. Another particularly desirable feature of the Divided Recoil is the minimizing of the "whip" or "jump" of the muzzle of the gun when shooting. This is due to the fact that the recoil of the Winchester Self-Loader expends its force lower vertically, nearer the horizontal center of the gun and in more direct line with the shooter's shoulder, instead of at the top and rear of the receiver, as is the case in other similar guns. This absence of "jump" or "whip" of the muzzle makes it much easier to shoot the second shot accurately with a Winchester Self-Loader than with any other recoil operated shotgun.

"The Winchester Self-Loading Shotgun will operate with complete certainty and safety with any properly loaded paper shell, from a "blank" to the maximum 12 gauge loads, either smokeless or black powder, loaded by this company, without the slightest change or readjustment. It requires no extra oiling to make it work with light loads nor the use of any additional parts to have it operate with heavy loads. It is a gun that requires no favoring. As it is often desirable to shift instantly from a heavy to a light load, sportsmen will welcome a recoil-operated shotgun with which this can be done without tinkering with the mechanism.

"The two part take-down system used in this gun is simple, strong, and handy. By turning the take-down screw at the rear of the receiver a few times the gun separates into two parts, the stock and guard being in one, and the barrel, magazine and receiver in the other. When taken down, the working parts of the action are accessible for cleaning. In taking down the Winchester Self-Loader, there are no parts separated from the guard, barrel or magazine, to be left behind or lost.

"There are no moving parts outside of the receiver to catch in the clothing, or any projections or sharp points to injure the hands of the user of a Winchester Self-Loading Shotgun. The bolt catch is located at the rear of the receiver where it is handy to reach without the user running any risk of having his fingers caught by the bolt as it moves forward. The receiver is entirely free from pins, screws or assembling holes to weaken it. In recoil-operated firearms the jar will shake loose receiver pins and screws almost invariably. This defect, common to this type of arms, has been overcome by the Winchester patented system of construction.

"The trigger lock on this gun operates crosswise, which makes it

The Model 50 was replaced by the Model 59, which was first described in the 1960 catalog. This was the first firearm in history to utilize fiberglass in the construction of its barrel. The unique Win-Lite barrel was an ingenious bonding of steel and glass fiber, finely polished and finished.

In manufacturing each Win-Lite barrel, 500 miles (that's 2,640,000 feet) of wound glass fiber were fused and bonded to a .020-inch thickness steel barrel liner. Factory photo from 1959 shows stages in the glass barrel manufacture. From left to right, filament-wound barrel, convolute-wrapped barrel, impregnated barrel, and the finished, polished and blued barrel. (Photo courtesy U.S. Repeating Arms, Co.)

impossible to be jarred out of place by the recoil. It is conveniently located in the guard so that it can be readily operated by the trigger finger. The position of the lock can be quickly told by sight or feeling. When the lock is off and the trigger can be pulled, the lock shows a red band of warning.

"By simply pressing in the bolt catch, the breech-bolt will be locked back and the gun remain open after the next shot is fired. This is a marked advantage over other recoil-operated firearms, which only remain open when there are no more shells in the magazine. Locking the bolt so that the gun will remain open at the option of the shooter, facilitates its use as a single loader, the changing of a shell or cleaning of the barrel, etc.

"Filling the magazine is not complicated by the necessity of pressing any carrier release. To throw the first shell into the chamber, the barrel is employed very much as it is in the loading of a double barreled gun. Instead of tipping down the barrel, it is drawn rearward as far as it will go. A band is knurled around the barrel, which affords a good grip, no matter what the condition of the hands or barrel may be.

"The trigger pull is short, smooth and light. An aperture in the forward end of the bolt makes it possible to see readily without opening the breech whether or not there is a loaded shell in the chamber. If there is any shell in the chamber, it must of necessity be a loaded one, for a shell as soon as it is fired in the gun is ejected by its own recoil.

"The releasing of the breech-bolt is not dependent upon a shell's emerging from the magazine. The bolt acts independently of the shell, thus assuring much greater reliability of the gun as a repeater.

"The extraction and ejection of the fired shells are absolutely positive in this gun.

"All springs used in this gun are made of special high tension wire, which makes them much more durable than ordinary flat springs.

"The front sight can be caught by the eye quickly and easily, as a bright point of tin is fused to the steel base. This construction prevents the sight tip from being jarred off.

"On all orders for Winchester Self-Loading Shotguns we will send guns made according to the following specifications, unless instructed to the contrary: Barrel: Full choke, 26 inch Nickel steel, chambered for 2-3/4 inch shells. Modified choke or cylinder bore barrels or barrels 28 inches long will be furnished without extra charge. Matted barrels will be furnished at the usual increased charge for this extra. Stock: Pistol grip, handsomely finished wood, 13-3/4 inches long with 1-5/ inches drop at comb and 2-3/8 inches drop at heel. Butt Plate: Rubber. Fancy walnut or plain wood handmade stocks of special lengths or

drops, straight or pistol grip, will be furnished at the regular increased charge for such extras. Receiver: Blued and matted on top along the line of sight.

"Interchangeable 26 or 28 inch Nickel steel barrels, full or modified choke or cylinder bore, can be furnished.

"Extra barrel complete with magazine, forearm, etc., $20.00. In all cases, extra barrels will have to be fitted at our armory."[1]

The Standard Gun, 12 Gauge, 26 inch Nickel Steel Barrel, and Pistol Grip Stock of plain wood was priced at.................................$38.00
Fancy Walnut Stock and Forearm $13.00
Checkered Stock and Forearm $5.00
Extra Length or Drop of Stock to order.......................$10.00
Matting Barrel $5.00
Interchangeable Barrel with Magazine and
Forearm complete $20.00

Following are the general specifications for the Model 1911:

TYPE

Self-loading repeating shotgun, recoil operated, hammerless, tubular magazine, takedown.

STYLE	YEARS PRODUCED	FEATURES
Standard Grade	1911 – 1926	
Fancy Finished	1911 – 1918	Fancy walnut, checkered stock and forearm. First listed at $56.00
Trap Grade	1913 – 1926	Matted barrel and selected fancy handmade, oil-finished checkered stock and forearm, (straight stock standard) or pistol grip style, checkered hard rubber butt plate. First listed at $70.00
Pigeon Grade	1912 – 1926	Same as Trap Grade with elaborate engraving on the receiver. First listed at $150.00

BARRELS AND CHOKES

26-inch and 28-inch, Full choke, Modified choke, or Cylinder bore.

[1] *Winchester Shotguns and Shotshells by Ronald W. Stadt, 1984, Armory Publications and The History of Winchester Firearms 1886-1992 by Thomas Henshaw, 1993 Winchester Press.*

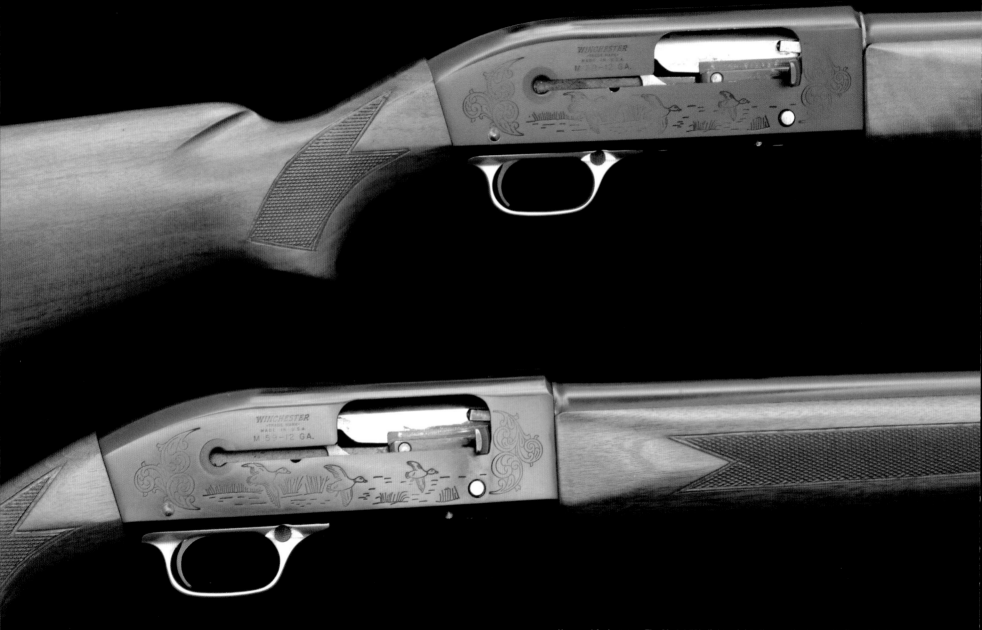

Here and facing page: The Model 59's lightweight alloy receiver was the first of its kind to be roll-engraved. Both sides were embellished with hunting scenes, the right with ducks in flight, and the left with a pointer flushing a quail. (U.S. Repeating Arms Co. Collection)

MAGAZINE

Tubular, capacity 5 shells.

CHAMBER

12 gauge, 2-3/4 inch shell

STOCK AND FOREARM

Standard Grade made of birch, laminated (3 pieces), pistol grip, hard rubber butt plate. Forearm made of birch with rock elm insert.

By the end of production in 1926 the Standard Grade gun had increased to $72.90, the Trap Grade to $120.20 and the Pigeon Grade to $234.80.[2]

Although the Model 1911 was Winchester's first hammerless shotgun, the Model 1912 almost immediately eclipsed the novelty. The Model 1911 was not a great success and always lived in the shadow of the Browning and Remington models, the basic designs of which have remained in production for over

100 years. In addition, there were early mechanical problems with the 1911's mechanism, which required a number of design changes during the first three years of production, and though Winchester had emphasized all of the Model 1911's safety features, the operation of the action was inherently dangerous if the shooter did not pay close attention when chambering the first round. One was supposed to hold the gun braced against the hip or in the off hand, and with the barrel pointed in a safe direction, grasp the knurled grip on the barrel with the strong hand and pull the barrel back to chamber the first round and cock the internal hammer. This was one of the solutions to avoid infringing on Browning's patent. Unfortunately, the Model 1911 could discharge accidentally if it was cocked improperly. Errors in judgment regarding this procedure resulted in fingers being shot off by pulling on the end of the barrel rather than the knurling, some six inches back from the muzzle, while inadvertently holding the trigger. But the worst case was when shooters got lazy, grabbed the barrel and pushed it back with the butt of the gun resting on the ground. Accidental

[2] Ibid

Rapid fire testing at Winchester in 1959 to illustrate how quickly the Model 59 could cycle. Note that there are two ejected shells in the air in this photo! (Photo by Sid Latham courtesy U.S. Repeating Arms Co.)

WINCHESTER MODEL 59 WITH VERSALITE CHOKE

In 1961 Winchester introduced "Versalite" chokes, which could be threaded into the barrel. Modified choke tubes were standard and Full and Improved Cylinder tubes were priced at just $4.45. The "Versalite" chokes, however, were only available for 26-inch barrels.

All of Winchester's claims about the Model 59 being lighter, easier to handle and having more manageable recoil were proven in the field by a 13-year old shooter. Note the ejected shell case coming toward the camera and the minimum of recoil being experienced by the young shooter. (Photo by Sid Latham courtesy U.S. Repeating Arms Co.)

discharges in this case were occasionally fatal, and the Model 1911 picked up the rather unwelcome nickname "head buster." After 15 years and 82,774 guns the Model 1911 went bust.[3] New Haven would not attempt to build another self-loader until 1940.

After a 14-year absence from the market, on January 2, 1940, Winchester introduced a new auto-loader, the Model 40. A year later it was discontinued after only around 12,000 were built.

The design of the receiver looked like a Model 12 in profile and it was Winchester's intention to design a self-loading shotgun that had more graceful lines, rather then the humpbacked styling that was prevalent in other semi-autos. Winchester had the shape right with the Model 40 but still had not worked out all of the mechanical problems. Weaknesses quickly devel-

oped in the guns. Priced at just $52.42 it was the shortest-lived model in Winchester history.

In its brief 12 months Winchester produced two versions of the Model 40, Field Gun and Skeet Gun, the latter retailing for $78.30. Field guns had pistol grip stocks and forearms of American walnut with a hard rubber butt plate. A straight stock could also be special ordered. The Skeet gun had checkered pistol grip and forearm and a plain un-choked barrel with a threaded on Lyman Style A compensator with Cutts Compensator body, and two choke tubes, one a spreader for Skeet and one .705 Full choke. A Modified choke could also be substituted for the Full choke at no additional charge.

John Olin, who was keen on Skeet shooting, encouraged development of the Model 40 as a Skeet gun but it just wasn't ready for production when Winchester

[3] While most sources agree on the number of Model 1911s produced and years of manufacture, it should be noted that the data in the 25th Edition Blue Book of Gun Values disputes the production number of 82,744 and states that production ran from 1911 to 1921 with some additional guns made between 1921 and 1928, for a total of 103,246 guns.

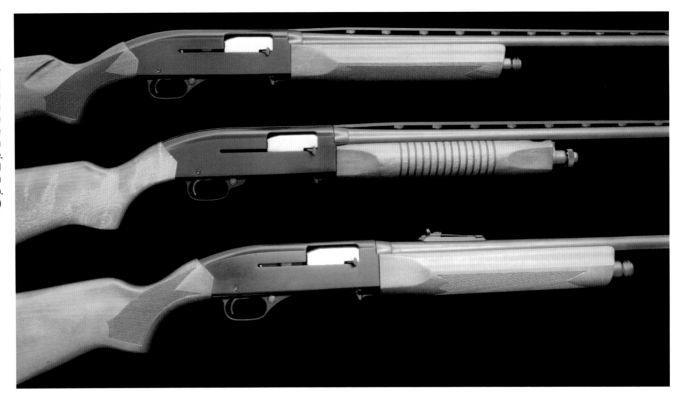

Introduced in 1964 the Model 1400 Automatic Shotgun featured a newly engineered rotating bolt head, locking lugs, and a gas-operated mechanism to extract, eject, and chamber a fresh shell when the gun was fired. The Model 1400 (and 1500 XTR) were the most successful auto-loaders in Winchester history up to that time. From 1964 to 1994, total combined production reached over 1.25 million guns! (U.S. Repeating Arms Co. Collection)

released it in 1940. Fraught with problems, which included premature firing before the action was completely closed, and a tendency for the magazine tube to bend, many Model 40s were recalled and owners who returned their guns were given new Model 12s.

According to Winchester historian Ronald W. Stadt, even though it was discontinued in 1941, the Model 40 was left in inventory until 1945, and actual assembly from remaining parts used to build guns during World War II brought production closer to 40,000 examples, although some were not fully assembled and others were scrapped because of serious faults.[4] A 100 percent example, which would be hard to find, is worth around $750 today, $250 more than a 100 percent Model 1911.

In 1954 Winchester finally got it right but it had taken New Haven half a century to catch up with Browning and Remington; that was the extent to which the rift between John Browning and T.G. Bennett had affected the company. In the January pricelist a new self-loading shotgun was announced, the Model 50,

available in both 12 and 20-gauge Field, Skeet, Trap, and Pigeon Grades.

Before getting into the specifics of each model, it can be said that the Model 50 was a success and between 1954 and 1961 nearly 200,000 were produced, the very first of which, serial number 1000, was presented to John M. Olin.

Winchester noted that the new Model 50 "…works through an entirely different and revolutionary principle. When the Winchester Automatic is fired, the barrel remains stationary, fixed, rigid. The chamber moves back a fraction of an inch and starts the action on its way. Surely and smoothly, the Winchester easy-action Automatic flips out the empty and picks up a loaded shell, and you're ready for a really fast second shot. The easy, positive action of the Model 50 does its fast, smooth job every time, in spite of weather, weed-seeds or dirt."

It was a very simple explanation for what was truly a revolutionary new design that simplified the operation of a semi-automatic shotgun. In its description of the Model 50, Winchester had used the word "Automatic," however "Automatic"

[4] Winchester Shotguns and Shotshells by Ronald W. Stadt, 1984, Armory Publications

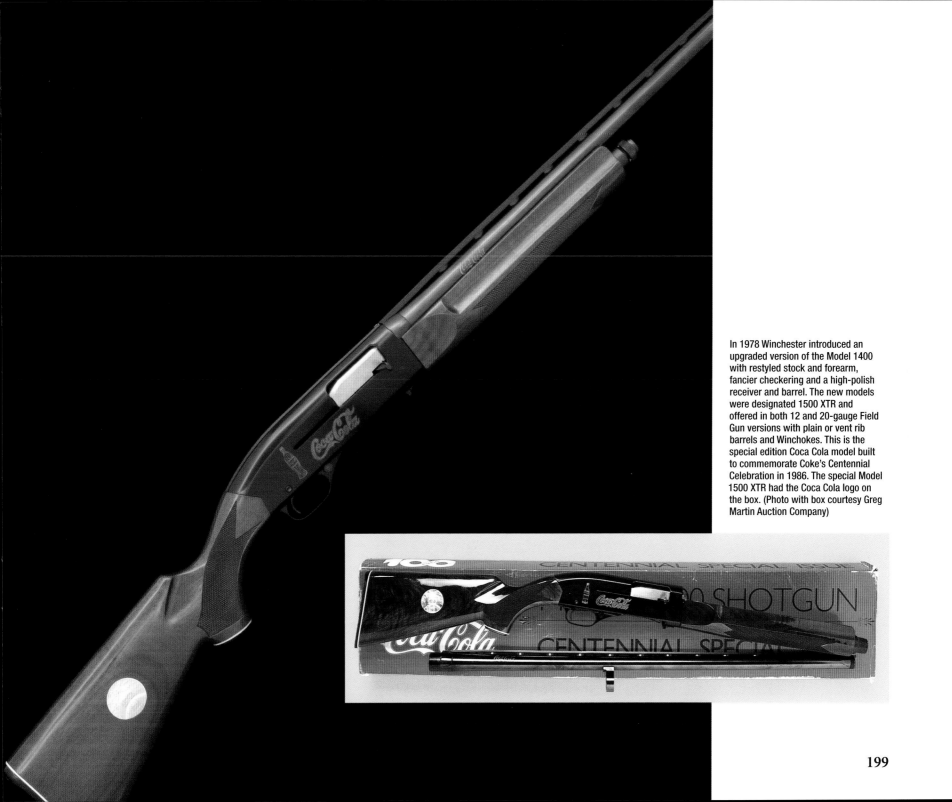

In 1978 Winchester introduced an upgraded version of the Model 1400 with restyled stock and forearm, fancier checkering and a high-polish receiver and barrel. The new models were designated 1500 XTR and offered in both 12 and 20-gauge Field Gun versions with plain or vent rib barrels and Winchokes. This is the special edition Coca Cola model built to commemorate Coke's Centennial Celebration in 1986. The special Model 1500 XTR had the Coca Cola logo on the box. (Photo with box courtesy Greg Martin Auction Company)

199

Among the special features of the 1500 XTR was an improved design cocking handle, a nickel plated carrier, and the high gloss XTR finished American walnut. The special Coca Cola model featured the logo and the trademark Coke bottle engraved in gold on the right side of the receiver. (U.S. Repeating Arms Company Collection)

The left side of the receiver on special Coca Cola Centennial models had the Coca Cola logo engraved in gold.

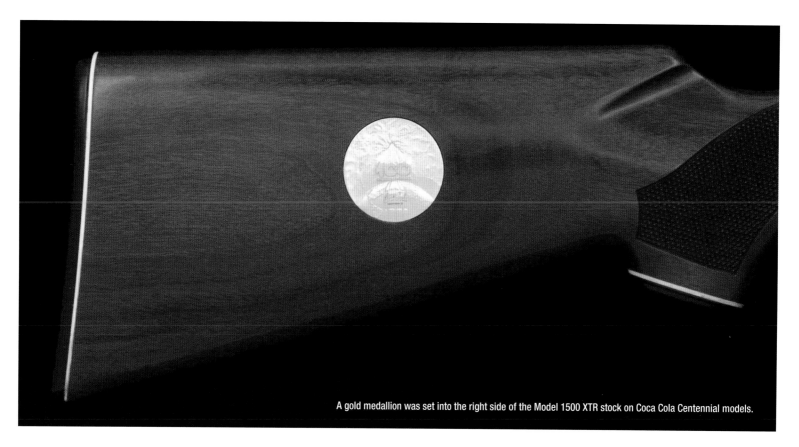

A gold medallion was set into the right side of the Model 1500 XTR stock on Coca Cola Centennial models.

and "semi-automatic" were considered interchangeable terms for the general public. Technically "Automatic" refers to a fully-automatic weapon, such as a machine gun, that fires continually as long as the trigger is held back. A "semi-auto" must have the trigger pulled each time it is fired. Only machine guns and machine pistols are truly "Automatic." The Winchester Model 50 employed an ingenious semi-automatic design based on the "short recoil" principle.

In this design a floating chamber moves back approximately 1/10th of an inch starting the action on its way to the rear. The bolt continues to the rear driven by its own momentum. During its travel the empty shell is extracted and ejected and new shell is lifted in line with the chamber. On the rebounding, or closing motion of the bolt, the new shell is seated into the chamber with the action locked and cocked behind it.[5]

[5] *The History of Winchester Firearms 1886-1992 by Thomas Henshaw, 1993 Winchester Press.*

Winchester used its patented *Winchester Proof Steel* for the Model 50's receiver, barrel, breech-bolt and other critical metal parts. Everything in the Model 50 was either milled from a solid block or bored from a solid bar. There were no metal stampings. Like the almost indestructible Model 12, the Model 50 was to become known for its strength and durability under heavy and prolonged use.

Following are the general specifications for the Model 50:

TYPE

Automatic (self-loading) recoil operated, non-recoiling barrel, repeating shotgun, hammerless, tubular magazine, takedown.

The Model 1500 XTR featured a raised ventilated rib. The Coke name was even engraved on the barrel of the special Centennial model.

In 1974 Winchester had introduced another upgraded Automatic, the Super X Model 1, offered in Standard, Skeet, Trap, and Custom Trap or Skeet models. The Super X line was also used for special Limited Editions, including a model for Ducks Unlimited. The Super X Model 1, Trap, and Skeet versions were built through 1981.

STYLES

Standard Field Gun; Field Gun with vent rib; Skeet Gun; Trap Gun; Pigeon Grade Standard or Featherweight in Field, Skeet or Trap; and Pigeon Grade special order.

BARRELS AND CHOKES

12 Gauge Standard Gun or with Winchester Special Ventilated Rib: 30-inch, Full choke; 28-inch Full or Modified choke; 26-inch, Improved Cylinder or Winchester Skeet choke. The Winchester Skeet choke was not offered with 26-inch ventilated rib barrel.

20 Gauge Standard Gun or with Winchester Special Ventilated Rib: 28-inch, Full or Modified choke; 26-inch, Improved Cylinder or Winchester Skeet choke. (All available early in 1956). The Winchester Skeet choke was again not offered with 26-inch ventilated rib barrels.

12 Gauge and 20 Gauge Skeet with Winchester Special Ventilated Rib: 26-inch Winchester Skeet choke. (20-gauge available early 1956)

12 Gauge Trap Gun: 30-inch, Full choke.

12 Gauge Featherweight Field Gun with plain or vent rib barrel: 30-inch, Full choke; 28-inch, Full choke or Modified choke; 26-inch, Improved Cylinder. (First listed in 1958)

20 Gauge Featherweight Field Gun with plain or vent rib barrel: 28-inch, Full choke or Modified choke; 26-inch Improved Cylinder choke. (First listed in 1958)

12 Gauge or 20 Gauge Featherweight Skeet Gun: 26-inch, Winchester Skeet choke.

12 Gauge or 20 Gauge Pigeon Grade: Available with any combination of barrels and chokes.

MAGAZINE

Tubular, capacity 2 shells plus one in the chamber.

CHAMBER

2-3/4 inch high-velocity long range and magnum shells.

STOCK, FOREARM, CARVING AND ENGRAVING

Hand checkered American walnut pistol grip stock with fluted comb, hand checkered American walnut forearm standard. Monte Carlo stocks available at extra cost. Trap and Skeet guns had three diamonds under the forearm, two checkered, one un-checkered. Trap, Skeet and Pigeon Grade guns came with steel Winchester pistol grip cap. Pigeon Grade came standard with extra fancy walnut and larger hand checkering pattern. Carving choices paralleled the Model 12. Pigeon Grade could also be ordered with hand engraving, gold and silver inlays, again in patterns similar to the Model 12. Pigeon was stamped near the serial number on the forward underside of the receiver.

Winchester's first successful auto-loader reached a production total of 196,402 before it was discontinued in December 1961. The Model 50 was replaced by the Model 59, which made its debut in 1959 and was first described in the 1960 catalog.

Winchester might have been a tad overzealous in their description of the innovative Model 59 when they proclaimed it, "The most significant advance in gun making techniques in more than 600 years." They were of course talking about manufacturing and not gun design, so it might not have been as farfetched as it sounded. The Model 59 was the first firearm in history to utilize fiberglass in the construction of its barrel.

Wrote Winchester: "Here is a most remarkable advance in the history of shotgun design and manufacture . . . the totally new Winchester Model 59 12-gauge, featuring the revolutionary, patented Win-Lite barrel! Here's an entirely new thrill in shooting pleasure—with the fastest-firing autoloading shotgun on the market, combined with fast-swinging, perfect-pointing lightness that's a pleasure to carry through the toughest days in the field. The heart of the Model 59 lies in the unique Win-Lite barrel—an ingenious bonding of steel and glass fiber...finely polished and finished...the lightest, strongest shotgun barrel ever made! Ideally balanced by a super-strength ultra-light aluminum alloy receiver, the Winchester Model 59 has everything you want in a fine shotgun.

NO POWER LOSS! The fixed barrel and floating chamber provide straight-line friction-free extraction and reloading with no loss of power in the system.

NON-RECOILING BARREL! This time and field-tested feature means you stay "on target" every time for a really fast second shot. No getting back on target as with some other autoloaders.

NO "DOUBLE SHUFFLE!" No forcing the shoulder into the stock to make the action work. The Model 59 action is smooth and unfailingly fast.

MAGNUM OR FIELD LOADS WITHOUT ADJUSTMENT! Shoots all 2-1/4" shells—regular field loads or super, long-range loads, including Magnum, without adjustment.

INSTANTLY INTERCHANGEABLE BARRELS! Change to any available Win-Lite barrel in seconds—anywhere, anytime—without tools.

20% LESS RECOIL EFFECT! A soft, steady push...not a sudden jab...with a measured 20% less recoil effect. Adds hours of shooting pleasure.

DAY-LONG CARRYING COMFORT! The ultra light weight of the Model 59 means more pleasant hours afield. Stay fresh, fast...and steady-on-target all day long!"

In its history, Ducks Unlimited has had a great number of special editions. The Super X Model 1 DU Missouri Flyaway was a 12-gauge in an edition of 500. Featuring deluxe wood and hand checkering, the left side of the receiver was handsomely engraved with the name, edition, and a duck in flight. (U.S. Repeating Arms Company Collection)

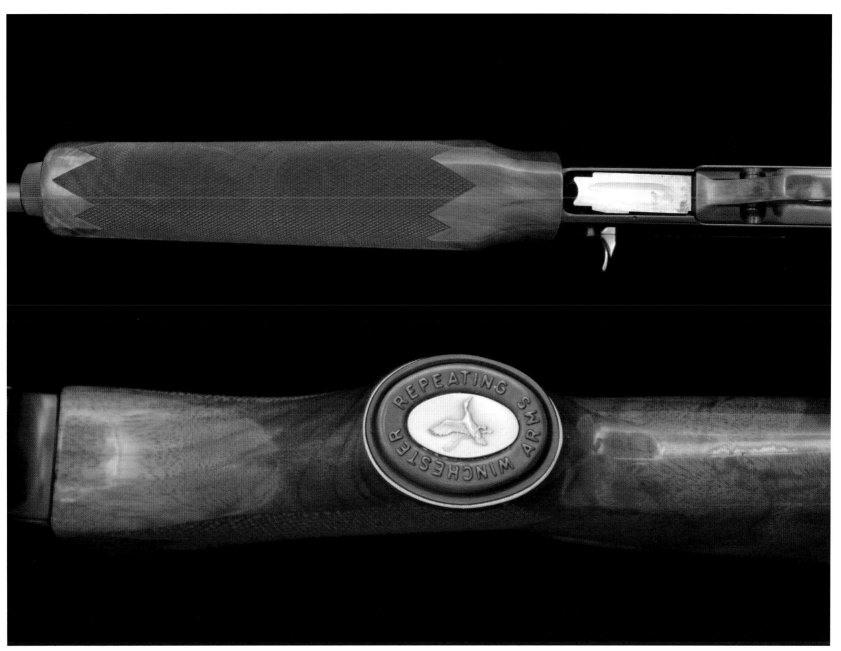

The DU special edition Super X Model 1 featured a special gold inlaid Ducks Unlimited grip cap, and beautiful hand checkering on the underside of the forearm.

Here & Facing: The popularity of the Super X Model 1 was not limited to the U.S. market. A European model was also produced with a highly polished receiver featuring a gray matte finish along the top, an engine turned bolt, the Winchester Rider logo and Winchester name on the right side, and European 1500 XTR on the left. (U.S. Repeating Arms Company Collection)

206

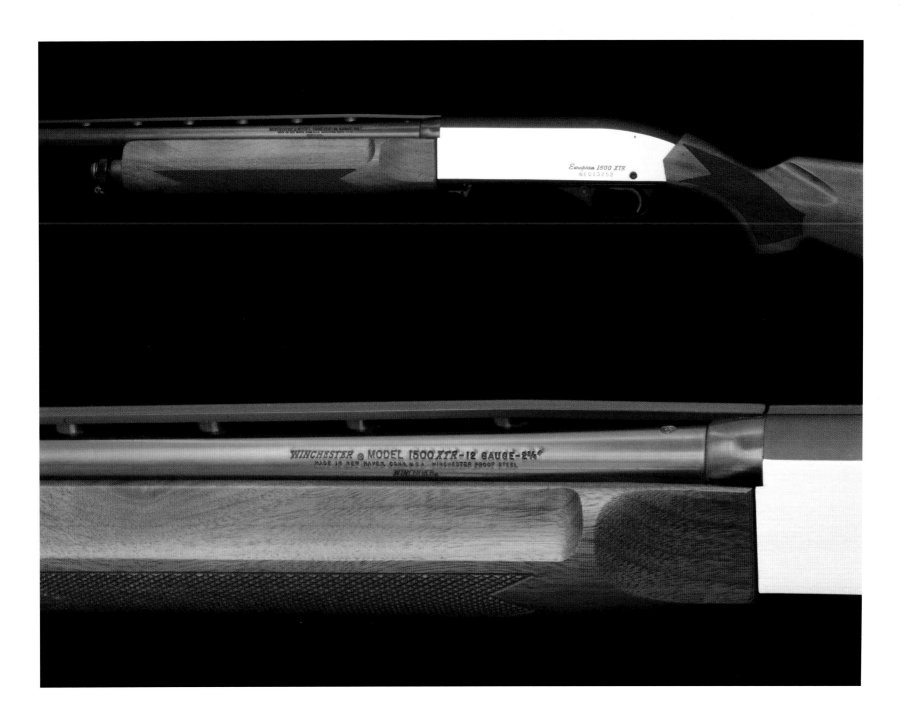

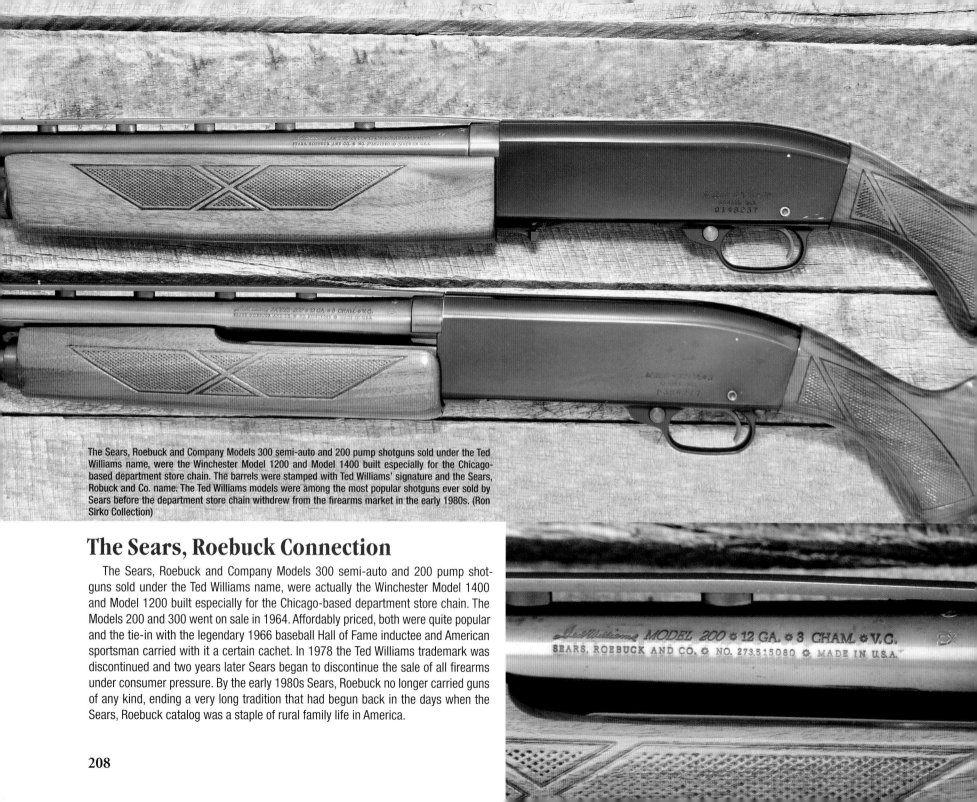

The Sears, Roebuck and Company Models 300 semi-auto and 200 pump shotguns sold under the Ted Williams name, were the Winchester Model 1200 and Model 1400 built especially for the Chicago-based department store chain. The barrels were stamped with Ted Williams' signature and the Sears, Robuck and Co. name. The Ted Williams models were among the most popular shotguns ever sold by Sears before the department store chain withdrew from the firearms market in the early 1980s. (Ron Sirko Collection)

The Sears, Roebuck Connection

The Sears, Roebuck and Company Models 300 semi-auto and 200 pump shotguns sold under the Ted Williams name, were actually the Winchester Model 1400 and Model 1200 built especially for the Chicago-based department store chain. The Models 200 and 300 went on sale in 1964. Affordably priced, both were quite popular and the tie-in with the legendary 1966 baseball Hall of Fame inductee and American sportsman carried with it a certain cachet. In 1978 the Ted Williams trademark was discontinued and two years later Sears began to discontinue the sale of all firearms under consumer pressure. By the early 1980s Sears, Roebuck no longer carried guns of any kind, ending a very long tradition that had begun back in the days when the Sears, Roebuck catalog was a staple of rural family life in America.

209

WEATHER-PROOFED! Forget the weather! The outside surfaces of the barrel and receiver won't rust or corrode, regardless of temperature or weather conditions.

These were very impressive claims, and nearly all of them were true. Some of the statistics behind the manufacturing of the Model 59, however, seemed even more astounding than Winchester's line about the most significant advance in gun making techniques in more than 600 years.

Point of fact: In manufacturing each Win-Lite barrel, 500 miles (that's 2,640,000 feet) of wound glass fiber were fused and bonded to a .020-inch thickness steel barrel liner. The lightweight alloy receiver was the first of its kind to be roll engraved, and all of the factory's claims about lighter, more manageable recoil were proven in the field by a 13-year old shooter.

Beginning in 1960, the Model 59 was offered in Standard Field Grade with 30-inch, 28-inch, and 26-inch Win-Lite barrels with Full, Modified, or Improved Cylinder chokes. A flyer listed both Full and Modified 28-inch barrels at $149.50.

A year later Winchester introduced "Versalite" chokes which could be threaded into the barrel. Modified choke tubes were standard and Full and Improved Cylinder tubes were priced at just $4.45. The "Versalite" chokes, however, were only available for 26-inch barrels. The Field Grade Model 59 was discontinued in 1965.

A Pigeon Grade Model 59 was built only in 1962 and 1963, and priced at $249.65. Like the Model 12 Pigeon Grade shotguns the Model 59 featured very fancy hand-checkered walnut stocks and forearms, hand-honed internal parts, and engine turned bolts and carriers. Because it had an alloy receiver, engraving was not offered for the Model 59 Pigeon Grade, they had the same roll engraved game scenes as the Field Grade.

Why only five years of production? It took that long to discover the few shortcomings the Model 59 possessed, none of which involved the gun's function or safety. With heavy use in the field, blueing on the alloy receivers began to rub off, leaving areas of white. The fiberglass-covered barrels were indeed weatherproof, but again the blueing began to fail and chamber areas of the barrels began to turn yellow. Both of these problems were common to guns getting heavy use, but in every other respect the Model 59 was all that Winchester had claimed. The real problem was the idea of the glass fiber barrel. Unlike a fiberglass bodied Chevrolet Corvette, which was all the rage in the 1950s, hunters really weren't warming up to a fiberglass barreled shotgun (unless maybe they owned a Corvette). After 82,085 guns were built, New Haven realized that the Model 59 would never be popular and it was not featured in the 1965 catalog.

Interestingly, the Model 59 has a very devoted following and used examples are worth upwards of $500 in very good condition today and as much as $750 for examples with all three "Versalite" chokes. Pigeon Grade models are very rare and have sold for over $2,000. Many of those guns with faded receivers and stained barrels are still out in the field every season, because the Model 59 really was one of the finest and most durable semi-automatic shotguns ever made.

In 1964 Winchester made significant changes in most of its product lines, thus the often referred to terminology for certain Winchesters as being *"Pre-'64"* models. In general, this indicates a model produced after 1963 through the use of investment casting, which eliminated much of the hand machining and handcraftsmanship that had distinguished Winchester arms since the 1850s. This does not mean that models built *after* 1963 are of lesser quality, they're just built through a more cost efficient process.

The first examples of this new technique were the Model 12 slide-action shotguns, and in the semi-autos the brand new Model 1400, also the first shotgun in Winchester history (along with the slide-action Model 1200) not to be designated by its initial year of manufacture.

Like the new Model 1200 pump, the 1400 Automatic Shotgun featured a newly engineered rotating bolt head, locking lugs, and a gas-operated mechanism to extract, eject, and chamber a fresh shell when the gun was fired.

Following are the general specifications for the Model 1400:

TYPE

3-shot, gas operated shotgun. Self compensation valve in the gas chamber automatically adjusts for standard magnum loads.

RECEIVER

Rust proof, high-strength aluminum alloy. Direct unloading from magazine. New push-button carrier release was introduced in 1968, designated as Model 1400 Mark II through 1972, after which the special designation was dropped. Left-handed versions of the Model 1400 were also available from 1968 through 1972. Approximately 1250 were made.

STYLES

Standard Field Gun (1964-1981); Field Gun with vent rib; Deer Gun (1965-1974); Slug Hunter (1990-1992); Trap Gun with ventilated rib and deluxe checkering (1965-1973); Trap Gun with Monte Carlo stock, ventilated rib and deluxe checkering; Skeet Gun with ventilated rib and deluxe checkering (1965-1973); New Model 1400 (1989-1994 standard with vent rib, Winchoke and three shell capacity magazine); 1400 Ranger (12- or 20-gauge with 26-inch barrel 1991-1993, 28-inch Winchoke barrel through 1994); Custom High Grade (special order only through Custom Shop with deluxe hand checkered walnut stock and forearm, and special engraving, 1991-1992 only).

BARRELS AND CHOKES*

12 Gauge: 30-inch Full choke; 28-inch, Full or Modified choke; 26-inch Improved Cylinder or Skeet bore; 22-inch special bore for Deer Gun (discontinued 1974), Slug Hunter, and Ranger.

16 Gauge: 28-inch, Full or Modified choke; 26-inch, Improved Cylinder choke. The 16-gauge models were discontinued in 1973.

20 Gauge: 28-inch, Full or Modified choke; 26-inch, Improved Cylinder or Skeet bore.

*Barrels within a gauge were interchangeable. Winchoke introduced on the Model 1400 for 12, 16, and 20-gauge models.

MAGAZINE

Capacity, Two 2-$^3/_4$ shells plus one in the chamber. Also from 1989 to 1994 models with three shell capacity magazine.

STOCK, FOREARM, CARVING AND ENGRAVING

Checkered American walnut pistol grip stock with fluted comb and Winchester recoil pad, checkered forearm. Trap and Skeet guns with deluxe checkering. Hydro-Coil stocks also offered beginning in 1964.

In 1978 Winchester introduced an upgraded version of the Model 1400 with restyled stock and forearm, fancier checkering and a high-polish receiver and barrel. The new models were designated 1500 XTR and offered in both 12 and 20-gauge Field Gun versions with plain or vent rib barrels and Winchokes. In 1982 U.S. Repeating Arms Co. added the Model 1500 XTR Waterfowl with a 30-inch vent rib barrel and Winchoke, and a 1500 XTR Deer Gun with 24-$^1/_2$ inch barrel and rifle sights.

Among the special features of the 1500 XTR was an improved design cocking handle, a fluted semi-beavertail forearm with deep cut checkering, a nickel plated carrier, and the high gloss XTR finished American walnut introduced on all XTR models in 1978. The 1500 XTR also featured white line spacers between the pistol grip cap and butt plate.

Following are the general specifications for the Model 1500 XTR:

TYPE

3-shot, gas operated shotgun. Self compensation valve in the gas chamber automatically adjusts for standard magnum loads.

RECEIVER

Rust proof, high-strength aluminum alloy. Direct unloading from the magazine, positive cross lock safety located in upper front of trigger guard.

STYLES

Field Gun, offered with plain barrel or vent rib, with or without Winchoke.

BARRELS

12 Gauge: 30-inch Full choke; 28-inch, Modified choke or Winchoke; 26-inch Improved Cylinder choke.

20 Gauge: 28-inch Full choke, Modified choke, or Winchoke; 26-inch Improved Cylinder.

MAGAZINE

Capacity, Two 2-$^3/_4$ shells plus one in the chamber.

STOCK, FOREARM, CARVING AND ENGRAVING

Checkered American walnut forearm and pistol grip stock with fluted comb, high-luster XTR finish, black serrated butt plate.

The Model 1500 XTR had a rather short production history, it was only available from 1978 to 1982, but it was really part of a much bigger picture. The Model 1400 and 1500 XTR were the most successful auto-loaders in Winchester history up to that time, and from 1964 to 1994, total combined production reached over 1.25 million guns!

In 1974 Winchester had introduced another upgraded Automatic, the Super X Model 1, offered in Standard, Skeet, Trap, and Custom Trap or Skeet models. The Super X Model 1, Trap, and Skeet versions were built through 1981, and Custom Trap or Skeet offered in limited quantities from 1987 through 1992. As such, the Custom models are more highly valued today and worth almost twice that of Trap and Skeet guns.

The Super X line was also used for special Limited Editions, including a model for Ducks Unlimited, and a limited number of custom guns with No. 5 engraving and gold inlays. The latter, according to the *25th Edition Blue Book of Gun Values*, is now worth $2,395. The last suggested retail in 1992 was $1,295.

After the Super X Model 1 Custom Trap and Skeet guns were discontinued, Winchester came back with the Super X2 series in 1999, which is still in production.

Chapter Nine
Late Model Slide-Action Shotguns
Model 1200 and Model 1300

As mentioned earlier, 1964 was a year that truly divides past from present in Winchester history. Although the Model 12 continued to be built after 1964, there was only one model offered, the Skeet Gun, which remained in the Winchester line until 1976. Beginning in 1964 a new line of slide-action shotguns was introduced to replace the discontinued Model 12s.

Had Winchester followed tradition with the naming of its shotguns, the new slide-action should have been the Model 64, but that number had already been used for a rifle back in 1933. Another option might have been, as Winchester had done with the Model 37, adding an A suffix, thus a Model 12A, but instead, the company went with a pair of zeros, and the Model 12's successor became the Model 1200.

Continuing New Haven's program to improve manufacturing and lower production costs, the Model 1200 took advantage of the latest developments in metallurgy with a high-strength aluminum alloy receiver. The all-new model also featured a rifle-type, head-locking, rotating bolt with four lugs that locked into the barrel extension. It was a vastly improved and more durable design that would set the standard for future models. The Model 1200 was the first truly "contemporary" slide-action shotgun to come from New Haven since the Model 1912.

There were five basic configurations for the Model 1200, the standard Model 1200 with plain barrel, Model 1200 with Winchester Recoil Reduction System and vent rib barrel, Model 1200 Trap Gun with vent rib, Model 1200 with Winchoke, and the Stainless Police Pistol model. There were, however, specific variations of each, plus a Deer Gun.

Following are the general specifications for the Model 1200:

TYPE
5-shot and 7-shot, slide-action shotgun. Front locking rotating bolt.

RECEIVER
Rust proof, high-strength aluminum alloy. Direct unloading from the magazine, positive cross lock safety located in upper front of trigger guard.

STYLES
Field Gun, offered with plain barrel or vent rib; Magnum Field Gun with plain or vent rib barrel; Deer Gun with rifle sights; Trap Gun with regular comb, vent rib, deluxe checkering, or Monte Carlo comb; Skeet Gun with vent rib and deluxe checkering.

BARRELS
12 Gauge: 30-inch, Full choke; 28-inch, Full or Modified choke; 26-inch, Improved Cylinder or Skeet bore; 22-inch, special bore for Deer Gun. The 30-inch Full choke was designed to handle both 3-inch magnum and all 2-$^3/_4$ inch shells interchangeably in the Magnum Field Gun added in 1966.

16 Gauge: 28-inch, Full or Modified choke; 26-inch, Improved Cylinder choke.

20 Gauge: 28-inch, Full or Modified choke; 26-inch, Improved Cylinder or Skeet bore. The 28-inch Full choke was designed to handle both 3-inch magnum and all 2-$^3/_4$ inch shells interchangeably in the Magnum Field Gun.

Pictured are a Model 1200 Riot with 18-inch barrel and 7-shot magazine, the Standard or Field Grade model with checkered pistol grip stock and checkered forearm, and the Model 1200 Defender which was offered only in 12-gauge with an 18-inch Cylinder bore barrel and 7-shot magazine. (U.S. Repeating Arms Company Collection)

Model 1200 Field Grade with Winchokes. The Winchoke barrels became available after 1969. Chokes were Improved Cylinder, Full, and Modified. The Model 1200 was also a take down gun that disassembled easily. (U.S. Repeating Arms Company Collection)

This is both an inexpensive and rare model at the same time. The basic gun would have been the Model 120 Ranger, a lower-priced 1200 that did not offer the checkered walnut stock and forearm of the Field Grade gun. This however is a 120 Ranger youth model in 20-gauge, and even more specifically, a Ducks Unlimited special edition known as the Whistler, named as one might expect, after a duck. (U.S. Repeating Arms Company Collection)

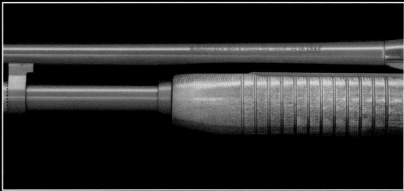

The Model 1300 offered many different variations on the improved Model 1200 design. Pictured are three very different examples. At the top a Ladies/Youth variation for wild turkey shooting, engraved on the receiver with a turkey and Wild Turkey Federation. Chambered in 20-gauge, 3-inch magnum, the model has the colorful laminated WinCam stock, grooved forearm, and camo sling. Manufactured only in 1992. Center, a Model 1300 Advantage Camo manufactured in 1978 in 12-gauge only with a 28-inch barrel, and bottom, the Model 1300 Slug Hunter with iron sights. This 12-gauge only model was offered with either a smooth bore or rifled 22-inch barrel. It was introduced in 1988. (U.S. Repeating Arms Company Collection)

Today's Model 1300 Sporting Field Gun is the latest version of a long-lived design that carries on the tradition of the hammerless, slide-action repeater established by the Model 1912. (Photo courtesy W.R.A. Co.)

Barrels within a gauge were interchangeable, except 3-inch magnums.

MAGAZINE

Capacity, four shells plus one in the chamber. (A factory installed, removable plug limited capacity to two shells). Riot and Defender, seaven shells.

STOCK AND FOREARM

Checkered American walnut forearm and pistol grip stock, with fluted comb, and Winchester recoil pad. Deluxe checkering on Trap and Skeet guns.

SIGHTS

Front metal bead on Field Guns; metal bead middle and red bead front on Trap and Skeet Guns; rifle sights front and rear on Deer Gun.

The Model 1200 had set the standard for American slide-action shotguns and in 1969 Winchester redefined the market again with the introduction of the Winchoke, a quickly interchangeable, screw in choke system that gave the Model 1200 (and Model 1400 semi-automatic) unprecedented versatility in the field and on the range.

The Winchoke was an improved variation of the Versalite interchangeable chokes introduced in 1961 for the Model 59. Winchokes were available in Improved Cylinder, Full, and Modified, and simply screwed into the muzzle of a Winchoke equipped model. A small spanner wrench was used to tighten down or remove the chokes and this was one tool you did not want to misplace! In 1971 the Winchoke became available for Trap Guns. The author's first shotgun was a Model 1200 with Winchoke and this was a popular and affordable model for Trap shooters, because the versatility afforded by the Winchoke system was like having three shotguns for the price of one.

The Model 1200 Field Grade was discontinued in 1981, the Magnum a year before, while the Skeet, Trap, and Deer Gun were all out of production by 1974. In their place Winchester had begun another transition beginning in 1979, with the Model 1300 series.

The first was the Model 1300 XTR "Featherweight" available in 12 and 20-gauge. Using the Model 1200 as a starting point, the stock and forearm were redesigned, new checkering patterns added, and a high-luster XTR finish was standard. The same year that the Model 1200 Field Grade was discontinued, Winchester introduced the first Model 1200 Ranger, which was listed in the 1982 catalog. A less expensive version of the Model 1200 (120), the Ranger did not have the highly polished receiver or engine turned bolt, the stock and forearm were not walnut, and the forearm was embellished only with grooves. Ranger models had no checkering.

The Model 1300 marked the beginning of a new Winchester shotgun dynasty that has continued for 27 years.

It was also during this period that Olin Industries decided to sell off its domestic firearms industry, and in 1981 a consortium made up of Winchester Repeating Arms Co. executives and employees took over operations under license from Olin. At the time John M. Olin was 89 years old and had owned Winchester for over half a century.

The new company would manufacture and sell Winchester rifles and shotguns produced in New Haven under the U.S. Repeating Arms Company name, while Olin Corporation would continue to manufacture Winchester ammunition and produce Winchester brand firearms in Japan at Olin-Kodensha. Thus from this point on there were Winchester shotguns manufactured in the United States and in Japan, both of which were sold here and abroad through U.S. Repeating Arms Co. in the United States and Canada, and by Olin's Winchester Group in the rest of the world.[1]

This arrangement continued until French munitions maker Giat acquired the U.S. Repeating Arms Co. along with Browning F.N. in Belgium in 1992. Since 1997 Fabrique Nationale (F.N.) Browning, and the U.S. Repeating Arms Co. have been under one parent company, each however, with its own autonomy and production facilities. Today, with the exception of Winchesters built by Browning F.N. in Belgium, and by Miroku in Japan (since 1976 for Browning and 1992 for Winchester)[2], the majority of shotguns bearing the historic name are still built in New Haven, Connecticut.

[1] Winchester An American Legend by R.L. Wilson.
[2] 25th Edition Blue Book of Gun Values by S.P. Fjestad.

Chapter Ten
Over-and-Under Shotguns for Game and Clays
Models 101, 91, 96 Xpert, 501, Presentation Grade, Shotgun/Rifle Combo, and 1001

As had been the case with Winchester's development of an auto-loading shotgun, New Haven did not exactly rush into the design and production of a superposed model. In fact, had it not been for Olin Industries and Olin-Kodensha, it is unlikely that the Model 101 over-and-under shotgun would ever have been built.

In the 1960s Browning and Remington owned the superposed market, at least in the United States. Both had been producing over-and-under design shotguns for more than 30 years. The first Browning superposed, a 12-gauge model with boxlock action, was introduced in 1931. Remington, one of America's oldest arms makers, also brought a superposed shotgun to market that year, the Model 32, a 12-gauge with double lock action. Thus Winchester's two greatest competitors had been building over-and-under shotguns for over three decades before New Haven leveled its sights on this long-established market.

By 1960, Winchester-Western and Olin-Mathieson were evaluating the possibility of offshore production to offset escalating costs in New Haven. After considering partnerships with manufacturers in Austria, Belgium, Germany, and Great Britain (where Winchester had turned for a double gun in the late 19th century), the best possible relationship appeared to be with Miroku Limited, in Japan. As noted by Winchester historian and author Herbert G. Houze, in

Winchester Repeating Arms Company Its History & Development from 1865 to 1981, a study had been commissioned to ascertain which company might be best suited to producing arms for the American market. "Ultimately, this research was to result in the selection of Miroku Ltd. in the Tochigi Prefecture as the best possible candidate. Shortly thereafter, Miroku and Olin-Mathieson agreed on a working relationship, and a new company called Olin-Kodensha Limited was established in 1961 to manufacture shotguns bearing the Winchester name."

At the same time, Winchester-Western was considering the production of a superposed model, and to their good fortune Miroku was already building one prior to the creation of Olin-Kodensha. Thus the Model 101 was almost entirely designed by Miroku. While there is often a stigma associated with Winchester shotguns made in Japan, R.L. Wilson notes that, "Despite the severe restrictions placed on gun ownership in Japan, Japanese mechanics rank among the best gunmakers in the world for factory mass production." The Model 101 was a finely crafted shotgun that, over the years, has proven its worth both in the field and on the secondary market.

The Model 101 was produced from 1963 through 1988 and remained a highly popular part of the Winchester line, leading the way to the current generation of Winchester superposed models built by Browning F.N. in Belgium.

The Model 101 was a handsome shotgun. Despite it being built in Japan (as were other Winchester models) the 101 was a high-quality firearm worthy of the Winchester name. Pictured (left to right) a Super Pigeon Grade, 12-gauge 101 Field Grade, and .410-gauge Skeet Grade. (Author's Collection)

Olin-Winchester sold a Model 91 superposed which was built in Spain for European sale only and through armed forces post exchanges. Seldom seen in the U.S. the Model 91 looked very similar to the Model 101, and came with scroll engraved receiver, 28-inch vent rib barrel, and walnut stock with checkered pistol grip. Chambered for 3-inch shells, the barrels were choked Full and Modified. (Photos courtesy Rock Island Auction Company)

There has always been some confusion regarding the Model 101 series, and R.L. Wilson briefly takes this to task in *Winchester An American Legend*. "Listed styles include Field, Magnum Field, Skeet, Trap Gun (with Monte Carlo or regular stocks), Trap Gun with single barrel, and Trap Gun with single and double-barreled combinations.

"Gauges were 12, 20, 28, and .410. The serial numbering was a bit odd, with the 12-gauge beginning at 50000 and going to 199999; then numbering began anew at 300000. The 101s in 20, 28, and .410 gauge were numbered from 200000." It is easy to misidentify the age of a Model 101, but with a little study and cross-reference from the *Blue Book of Gun Values* owners can usually find where their particular model falls in the procession of guns produced from 1963 to 1988.

In addition to the standard models, there were Pigeon Grade, Golden Pigeon, Diamond Grade, and Presentation Grade guns, the 501 Grand European, and Model 101 Shotgun/Rifle combinations.

For Winchester-Olin's European sales, the Model 101 was produced in a Super Grade with a silver gray nitrite receiver, double triggers, and a straight English or rounded pistol grip style stock. As noted by Winchester-Olin:

"For markets in Europe, Australia, Canada, South and Central America, Winchester offers a special line of over-and-under shotguns. The Super Grade series includes seven field guns (six 12 gauge and one 20 gauge), three trap guns and a skeet gun. The series features oil-finished, semi-fancy American walnut stocks with full pistol, semi-pistol, or English straight grip and silver gray nitrite receivers with fine engraving. The Model 101 Lightweight series includes five field guns in 12-gauge and one field gun in 20-gauge. The Lightweight guns are

available with single and double triggers with a choice of full pistol, semi-pistol or English straight grips. The wood is oil-finished American walnut and the sides and bottom of the receiver feature engravings of game birds. The Model 101 Winchoke field gun, in 12 gauge, comes with six interchangeable Winchoke tubes (two each in Improved Cylinder, Modified, and Full). The gun is available with or without a recoil pad. The wood is oil-finished American walnut and the grip is full pistol. Fine engraving on the receiver."

For the American market, the magnum Field Gun, introduced in 1966 in both 12 and 20-gauge, would take either 3-inch magnum or 2-3/4 inch standard shells. Notes Thomas Henshaw in *The History of Winchester Firearms, Sixth Edition*, "…it is not commonly known, but all 20-gauge Model 101 shotguns are chambered for 3-inch shells, even the skeet versions."

The Model 101 Trap Gun with Monte Carlo stock was introduced in 1967 and came choked Full and Improved-Modified. A 20-gauge Skeet Gun with 26-1/2 inch barrels was also introduced in 1967, and a year later .410 and 28 gauge models were added. Both were offered in Field or Skeet Gun, or in a special combination cased skeet set, featuring .410, 28-gauge, and 20-gauge barrel sets furnished with one Model 101 frame. The 28-gauge models were chambered for standard 2-3/4 inch shells in both Skeet and Field Gun, the .410 for 3-inch shells.

The most unusual Model 101 was the "single barrel" Trap Gun introduced in 1968. The single shot 101 was offered with a choice of 34-inch Full choke, 32-inch Full choke, or 32-inch Improved-Modified choke barrels, complete with vent rib. The Model 101 single was also offered in three different combination sets, and here the logic finally came to light. One consisted of a 34-inch Full

The Lower-Priced Spread
Winchester's Xpert Model 96

Irony. That's when something you plan to make things better eventually has the opposite result. For Winchester, the idea of producing the Model 101 in Japan had been to reduce manufacturing costs. And in fact that was the result achieved by Olin Industries in the 1960s. By the late 1970s, however, the success of the Model 101 for hunting and sports shooting had driven the average price just out of reach for a lot of Winchester customers. Thus, responding to customer requests for a more economical over-and-under, Winchester introduced a lower-priced superposed in 1976, the Xpert Model 96. The new shotgun was offered in traditional field, trap and skeet versions with a blued plain receiver and ventilated rib barrels. The walnut stock and forearm were still hand checkered and high-gloss finished, so the even though the Xpert was lower priced, it didn't look it. All versions featured a single trigger and a safety selector plus automatic ejectors, just like the Model 101.

All three models were available in 12 and 20-gauge versions. The Field Gun came with 3-inch chambers. The Xpert Trap Gun, with 2-$\frac{3}{4}$ inch chambers, was introduced in 30-inch Full and Full with regular and Monte Carlo stocks (dropped in 1978). The Xpert Skeet Gun was offered with 2-$\frac{3}{4}$ inch chambers and 27-inch barrels choked Skeet and Skeet.

In 1977 an Xpert trap gun choked Improved-Modified and Full, with 30-inch barrel and a choice of regular or Monte Carlo stock was added to the line, and in 1980 32-inch barrels as an option.

There was yet another irony. Winchester did not attain the desired result with the Model 96 Xpert, which picked up the rather unflattering nickname, "Poor Man's 101." In 1982 the line was discontinued.

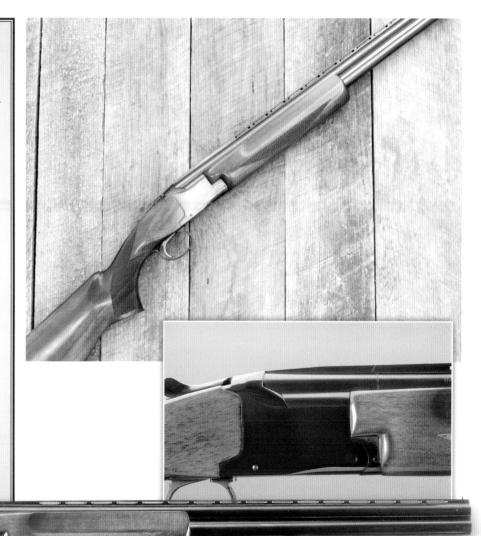

In response to customer requests for a more economical superposed, Winchester introduced the lower-priced Xpert Model 96 in 1976. The new shotgun was offered in traditional field (shown), trap and skeet versions with a blued plain receiver and ventilated rib barrels. The walnut stock and forearm were still hand checkered and high-gloss finished. It was not a great success and the model line was discontinued in 1982.
(Model 96 courtesy W.R.A. Co. Collection, additional photos courtesy Rock Island Auction Company)

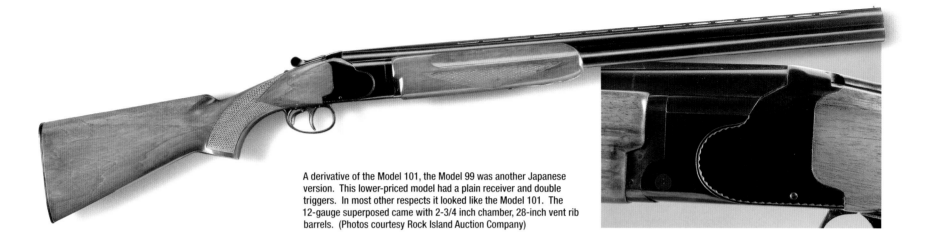

A derivative of the Model 101, the Model 99 was another Japanese version. This lower-priced model had a plain receiver and double triggers. In most other respects it looked like the Model 101. The 12-gauge superposed came with 2-3/4 inch chamber, 28-inch vent rib barrels. (Photos courtesy Rock Island Auction Company)

choke single barrel, plus a Model 101 interchangeable over-and-under barrel set with forearm. A second combination offered 32-inch single and 30-inch over-and-under barrel sets and the third combination consisted of a 32-inch Full choke single plus two sets of over-and-under barrels with forearms. This deluxe set came in a fitted trunk case.

By 1974 Winchester had phased out a number of 101 model choices and completed a reorganization of the trap line by discontinuing all previous models and introducing one Pigeon Grade Trap Gun, offered with either a 30-inch or 32-inch set of barrels choked Improved-Modified and Full choke. This new Pigeon Grade Trap Gun featured a finely detailed, hand engraved and polished receiver, and a fancy grade French walnut stock and forearm with special hand checkering. The Pigeon Grade Trap Gun stocks were offered in both regular and Monte Carlo styles.

A 12-gauge Pigeon Grade Field Gun was made available in 1976 with 26-inch or 28-inch barrels, also a Pigeon Grade Skeet Gun in 12 or 20 gauge with 2-3/4-inch chambers and 27-inch barrels choked Skeet and Skeet. A new Pigeon Grade Skeet Set also

replaced the original 20, 28 and 410 gauge set.

The new Pigeon Grade models featured finely detailed hand engraving on both sides of gray, satin-finished receivers. A specially engineered ventilated rib with metal front and middle sight provided an improved sighting plane and the trigger was designed with a single inertia system for a light, crisp pull.

To further distinguish its line of premium over-and-under shotguns, beginning in 1980 every Pigeon Grade Model 101 came packed in a custom-crafted case, complete with brass-plated hardware and combination lock.

In 1981 the 501 Grand European was added to the superposed line in both Trap Gun and Skeet Gun grades. Both featured a semi-fancy American walnut stock and Schnabel forearm with hand-cut checkering at 22 lines to the inch. The receivers had a silver-nitrite finish with fine scroll engraving and a Grand European logo etched on both the frame and barrels. Available in 12-gauge Trap Gun or 20-gauge Skeet Gun, barrel selections were 27, 30, or 32-inches. A 20-gauge Grand European Feather-weight with straight grip stock and 25-$^1\!/_2$ inch vent rib barrel was also available from 1981 to 1986.

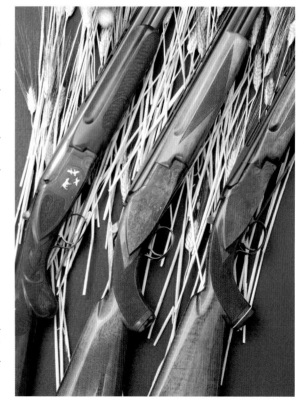

Here & left: The Model 101 was a great success for Winchester-Olin and Winchester-Western, as well as the U.S. Repeating Arms Company. Produced from 1963 to 1988 the 101 superposed was offered in a variety of models ranging from Field Grade (right and center) to deluxe models with fine hand engraving, gold inlays, and beautifully carved fancy walnut stocks and forearms.

The most popular of 101 variations was the Field Grade in 12-gauge. Produced from 1963 to 1987, it was a handsome, well-built shotgun that has withstood the test of time. Today, Model 101 values are rising on the secondary market as collectors have finally come to embrace the Japanese Winchesters. Note the red W on the metal grip cap, engraved trigger guard and fine hand checkering. (Author's Collection)

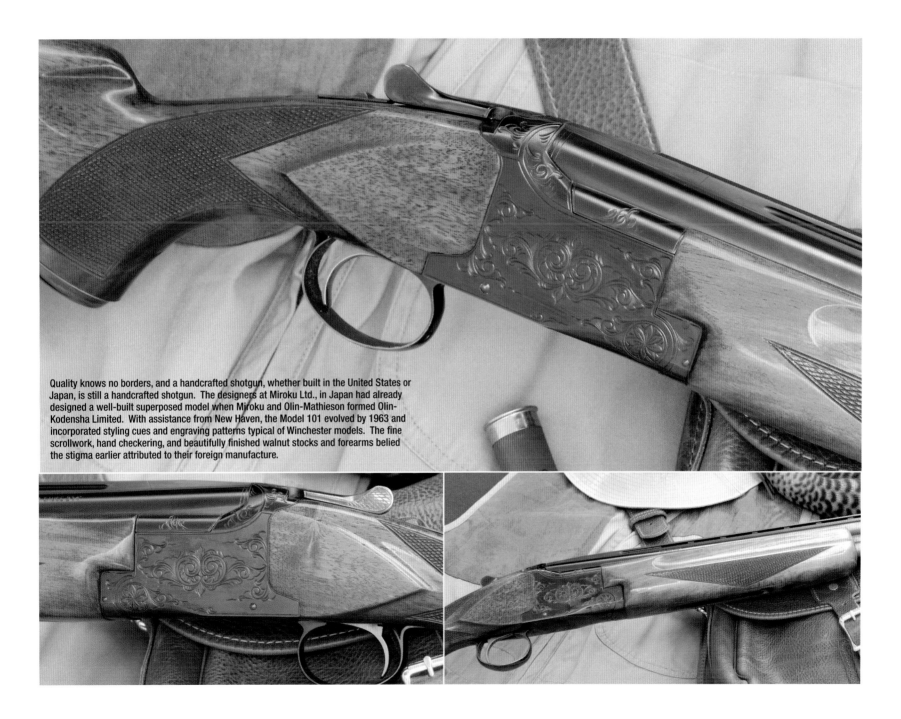

Quality knows no borders, and a handcrafted shotgun, whether built in the United States or Japan, is still a handcrafted shotgun. The designers at Miroku Ltd., in Japan had already designed a well-built superposed model when Miroku and Olin-Mathieson formed Olin-Kodensha Limited. With assistance from New Haven, the Model 101 evolved by 1963 and incorporated styling cues and engraving patterns typical of Winchester models. The fine scrollwork, hand checkering, and beautifully finished walnut stocks and forearms belied the stigma earlier attributed to their foreign manufacture.

The boxlock action of the Model 101 was sturdy and beautifully finished with polished engine turned surfaces. This was the kind of quality Winchester owners expected.

226

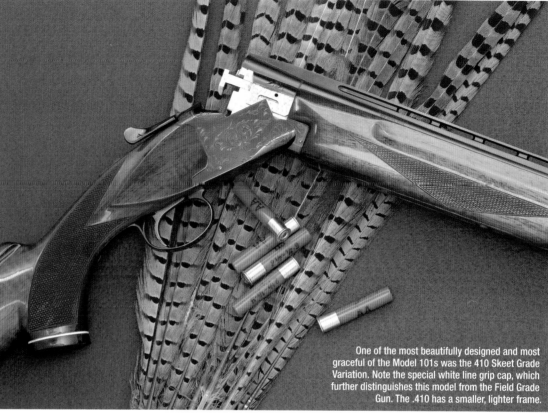

One of the most beautifully designed and most graceful of the Model 101s was the 410 Skeet Grade Variation. Note the special white line grip cap, which further distinguishes this model from the Field Grade Gun. The .410 has a smaller, lighter frame.

Following the transfer of its New Haven Arms operations to the U.S. Repeating Arms Company in mid 1981, Olin Corporation continued to manufacture various over-and-under models in Japan. Beginning in 1981 Olin-Kodensha introduced the Pigeon Grade XTR Lightweight with Winchoke. In 1982 the Super Grade, rifle/shotgun combination (12-gauge over and 30-06 under), the Double Express over-and-under rifle in 30-06, and Diamond Grade superposed Trap and Skeet Guns. In 1983 the Presentation Grade over-and-under with hand engraving and gold inlays was introduced. The next year Trap sets were introduced in 12-gauge single barrel plus over-and-under barrels with Winchoke. In 1986, one year before most of the Model 101 line was discontinued, a Quail Special 12-gauge over-and-under with 25-$^1/_2$ inch barrels and Winchoke was introduced along with the Super Pigeon, a 12-gauge superposed with 27-inch Winchoked barrels, a hand engraved receiver with gold inlays, and (B-style) carved American walnut stock and forearm. A two-barrel Hunting Set was also made available with 28-gauge, 27-inch barrels and .410 bore 27-inch barrels. Winchester also built a special ATA Hall of Fame Set, a 12-gauge Trap Gun with 30 and 34-inch Winchoked barrels. The entire Model 101 line was discontinued in 1987, but a year later Winchester introduced the 25th Anniversary Model in 12-gauge with 32-inch barrels choked Full and Modified. The cased Anniversary Model 101 was engraved "1 of 101" and manufactured only in 1988.

Mechanical features of the Model 101 included automatic ejectors and single selective triggers (the tang-mounted safety doubling as the selector), and boxlock action. Select walnut stocks and forearms were standard with fancy walnut, hand engraving with gold inlays, and stock/forearm carving standard on deluxe models such as Super Pigeon.

The Model 101 was one of the most successful lines in modern day Winchester history, and now, almost 20 years since being discontinued, the first Winchester superposed models are becoming very collectible.

Two views show the
extractors in operation as
the gun is opened.

228

Detail shows the elegant engraving on the receiver of a Model 101 in .410-gauge. Note that the chamber is marked 2-1/2 inch, which indicates a Skeet Grade Gun. Field Guns had 3-inch chambers.

Following are the general specifications for the Model 101:

TYPE

Over-and-under double barrel shotgun, hammerless, breakdown, ventilated rib, automatic ejectors, single selective trigger. Double trigger offered on some European models.

STYLES

Field Gun: available 1963 to 1987 also Field Gun two-barrel hunting set. Special 25th Anniversary model engraved "1 of 101" with silver inlays. Manufactured only in 1988.

Magnum Field Gun: available June 1966 (12 gauge only).

Lightweight Field: coin-finished receiver.

Field Special: 27-inch barrels with Winchokes, scroll engraved blued receiver.

Waterfowl Model: 12-gauge only with 3-inch chambers, 30 or 32-inch Winchoke barrels.

National Wild Turkey Federation Commemorative: Only 300 produced.

American Flyer Live Bird: 12-gauge only, 28-inch or 29-$^1/_2$ inch separated barrels with special raised vent rib, blue frame with gold borders, gold pigeon inlay and Live Bird engraved on underside of receiver. Only manufactured in 1987.

Quail Special: 12-gauge, 20-gauge (discontinued in 1984), 28-gauge and .410-gauge, both introduced in 1987. Straight stock, engraved coin finish receiver. Limited to 500 examples of each gauge.

Skeet Gun, Triple Barreled Skeet Set: .410, 28 and 20 gauge on same frame, cased. Manufactured from 1974 to 1984.

230

There was little to compare with the Model 101 Pigeon Grade Guns. This beautiful cased example in 28-gauge with 28-inch barrels choked Improved Cylinder and Modified is exemplary of the high quality fit and finish Olin-Kodensha provided. (Courtesy Dave Riffle)

231

One of the more rare Model 101 variations, this is a 12-gauge, two barrel, American Flyer Live Bird Combo. Offered with 28-inch or 29-1/2 inch separated barrels with special raised vent rib, the frame on the Live Bird was outlined with a gold border. A gold pigeon was inlaid on the underside of receiver, and each gun was marked Winchester Live Bird. This version was only manufactured in 1987. (Courtesy Dave Riffle)

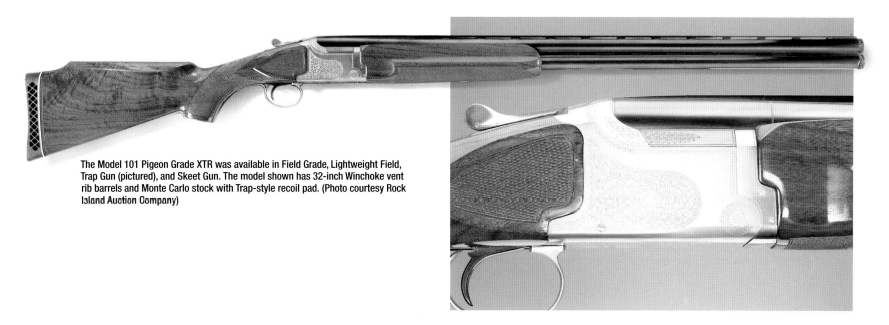

The Model 101 Pigeon Grade XTR was available in Field Grade, Lightweight Field, Trap Gun (pictured), and Skeet Gun. The model shown has 32-inch Winchoke vent rib barrels and Monte Carlo stock with Trap-style recoil pad. (Photo courtesy Rock Island Auction Company)

Trap Gun: Monte Carlo stock or regular stock. Manufactured 1966 to 1984.

Pigeon Grade XTR, Field Grade, Lightweight Field, Trap Gun, Skeet Gun: Manufactured 1974 to 1987.

Single Barrel Trap Gun: Also sold in combination Single Barrel and Double Barrel Trap Gun. Cased.

Super Pigeon Grade: 12-gauge only. Deluxe model with hand-engraved receiver featuring gold inlaid hunting dog and pigeons on right panel and ducks on left panel. Extra select walnut stock and forearm with style B carving. Manufactured 1985-1987.

Diamond Grade: Trap or Skeet Gun, Trap 12-gauge only, Skeet in 20, 28, or .410-gauge, engraved satin-finish receiver.

Grand European: Also known as 501 Grand European, Trap or Skeet Gun. Also offered in Featherweight model.

Presentation Grade: 12-gauge only, Trap or Skeet Gun. Highly engraved receiver, gold inlays, silver wire borders, special crotch walnut stock and forearm. Manufactured 1984-1987.

Grand European Shotgun/Rifle Combination Gun: 12-gauge combined with choice of .222 Remington, .223 Remington, .243 Winchester, .270 Winchester, .30-06, .308 Winchester, .300 Winchester magnum, 5.6x57R, 6.5x55mm, 7x65R, 7x57 Mauser, or 9.3x74R caliber rifle. Only with 25-inch barrels, top barrel with Winchoke. Grand European engraving and finish. Manufactured 1983-1985. Mostly European sales.

BARRELS AND CHOKES

Field Gun: 30-inch, Full and Full choke; 30-inch Modified and Full; (12 gauge only); 28-inch, Modified and Full; 26-inch, Improved Cylinder and Modified choke; 26-1/2 inch, Improved Cylinder and Modified choke, (20, 28 and .410 gauge only).

Magnum Field Gun: 30-inch Full and Full choke (12 gauge only).

Skeet Gun: 26-inch, Skeet I and Skeet 2 (12 gauge only), Skeet Gun, 26-^{1}/$_2$ inch, Skeet I and Skeet 2 (20 gauge only), Skeet Gun, 28-inch, Skeet I and Skeet 2 (all gauges), Skeet Set, 28-inch, Skeet I and Skeet 2 (20, 28 and .410 on same frame).

Trap Gun: 30-inch, Full and Full choke (12 gauge only),

Single Barrel Trap Gun: 34-inch Full, 32-inch Full, and 32-inch Improved-Modified choke barrels with ventilated rib. (Also available as part of trap combination with set of double barrels, 32-inch choked Improved-Modified and Full, on same frame).

CHAMBERING

12 gauge: 2-^{3}/$_4$-inch shells, except Magnum Field Gun which has 3-inch chambers.

20 gauge: standard chambers handle 2-^{3}/$_4$ and 3-inch shells.

28 gauge: standard 2-^{3}/$_4$-inch chamber in Skeet version, 3-inch chamber in Field Gun.

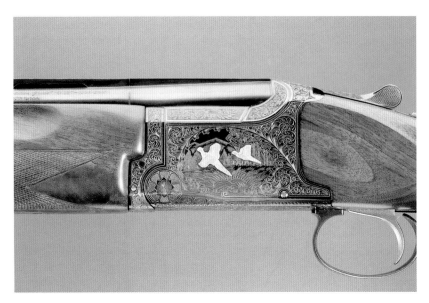
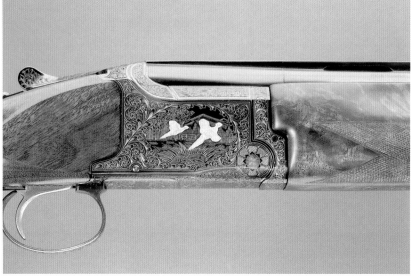

Above: The Model 101 Presentation Grade Gun was the most lavishly embellished production model with full coverage on the receiver, and gold inlays. Both sides have gold inlaid pheasants taking flight with a forest scene engraved in the background. The engraving was identical on both panels. The top of the barrel was marked Presentation Grade. Fitted with 27-inch barrels choked Skeet and Skeet. (Photos courtesy Rock Island Auction Company)

The Super Pigeon Model 101 is one of the more desirable variations due to the extra select walnut used, the B-style carving, elegant round pistol grip, and intricate gold inlays on the receiver. Unlike the Presentation Grade, the Super Pigeon featured a different scene on each panel. (Author's Collection)

235

The gold inlays on Super Pigeon Guns harkened back to the days of the Winchester Custom Shop and the beautiful work done by John and Nick Kusmit. Underside of the Super Pigeon has a gold pigeon and Super Pigeon inlaid in gold script within a gold oval.

Left: Super Pigeon barrel design was different from other grades with smaller vents between the barrels, and distinctive vents at the top of the rib behind the muzzle. This was and still is the most expensive Model 101, with the exception of the Four Gauge Skeet Set. Price today for a Super Pigeon averages $4,500.

Below & bottom: Definition of an oxymoron: A single barrel over-and under. The Model 101 single shot was offered with a choice of 34-inch Full choke, 32-inch Full choke, or 32-inch Improved-Modified choke barrels, complete with vent rib. It was also offered in three different combination sets, which included a single barrel and either one or two pairs of superposed barrels, making this one of the most versatile of all 101 models. (Photos courtesy Rock Island Auction Company)

There was yet another superposed model, the 1001 built in Italy by Marocchi. Available in Field Grade, Sporting Clays, and Sporting Clays Lite, the Field Gun (pictured) was available only with a 28-inch vent rib barrel, 3-inch chambers and WinPlus chokes. Neither plain nor overly fancy, the receiver had 40 percent engraving coverage and a high luster blue finish. (U.S. Repeating Arms Company Collection)

The Italian Job
Winchester's Model 1001

In 1993 Winchester introduced a new superposed model built in Italy by Marocchi. Like the Model 96 Xpert, the Model 1001 hit the ground running with a full lineup including Field Grade, Sporting Clays, and Sporting Clays Lite. The Field Gun was available only with a 28-inch vent rib barrel, 3-inch chambers and WinPlus chokes. Neither plain nor overly fancy, the receiver had 40 percent engraving coverage and a high luster blue finish.

With sporting clays having become one the most popular shooting sports in the world by the 1990s, playing on the "sporting clays" name was a very good idea, and both Model 1001 Sporting Clays guns were handsomely finished with full engraving and a combination of a silver nitrate receiver and bright blued barrels. The stocks and forearms were Grade II and Grade III with a beautiful finish. The Sporting Clays model offered a choice of 28-inch or 30-inch vent rib barrels with 2-$\frac{3}{4}$ inch chambers and the WinPlus chokes.

The Sporting Clays Lite model was added in 1995 with 3-inch chambers, and 28-inch vent rib barrels with WinPlus chokes. All three models were discontinued in 1998.

If a single shot over-and-under weren't confusing enough, Winchester added another model that left folks taken aback, the Grand European Combination Gun, a latter day Drilling, combining a 12-gauge with a choice of a dozen rifle calibers from .222 Remington to .30-06 (pictured) and .300 Winchester magnum. Available only with 25-inch barrels, the shotgun barrel was equipped for the Winchoke. The Combination Guns featured a silver gray nitrite receiver with game scenes and fine scrollwork. Manufactured 1983-1985, the guns were mainly sold in Europe where they were chambered for a variety of metric calibers. (Photos courtesy Rock Island Auction Company)

RECEIVER

Machined from solid block of high strength Winchester proof steel, hand engraved. All visible internal surfaces engine turned.

STOCK AND FOREARM

Walnut, fluted comb, pistol grip and beavertail forearm checkered. Straight English stocks on specific models and special orders.

SIGHTS

Field Gun, metal front; Skeet and Trap Guns, metal front and middle.

STANDARD MODEL WEIGHTS

30-inch barrel, 7-$^3/_4$ lbs. (12 gauge only), 28-inch barrel, 7-$^5/_8$ lbs. (12 gauge only), 26-inch barrel, 7-$^1/_2$ lbs. (12 gauge only), 20 gauge versions, 6-$^1/_2$ lbs, 28 gauge version, 6-$^1/_4$ lbs, .410 gauge versions, 6-$^1/_4$ lbs.

SERIAL NUMBERS

Located on upper tang. [1]

[1] Model specifications and production numbers compiled from The History of Winchester Firearms, Sixth Edition by Thomas Henshaw, and the 25th Edition Blue Book of Gun Values, which lists all 101 models in detail along with current values.

Winchester calls it the Super X2 Greenhead, but hunters call it the 3 $\frac{1}{2}$ inch, all-weather, semi-auto, that's indestructible. This is one of 51 shotguns offered by U.S. Repeating Arms Company today.

Chapter Eleven
Contemporary Models
Models 1300, Super X2, Select Elegance, Select Energy and 9410

All photos courtesy U.S. Repeating Arms Company

With nearly 150 years of history behind it, Winchester has had an opportunity to establish more than a few benchmarks in firearms design and many of today's Winchester shotguns have their designs well rooted in that great history.

Interestingly, one of the latest, the Model 9410 introduced in 2001, and winner of the Shooting Industry Academy of Excellence "2001 Shotgun of the Year" award, has its design grounded in the very first New Haven-built shotgun, the Model 1887. The Model 9410 is a lever-action repeater chambered in .410-gauge. The "94" prefix tells you from the start that this shotgun looks like the famed Winchester rifles of the old west.

There are seven versions of the Model 9410, so the gun can really be tailored to anyone's specific hunting or sport shooting needs. First is 9410 Traditional with a straight grip stock and tang safety that brings back the long overdue looks and feel of the original Model 94s. The Traditional is designed with the kind of handling necessary when hunting fast-moving game. The 24-inch barrel, with interchangeable Invector™ chokes, handles all current factory 2-$^1/_2$ inch .410 bore shotgun loads, including Foster-type rifled slugs (for larger varmints). A modified shallow "V" adjustable rear sight is paired with a fiber optic TRUGLO® front sight for fast target acquisition.

For field hunting or just as a lightweight shotgun on back country hikes, the more compact 9410 Packer with the Invector™ choke system is a step forward in the evolution of this unique firearm. Made especially for those who require the additional versatility a choke system provides — in a smaller, lighter package, the Packer features a 20-inch barrel equipped with essentially a cylinder

bore choke capable of accurately firing dense, mid-range patterns, depending on the load, and three-quarter magazine for a compactness and a feel you'll appreciate on your next squirrel or cottontail hunt. It has a semi-pistol grip walnut stock and forearm with distinctive forearm. Since this is a gun designed for the field, sling posts are included.

There's an even smaller version, the Packer Compact, with reduced stock dimensions (12-$^1/_2$ inch length of pull), plus light weight and low recoil, this is the perfect first gun, especially for the younger or smaller shooter. Look closely and you'll notice all the features found on the full size models are here: TRUGLO® fiber optic front sight with modified shallow "V" adjustable rear sight, walnut stock and forearm with distinctive end-cap. In addition, the Compact has the Invector™ choke system for increased versatility in providing the patterns you want to shoot. Top-tang safety is conveniently placed and perfect for small hands to operate. You can count on doing a lot of walking when you're after rabbits, squirrels or doves. The Packer Compact weighs only 6-pounds, making it easy to carry, easy to shoulder and swing. This model won't be caught short, however, where important features are concerned.

The Model 9410 Ranger is the award-winning Model 9410 Traditional in a value priced, feature-packed Ranger version. The reliable action and 24-inch smoothbore barrel readily handles all current factory 2-$^1/_2$ inch .410 bore shotgun loads, including Foster-type rifled slugs. The full-length tubular magazine allows for a full nine-shot capacity. The cylinder bore choke produces excellent mid-range patterns and a straight grip stock makes it easy to shoulder.

If you're after a little more gun, rather than a little less, Winchester has the deluxe Model 9410 Semi-Fancy Traditional. The Traditional is dressed for the dance with the addition of a new semi-fancy walnut stock, fit nicely to a blued receiver and barrel. This slick little .410 bore shotgun has earned its place alongside the timeless models of the Winchester Rifle and Shotgun line. Whether you are shooting clay targets or hunting cottontails or doves, pattern performance is optimized by the Invector™ choke system. And, with the array of high-performance shotshells and slugs available, the new Invector-equipped Model 9410 Semi-Fancy Traditional could be the most versatile and beautiful combination gun ever produced.

Another historic Winchester was the Model 1912, the first truly modern slide-action shotgun, and the best selling and most revered American shotgun ever built. Today the heritage of the first Winchester slide-action repeaters lives on in the Model 1300 series, one of the most varied, all-around, all-season shotguns made today. There are a remarkable 18 different shotguns available with the Model 1300 designation.

The Model 1300 New Shadow Grass is a Speed Pump™ built just for waterfowl hunters. The Mossy Oak® New Shadow Grass™ finish applied to this rugged shotgun is designed to blend in with the surroundings, better concealing you to bring the birds in close. Like all Speed Pump shotguns, this model features Winchester's tough rotary bolt design to work in the nastiest conditions and, thanks to inertia-assisted pumping, you can count on it to work fast. The action is compatible with all factory 2-3/4 inch and 3-inch magnum loads. The versatile WinChoke® choke system is steel, tungsten, bismuth and lead shot compatible. It also features a composite stock and forearm. There are two barrel lengths from which to choose, 26 or 28-inch.

The Model 1300 Universal Hunter Field Gun is another versatile shotgun designed to hunt game and work under the nastiest conditions. The Universal Hunter Field features a durable finish in Mossy Oak New Break-Up camo, maneuverable 26-inch vent rib barrel with WinChoke tubes and a composite stock and forearm. The lightweight alloy receiver is drilled and tapped to accept a scope or red dot sight.

The Upland Special Field Gun is claimed by Winchester to be the most maneuverable speed pump ever. Highlighted by an English-style, straight

Recalling the days of the first lever-action Winchester shotguns, the Model 9410 is a .410-gauge version of the venerable Model 94. For 2005, a custom Model 9410 is also available with a case colored frame.

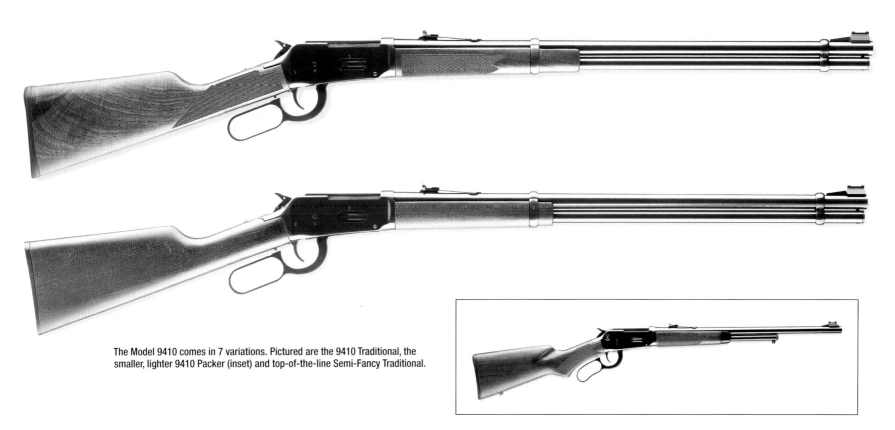

The Model 9410 comes in 7 variations. Pictured are the 9410 Traditional, the smaller, lighter 9410 Packer (inset) and top-of-the-line Semi-Fancy Traditional.

grip stock with new gloss finish, the Upland Special is designed to come to the shoulder quickly and get you on target fast. A compact 24-inch vent rib barrel and a slim, cylinder-style forearm move your hand closer to the bore center-line for better balance. The Upland Special is available in both 12 and 20 gauge models and features the excellent patterning WinChoke® system, with three chokes as standard equipment.

The Ranger name is another constant in Winchester history and there is a Model 1300 Ranger. With all of the most important features necessary in a fine field shotgun — speed, reliability, balanced handling — the Ranger® Speed Pump™ is one of the world's most popular field guns. The satin-finished hardwood stock and forearm are the perfect mix of rugged good looks and value. Offered with the proven and versatile WinChoke® system, the Ranger comes with a 28-inch ventilated rib barrel, and shoots all factory 2-³/₄ inch and 3 inch magnum loads. Available in 12 and 20-gauge models.

The Model 1300 Ranger® Compact & Ranger® Deer Compact offer two smaller versions ideally suited to the field. Just like its full-sized sibling, the Ranger® Compact has everything you need in a shotgun — just in a smaller package. With a length of pull of just 13 inches and a drop at heel of 2-³/₈ inches, speed to the shoulder and rib alignment are ideal for smaller shooters. The inertia-assisted Speed Pump™ rotary bolt makes pumping not only much faster, but much easier as well. The forearm is positioned rearward for a shorter reach, making it easier to work the action. The grip area is smaller for better finger-to-trigger fit. It's complete with the interchangeable WinChoke® system for excellent shot patterns. It is available in 12 or 20-gauge models.

The Deer Compact is a high-performance, lightweight, fast-handling 20-gauge slug gun with a 13-inch length of pull and 22 inch barrel. The Ranger® Compact Deer is designed to allow smaller or younger hunters to take full advantage of the superb ballistic performance afforded by modern 20 gauge slugs. The rifled barrel is especially designed for accurate, hard-hitting results with today's 20-gauge sabot slugs. Adjustable rifle-type sights and a non-glare

243

The need for speed is fulfilled by Winchester's Model 1300 series
Speed Pumps. Count the ejected shells…that's three still in the air!

244

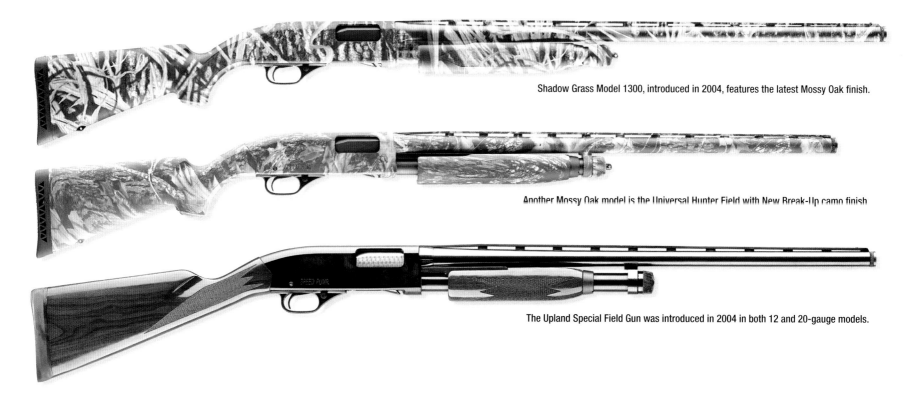

Shadow Grass Model 1300, introduced in 2004, features the latest Mossy Oak finish.

Another Mossy Oak model is the Universal Hunter Field with New Break-Up camo finish.

The Upland Special Field Gun was introduced in 2004 in both 12 and 20-gauge models.

finish on metal surfaces make this an ideal gun for inclement weather.

The Model 1300, Ranger® Deer has all the same features: speed, reliability, balanced handling and strength plus the availability of either the 12-gauge or new 20- gauge model. The receiver is drilled and tapped to readily accept a scope or use the included, adjustable, metal Truglo® rifle sights to provide excellent low-light target acquisition. The satin-finished hardwood stock and forearm features cut checkering.

Next are the Model 1300 Black Shadow® Deer & Black Shadow® Cantilever models. The Winchester® Black Shadow® Deer is available in a rifled barrel for shooting sabot slugs (available in 12 or 20 gauge). This model has the non-glare finish of the composite stock, forearm and exposed metal surfaces and a receiver that is drilled and tapped for mounting a scope. Adjustable rifle sights and sling swivel posts are included. A 12-gauge model is also available as a combo that includes both a rifled barrel and a 28-inch vent rib field barrel. The Black Shadow® Cantilever adds a sturdy cantilever scope mount and fully rifled 22-inch barrel. The cantilever mount keeps the scope connected directly

to the barrel, ensuring the scope stays sighted in while allowing the shotgun to easily be taken down for cleaning without compromising accuracy. The special customized composite stock features a raised comb to allow better alignment with a scope. Available in 12-gauge only, the Cantilever model does not include a scope.

Basic black is the rule of thumb for Winchester's Model 1300, Black Shadow® regarded as the toughest, most reliable pump shotgun in the series. The non-glare black finish of the barrel and receiver won't give away your position to lighting waterfowl and the rugged composite stock and forearm are up to the abuse a day afield can dish out. The fast, hardworking Speed Pump™ action shoots all factory 2-³/₄ inch and 3-inch magnum loads. The versatile WinChoke® system is steel, tungsten, bismuth and lead shot compatible. The Black Shadow is available in both 12 and 20-gauge models.

The Model 1300 Camp Defender is a true do-it-all shotgun. With an accurate 22-inch barrel, adjustable open sights, satin-finished hardwood stock and forearm and versatile WinChoke® system, it's perfect for camping in bear coun-

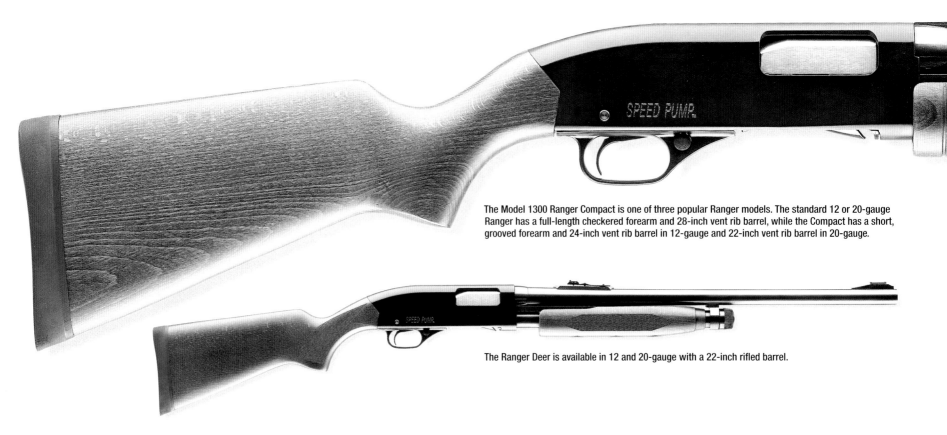

The Model 1300 Ranger Compact is one of three popular Ranger models. The standard 12 or 20-gauge Ranger has a full-length checkered forearm and 28-inch vent rib barrel, while the Compact has a short, grooved forearm and 24-inch vent rib barrel in 12-gauge and 22-inch vent rib barrel in 20-gauge.

The Ranger Deer is available in 12 and 20-gauge with a 22-inch rifled barrel.

try or for an occasional grouse hunt. Additionally, the Camp Defender can accurately fire Foster slugs or sabots when using a WinChoke® rifled choke tube (available separately) for deer hunting. The Camp Defender features an eight-round magazine.

The Defender 8-Shot is anther great all-around camp gun. It's easy to pack and carry and handles both buckshot and rifled slugs easily. The rugged Defender 8-Shot features an eight-shot magazine; 18-inch cylinder bore barrel, non-glare metal surfaces and a composite stock and forearm. Choose from the full stock version with a removable front Truglo® fiber optic sight, the pistol grip model, or the combo version with both pistol grip and full stock included. The full stock model is available in both 12 and 20-gauge.

The Model 1300 NWTF Short Turkey is the most specialized turkey gun built — ever. A highly maneuverable, 18-inch barrel is a benefit when moving through thick brush and the adjustable Truglo® fiber optic sights provide excellent low light performance. Or, if you prefer, the receiver is drilled and tapped

for mounting a scope or red dot type sight. The top performing Extra-Long, Extra-Full Extended Turkey tube is included and yields extremely tight patterns. Mossy Oak® New Break-Up™ camo keeps you hidden from wary eyes. The rugged composite stock is finished with a National Wild Turkey Federation medallion on the grip cap. Magazine cap and stock sling studs are standard.

Whitetail and turkey can move fast. That's why the NWTF Buck and Tom is exactly what you need in a shotgun. The inertia-assisted Speed Pump™ action gives you impressively fast follow-up shot capabilities and excellent reliability. A rugged composite stock and forearm, fully covered in Mossy Oak® New Break-Up™ camo keeps you hidden when the action is close. Whether you are using the included, extended rifled choke tube for deer, or the Hi-Density WinChoke® Extra-Full Turkey tube on big toms, the smooth bore 22-inch barrel is impressively accurate. Includes adjustable metal Truglo® fiber optic sights or mount-up a scope or red dot type sight on the drilled and tapped receiver. Authorized and endorsed by the National Wild Turkey Federation.

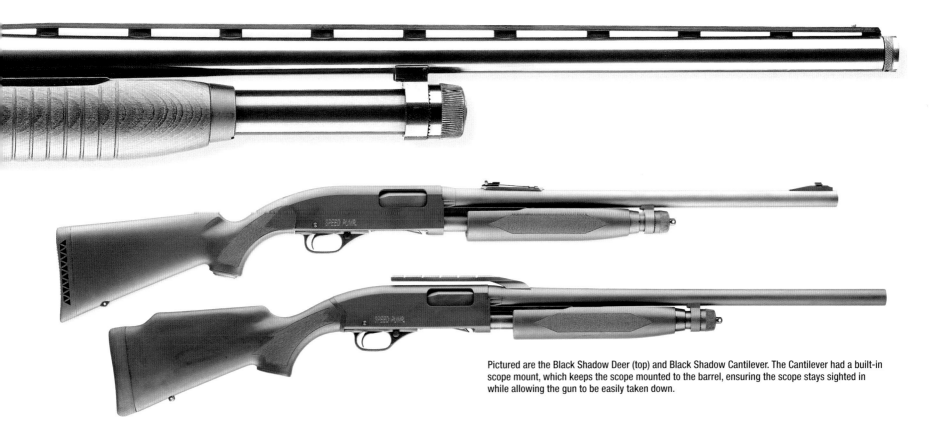

Pictured are the Black Shadow Deer (top) and Black Shadow Cantilever. The Cantilever had a built-in scope mount, which keeps the scope mounted to the barrel, ensuring the scope stays sighted in while allowing the gun to be easily taken down.

What are you hunting today? With the proven Speed Pump™ rotary bolt action and a list of accessories a mile long, versatile is the best word to describe the Universal Hunter Turkey. Turkeys, ducks, pheasants ... this shotgun can handle it all. It features a versatile 26-inch ventilated rib barrel with Extra-Full Turkey, Improved Cylinder, Modified and Full WinChoke® tubes included. A drilled and tapped receiver makes it easy to select a scope or red dot sight, or the easily removable metal Truglo® three dot sights. Full coverage Mossy Oak® New Break-Up™ camo, composite stock and forearm with magazine cap and stock sling studs come standard.

Looking for a single, versatile shotgun to perform on the range as great as it does in the field? Then look no further than the Model 1300 Sporting/Field. The Sporting/Field is loaded with features like a TRUGLO® TRU-BEAD™ front sight with mid bead for fast target acquisition and a great looking walnut stock and forearm with a satin finish and cut checkering. A Pachmayr® Decelerator® recoil pad tames recoil effectively. The 28-inch barrel features the WinChoke®

System and five choke tubes to accommodate any hunting or range situation.

The 1300 Sporting/Field Compact adds another level of versatility to the Winchester line of shotguns with a quality model that builds confidence on the range and in the field. The combination of a smaller stock, a rear-positioned forearm, special dimensions and naturally fast handling makes the Sporting/Field Compact the ideal gun for the smaller shooter. This Speed Pump™ comes complete with high-performance features like a Truglo® Tru-bead™ fiber optic front sight, five WinChoke® tubes and a Pachmayr® Decelerator® recoil pad to make shooting all day long a pleasurable experience. A 24-inch barrel allows for a fast swing with manageable weight. (Four extra fiber optics in different colors are included.)

When you hear the word "coastal," you think salt water and salt air. Not the best environment for a shotgun. That's why Winchester built the Model 1300 Coastal Marine just for saltwater environments. Designed specifically to meet the rigors of the harsh marine environment, it has an 18-inch nickel-plated,

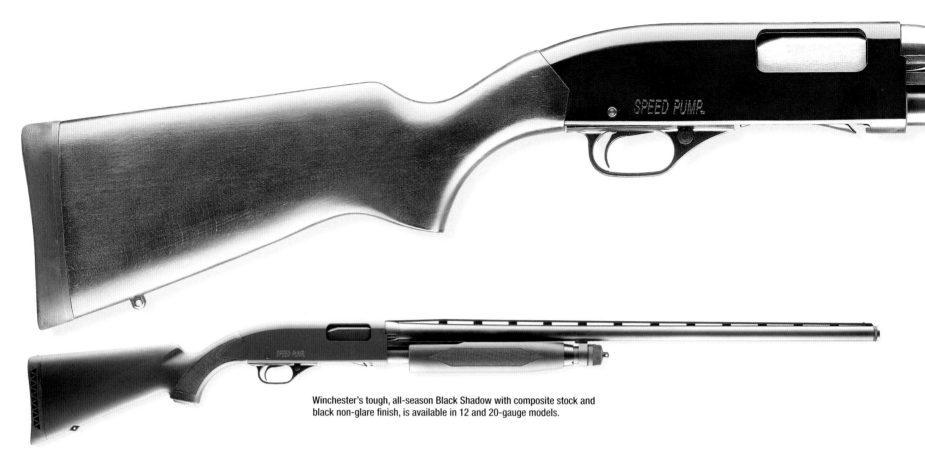

Winchester's tough, all-season Black Shadow with composite stock and black non-glare finish, is available in 12 and 20-gauge models.

stainless steel barrel, anodized aluminum alloy receiver and key parts plated for corrosion resistance. In 2004, Dura-Touch® was added to this rugged shotgun to improve grip in the harshest weather. Cylinder bore, eight-shot magazine capacity and sling swivel studs included. Removable front Truglo® fiber optic sight.

At the opposite end of the field, literally, is the elegant Model 1300 Walnut Field Gun. The original Winchester® Speed Pump™, the latest version looks better than ever with an elegant gloss-finished walnut stock and forearm with cut checkering. But don't let the handsome new look of the Walnut Field fool you, it's just as hardworking, versatile and dependable as the original. You can count on the 12 gauge Walnut Field to easily handle any hunt dependably — from duck to pheasant to clay birds — and because it's a Speed Pump, you can bet it will get the job done fast. The ventilated rib barrel utilizes the WinChoke® threaded choke system and is available in 26 and 28-inch lengths and a 3-inch

chamber.

Back in 1974 Winchester introduced a new, upgraded semi-auto, the Super X Model 1, offered in Standard, Skeet, Trap, and Custom Trap or Skeet models. The Super X Model 1, Trap, and Skeet versions were built through 1981, and Custom Trap or Skeet offered in limited quantities from 1987 through 1992. After the Super X Model 1 was discontinued Winchester came back with the Super X2 series in 1999. Today, this is the American standard in high-power semi-auto field guns.

Over the years the SX2 has become famous for its reliability, but its true advantage is its handling. Take the reliable, extremely fast Super X2™ 3-inch action, match it with a walnut stock and forearm and you have a classic-looking autoloader built to perform. The 3-inch Field model features a deeply blued receiver and anodized barrel. The back-bored barrel with ventilated rib is available in both 26 and 28-inch lengths and includes three Invector-Plus™ choke

The 8-shot Model 1300 Camp Defender features a short 22-inch barrel and adjustable open sights. The Camp Defender can accurately fire Foster slugs or sabots when equipped with the optional WinChoke rifled choke tube.

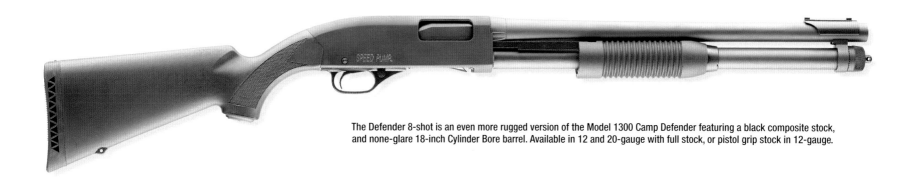

The Defender 8-shot is an even more rugged version of the Model 1300 Camp Defender featuring a black composite stock, and none-glare 18-inch Cylinder Bore barrel. Available in 12 and 20-gauge with full stock, or pistol grip stock in 12-gauge.

tubes that give you the patterns you need.

Whether for serious competition or simple enjoyment, the Super X2™ Sporting Clays is the right gun for one of the fastest-growing shooting sports in the world. Built around the reliable, lightning fast Super X2™ 3-inch action, this model features a specially designed, shim adjustable stock for a custom fit. The low luster finish of the receiver and Invector-Plus™ ventilated rib barrel reduce glare and complement the satin finish of the walnut stock and forearm. Two interchangeable gas pistons are provided to cover the extremes of factory ammunition loads. No longer do you need worry about light loads cycling. Five Invector-Plus™ choke tubes included.

If you love mixing it up in hot competition, then the SX2™ Practical MK II is your shotgun. This nimble handling Practical model is built around the Super X2 3-inch action for unequaled speed and reliability plus reduced recoil to put you back on target fast. Dura-Touch® Armor Coating improves the feel

and grip of the black composite stock and forearm. The easily removable LPA ghost-ring type rear sight mounts to a newly designed picatinny rail cantilever. TRUGLO® fiber optics are found in both the LPA rear and front sights. The MK II features a 22-inch barrel; 8-round extended magazine tube and the Standard Invector™ choke system for performance with slugs or shot.

Ready for USPSA Limited Division competition right from the box, the SX2 Practical MK I has the features and performance that will lower your times. The Super X2™ 3-inch action is proven fast — five shots in .51 of a second — while taming recoil to help get those shots on target. In addition, the MK I features a 22-inch barrel, 8-round extended magazine tube with titanium nitride treatment to eliminate wear, plus a black composite stock and forearm. Features the Standard Invector ™ choke system for accurate performance with rifled slugs when needed.

Sure, you can buy any shotgun for hunting, but the Greenhead is the shot-

249

The NWTF Short Turkey is the most specialized Winchester turkey gun built—ever. Fitted with a highly maneuverable 18-inch barrel with extra-long, extra-Full choke tube, the Model 1300 is finished in Mossy Oak New Break-Up camo and comes with adjustable TRUGLO® fiber optic sights. Every gun has a National Wild Turkey Federation medallion on the grip cap.

gun for mallards. Take the proven, reliable Super X2™ 3-¹/₂ inch action, add a 28-inch Invector-Plus™ ventilated rib barrel fitted with a white front bead and head to the wetlands. Add a composite stock and forearm treated with Dura-Touch® in the symbolic "Greenhead" finish and don't worry. With that list of features, you know this shotgun will take whatever you — or nature — can throw its way. Three choke tubes and sling swivel studs are included.

If heavy geese and other waterfowl are on the menu, the Super X2, 3-¹/₂ inch Camo Waterfowl is the shotgun you need. It is made specifically for waterfowl hunters and reliably shoots factory field loads from 2-³/₄ inch (1-¹/₈ oz.) to 3-¹/₂ inch magnums. This Mossy Oak® New Shadow Grass™ model features a composite stock and forearm with the grip enhancing Dura-Touch® Armor Coating finish. The barrel is back-bored, has an improved, more durable, ventilated rib configuration and features the Invector-Plus™ interchangeable choke system. Sling swivel studs included.

The Super X2™ 3-inch and 3-¹/₂ inch Magnum Composite models are the original workhorse semi-autos that started the SX2 revolution. Protected with a sleek, low luster black finish under a tough Dura-Touch® coating on the composite stock and forearm, the Super X2™ 3-¹/₂ inch Composite is built to perform in the worst conditions. The reliable Super X2 3-¹/₂ inch action is built to shoot factory field loads from light 2-³/₄ inch (1-¹/₈ oz.) to heavy 3-¹/₂ inch magnums, thanks to efficient gas operation. This model also has a back-bored, Invector-Plus™ ventilated rib barrel with a white bead front sight. Sling swivel studs are included.

The 3-inch Composite Super X2™ is a tough, reliable shotgun. The simple gas-operated action allows you to shoot the heaviest factory 3-inch magnums, light 2-³/₄ inch (1-oz.) field loads and everything in between. The gas opera-

NWTF Buck and Tom model comes with a 22-inch barrel with an extended rifled choke for deer and a Hi-Density WinChoke Extra-Full Turkey tube for those big toms.

tion reduces recoil and allows for unbelievably fast follow-up shots. Sling swivel studs are included.

If you're a die-hard turkey hunter, you'll appreciate helping to support the most regal of all birds. Endorsed by the National Wild Turkey Federation, the Super X2™, 3-$^1/_2$ inch NWTF Turkey features Mossy Oak® New Break-Up™ and Dura-Touch® on the composite stock and forearm. A 24-inch barrel with Extra-Full Extended Invector-Plus™ Turkey choke tube is standard. The reliable gas operation reduces recoil for fast, accurate follow-up shots. Shoots all factory field loads from 2-$^3/_4$ inches (1-$^1/_8$ oz.) to the heaviest 3-$^1/_2$ inch magnums. Durable, screw-on type three-dot TRUGLO® sights and sling swivel studs are standard. The receiver is drilled and tapped for a scope or red dot type sight. An attractive brass medallion on the pistol grip cap completes the package and a portion of all sales of this shotgun helps support the NWTF.

The most versatile, reliable autoloader ever, the SX2 Universal Hunter Turkey means greater confidence when hunting these hearty birds. A 26-inch barrel with Extra-Full Extended Invector-Plus™ Turkey choke tube, plus three field Invector-Plus tubes and easily removable TRUGLO® sights also make it ideal for upland game or waterfowl hunting, too. Extra fine features include Mossy Oak® New Break-Up™ camo with the protective Dura-Touch® Armor Coating. Sling swivel studs standard. The receiver is drilled and tapped for mounting a scope or red dot type sight.

The Super X2™ 3-$^1/_2$ inch Universal Hunter Field is versatile, fast, reliable... the one gun that can do it all. Clad in Mossy Oak® New Break-Up™ camo, it's built to hunt waterfowl, upland game and even shoot clay targets in the most severe conditions, thanks to the award-winning, gas-operated Super X2™ action. The composite stock and forearm are coated with Dura-Touch® for unequaled grip and feel. Fast swinging 26-inch barrel features the Invector-Plus™ choke tube system and three choke tubes are included. Sling swivel studs standard.

The best game-getting features you'll ever need in a deer slug gun are now found on the SX2 3-inch Cantilever Deer. The new Dura-Touch® coating on the composite, matte black stock and forearm gives you quicker, greater handling control than ever before, especially with its fast, 22-inch barrel. The unique cantilever design allows you to aim with the rear adjustable sight using the TRUGLO® fiber optic front sight. Or, fold down the rear sight and instantly sight down the lengthwise groove in the cantilever for quick, close action. And, of course, you can easily fasten a red dot or conventional scope to the picatinny rail on the cantilever.

The Super X2™ Signature Red Sporting is designed specifically for the serious sporting clays contender. The foundation is its fast and reliable action, giving sure confidence that helps you concentrate on the targets during competitive shooting. Dura-Touch® Armor Coating improves your grip, meaning a more controlled, fluid swing. If the gun feels better, you'll shoot better. Dura-Touch

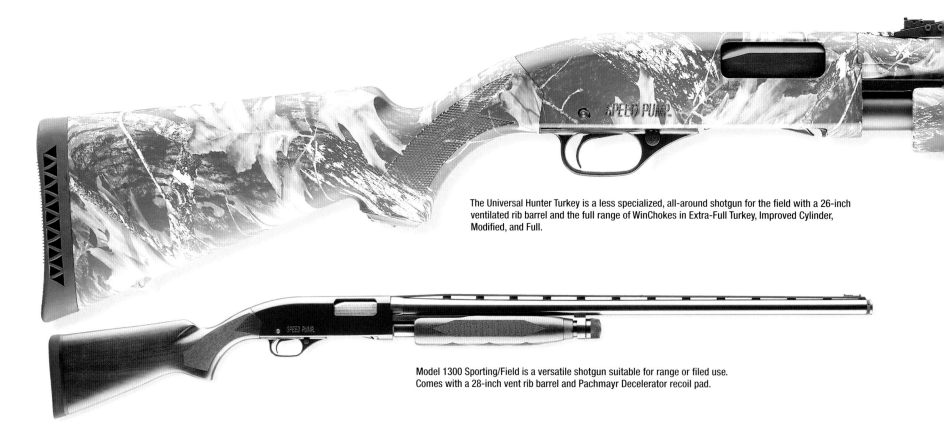

The Universal Hunter Turkey is a less specialized, all-around shotgun for the field with a 26-inch ventilated rib barrel and the full range of WinChokes in Extra-Full Turkey, Improved Cylinder, Modified, and Full.

Model 1300 Sporting/Field is a versatile shotgun suitable for range or filed use. Comes with a 28-inch vent rib barrel and Pachmayr Decelerator recoil pad.

also protects the red finish that's all Winchester®. The specially designed hardwood stock is shim adjustable for a custom fit. Five Invector-Plus™ choke tubes are included, plus two gas pistons to cover the extremes of sporting ammunition loads. Select a 30 or new 28-inch barrel.

In 2005 Winchester introduced two new Super X2 shotguns, the Light Field and the Sporting Clays Signature II. The new Light Field model is a gas operated semi-auto chambered in 3-inch magnum with a lightweight rib configuration, and an alloy receiver and magazine. The Sporting Clays Signature II features a red-anodized receiver with black metallic fleck paint on the stock.

Winchester's Select Series superposed models continue the fine tradition established more than 40 years ago with the Model 101. The Select Series are improved shotguns whose performance is only matched by their impressive appearance. There are six models, each with distinctive features.

The new Select™ Energy Sporting is easily the most innovative, most exciting Winchester® target gun in a long time. Here is a new shotgun (introduced in

2004) that instills confidence because of extraordinary balance and fit. Ported barrels with vented side ribs offer less recoil, more control, quick handling and fast swinging. The butt stock provides instant and definite rib/sight alignment. You'll appreciate the looks and feel of the distinctive oval checkering on the walnut stock and forearm. It carries the most popular choke system ever, the Invector-Plus™. A TRUGLO® TRU-BEAD™ competition front sight and a mid bead pick-up clays instantly. Each model has a comfortable, slight right-hand palm swell. Select 28, 30 or 32-inch barrels.

Claiming all of the top features you need for shooting excellence, the Select™ Energy Sporting with adjustable comb is ready to be tailored for your personal fit. If you need your sporting gun to fit perfectly, then this is the model from the Energy series you need. The comb area can be raised and moved left or right for cast on/off. Using a small wrench, it takes only seconds to customize the comb. The Select Energy Sporting has all of the features found in the new Energy series, including 2-3/4 inch chambers and Invector-Plus™ choke tubes for opti-

The Sporting/Field Compact offers the same confidence for range or field use in a smaller model with 24-inch vent rib barrel and short forearm.

mum shotshell performance, new oval checkering, lighter barrel profile, adjustable trigger for length of pull, and your choice of 28 to 32-inch barrel lengths.

Shooting trap is contagious. Even if you score high, the challenge always welcomes you again to the range. And now, a new high performance trap gun is in order. The Select™ Energy Trap features ported barrels that tame second shot recoil and vented side ribs to improve balance and make it easier and quicker to swing. A TRUGLO® TRU-BEAD™ front sight pairs with the mid bead in acquiring clays immediately, and the Monte Carlo stock comes to your shoulder effortlessly, aligning your eye along the wide, runway rib. The slight, right-handed comfortable palm swell will clinch the deal. The Select™ Energy Trap features the Invector-Plus™ choke system and back-bored 30 or 32-inch barrels.

Serious trap shooters are fussy. If a gun accessory or feature will help boost their score, they're on to it. The new Select™ Energy Trap Select™ with adjustable comb totally fills the bill. Along with the new, wide runway rib, mid bead sight and TRUGLO® TRU-BEAD™ interchangeable fiber optic front sight, the comb is adjustable to whatever position you need. You can raise the comb and move it for cast on/off in seconds. All Select Energy models are ported, have vented side ribs, adjustable trigger shoes and a slight right-handed palm swell. Trap models are available with 30 or 32-inch barrels.

The new Extreme Elegance (introduced in 2004) is a fine shotgun, stunning in both quality and appearance. Full coverage engraving of wild bird scenes and fleur-de-lis patterns, lightly inked, show the true elegance of this shotgun and give credence to its name. Low profile receiver and lightweight barrel contours put you on target quickly. Plus, the unique oval checkering pattern enhances grip and adds a distinct appearance you'll appreciate for years to come. Strong, crisp ejectors elevate unfired shells and eject fired shells with purpose. The dual, tapered locking lugs, aided by a third, fixed lug mean strength on the inside and unbridled confidence on the outside. Choose 26 or 28-inch barrels. Every Select™ Elegance Shotgun comes with a durable hard case imprinted with the Winchester® horse and rider.

The Select™ Traditional Elegance features a fully engraved receiver and trigger guard with game birds adorning the sides and bottom. Each line is lightly inked, enhancing the scene and fleur-de-lis borders. Opening the receiver reveals positive ejectors and strong locking, dual tapered lugs with a third lug that guards against stress from recoil. Checkering is in traditional styling. A high performance recoil pad is fitted. You'll immediately notice the Traditional Elegance comes quickly to the shoulder, pointing naturally due to the conveniently low receiver profile and barrel contour. Here is an over and under gun that you'll be proud to own and anxious to shoot, season after season. Either 26 or 28-inch barrels available. Every Select™ Elegance Shotgun comes with a durable hard case imprinted with the Winchester® horse and rider.

Perhaps you have always wanted an over and under shotgun. After all, the superposed barrels create an image of a romantic gun, an expensive gun. Fortunately, with the Select™ Field, you can have all the romance and keep much of your hard-earned cash. The Field is built with the same internal integrity as all the Select series. It features an engraved receiver and dramatic new oval style checkering. The low profile barrels fit precisely and solidly with the receiver. Ejectors are sure and crisp, extracting and ejecting shells with authority. The Invector-Plus™ choke system keeps any shot pattern you need right in your pocket. With the Select Field, romance is very much alive, and has never been so affordable. The Select Field comes with either 26 or 28-inch barrels.

The story of The Shotguns of New Haven began with the British double guns imported in 1879, and has continued, uninterrupted for over 125 years. Today, fine, high-quality Winchester shotguns are still manufactured in New Haven, Connecticut, just as they have been since 1887. And while the names have changed, and partnerships have come and gone, when all is said and done, Winchester is still the most famous name in rifles and shotguns the world has ever known.

Durability has long been a Winchester hallmark, but the Model 1300 Costal Marine raises the bar with an 18-inch nickel-plated stainless steel barrel and anodized aluminum alloy receiver. Designed for marine use this is the most rugged shotgun Winchester has ever built. Also available with a pistol grip.

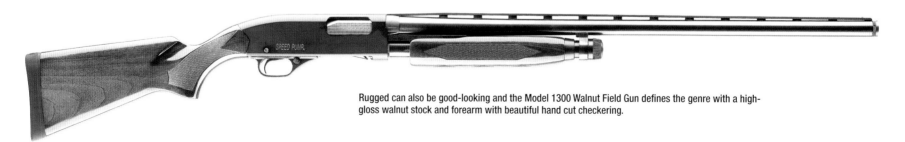

Rugged can also be good-looking and the Model 1300 Walnut Field Gun defines the genre with a high-gloss walnut stock and forearm with beautiful hand cut checkering.

Winchester's got your goose with the Super X2 series semi-automatics featuring 3-$\frac{1}{2}$ inch chambers.

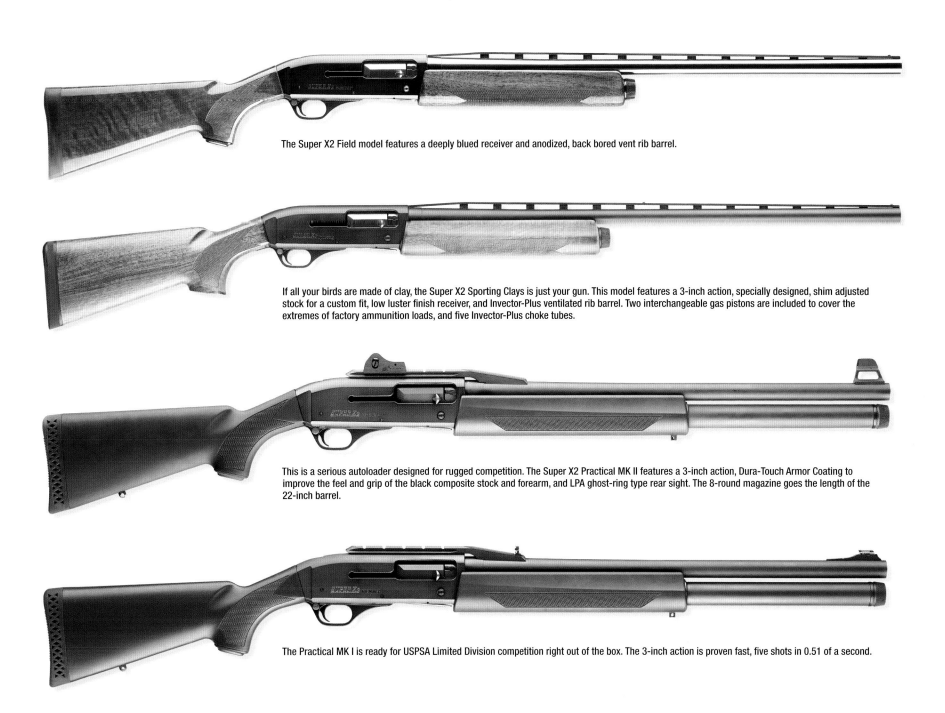

The Super X2 Field model features a deeply blued receiver and anodized, back bored vent rib barrel.

If all your birds are made of clay, the Super X2 Sporting Clays is just your gun. This model features a 3-inch action, specially designed, shim adjusted stock for a custom fit, low luster finish receiver, and Invector-Plus ventilated rib barrel. Two interchangeable gas pistons are included to cover the extremes of factory ammunition loads, and five Invector-Plus choke tubes.

This is a serious autoloader designed for rugged competition. The Super X2 Practical MK II features a 3-inch action, Dura-Touch Armor Coating to improve the feel and grip of the black composite stock and forearm, and LPA ghost-ring type rear sight. The 8-round magazine goes the length of the 22-inch barrel.

The Practical MK I is ready for USPSA Limited Division competition right out of the box. The 3-inch action is proven fast, five shots in 0.51 of a second.

257

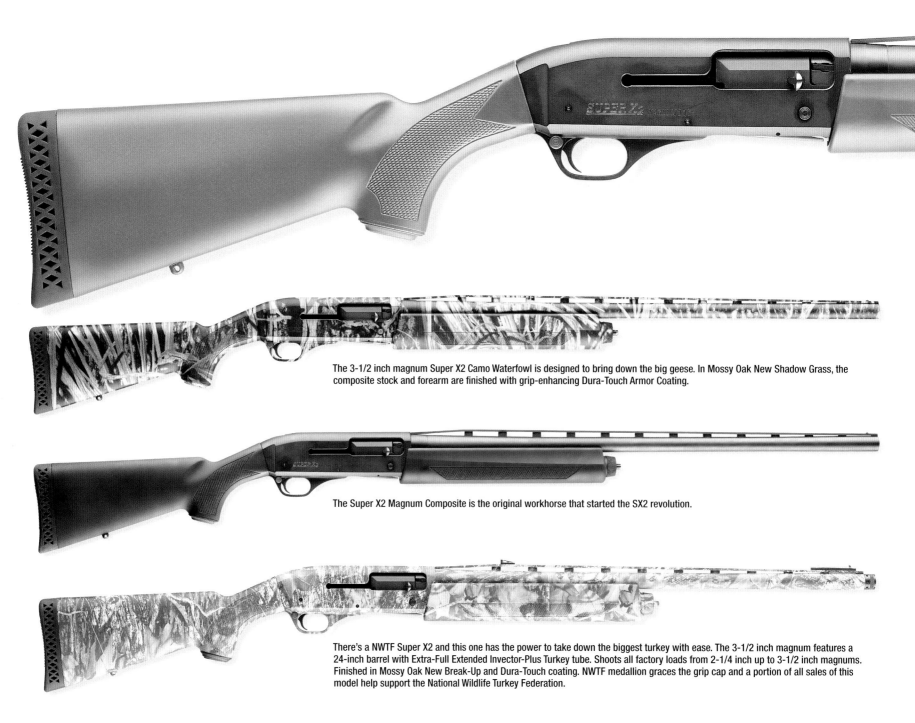

The 3-1/2 inch magnum Super X2 Camo Waterfowl is designed to bring down the big geese. In Mossy Oak New Shadow Grass, the composite stock and forearm are finished with grip-enhancing Dura-Touch Armor Coating.

The Super X2 Magnum Composite is the original workhorse that started the SX2 revolution.

There's a NWTF Super X2 and this one has the power to take down the biggest turkey with ease. The 3-1/2 inch magnum features a 24-inch barrel with Extra-Full Extended Invector-Plus Turkey tube. Shoots all factory loads from 2-1/4 inch up to 3-1/2 inch magnums. Finished in Mossy Oak New Break-Up and Dura-Touch coating. NWTF medallion graces the grip cap and a portion of all sales of this model help support the National Wildlife Turkey Federation.

258

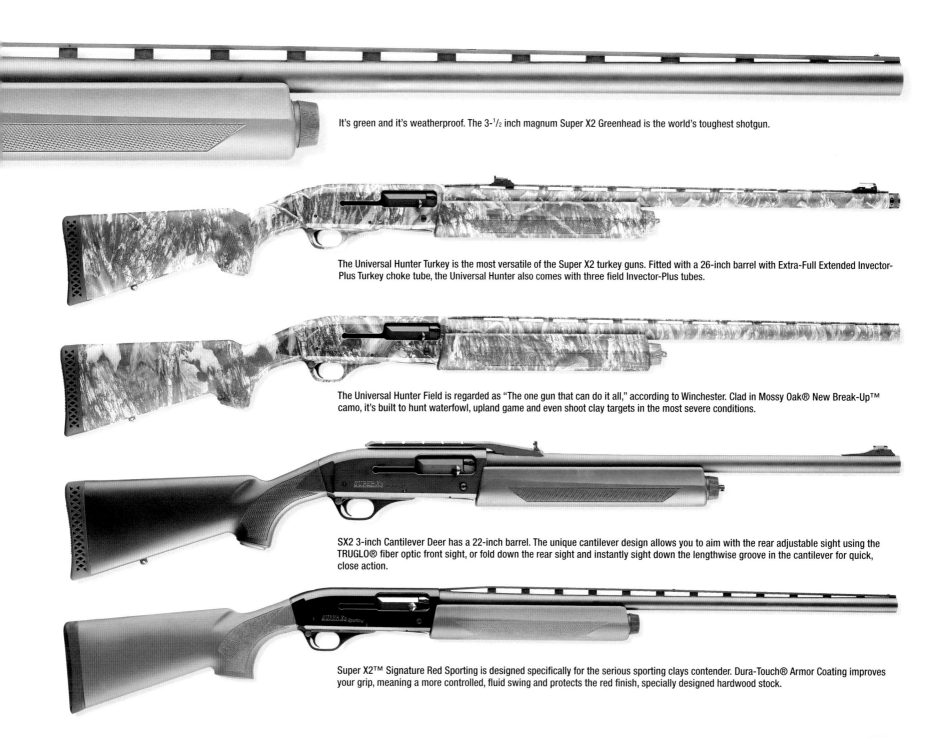

It's green and it's weatherproof. The 3-$\frac{1}{2}$ inch magnum Super X2 Greenhead is the world's toughest shotgun.

The Universal Hunter Turkey is the most versatile of the Super X2 turkey guns. Fitted with a 26-inch barrel with Extra-Full Extended Invector-Plus Turkey choke tube, the Universal Hunter also comes with three field Invector-Plus tubes.

The Universal Hunter Field is regarded as "The one gun that can do it all," according to Winchester. Clad in Mossy Oak® New Break-Up™ camo, it's built to hunt waterfowl, upland game and even shoot clay targets in the most severe conditions.

SX2 3-inch Cantilever Deer has a 22-inch barrel. The unique cantilever design allows you to aim with the rear adjustable sight using the TRUGLO® fiber optic front sight, or fold down the rear sight and instantly sight down the lengthwise groove in the cantilever for quick, close action.

Super X2™ Signature Red Sporting is designed specifically for the serious sporting clays contender. Dura-Touch® Armor Coating improves your grip, meaning a more controlled, fluid swing and protects the red finish, specially designed hardwood stock.

259

In the field or shooting clays, the new Traditional Elegance superposed built for Winchester by F.N. is one of the most beautiful shotguns in Winchester history. Checkering is in traditional style and the fully engraved receiver is lightly inked to enhance the game scenes and scrollwork. This handsome new model was introduced in 2004.

Open and out. The Select
Elegance and Select Energy series
superposed shotguns are ready for
reload in an instant.

Select Energy Sporting models
come in two versions, one with an
adjustable comb.

261

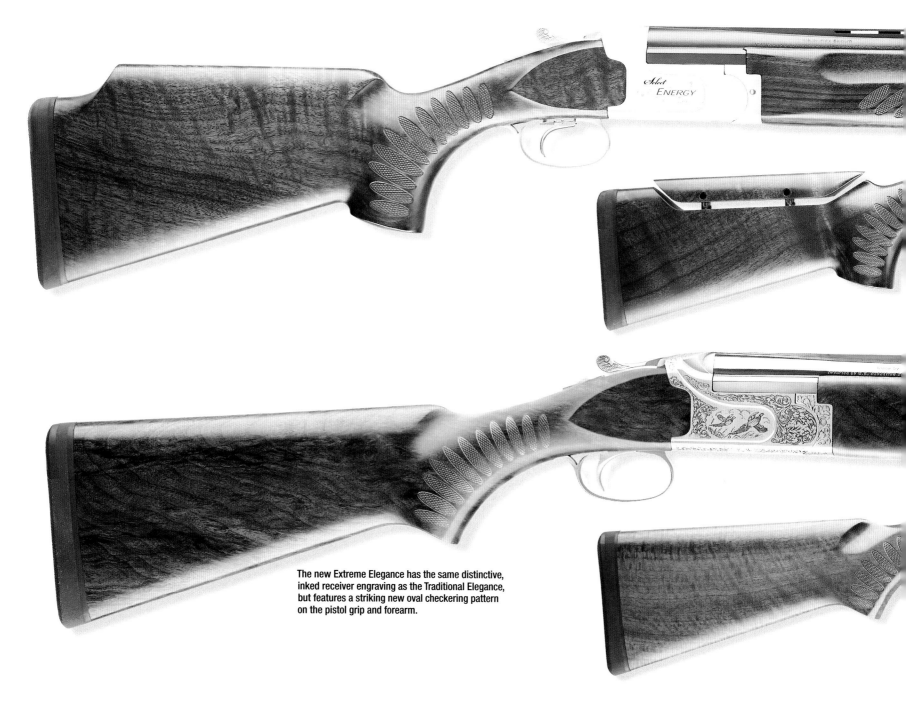

The new Extreme Elegance has the same distinctive, inked receiver engraving as the Traditional Elegance, but features a striking new oval checkering pattern on the pistol grip and forearm.

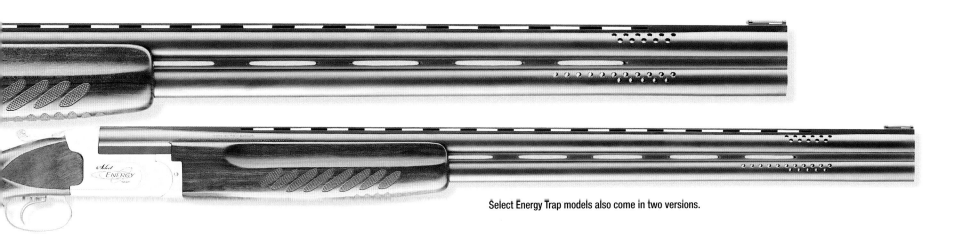

Select Energy Trap models also come in two versions.

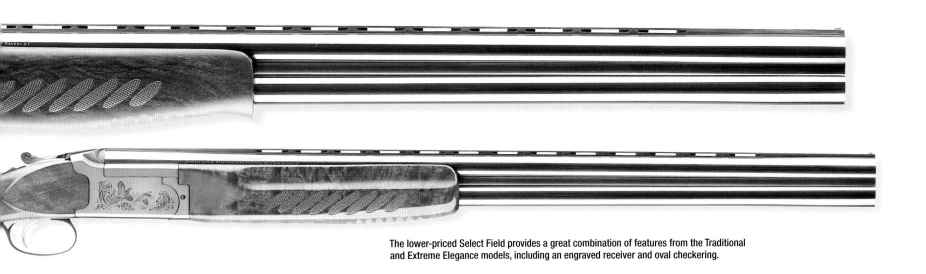

The lower-priced Select Field provides a great combination of features from the Traditional and Extreme Elegance models, including an engraved receiver and oval checkering.

Chapter Twelve
Winchester Art
Advertising and Sales Brochures

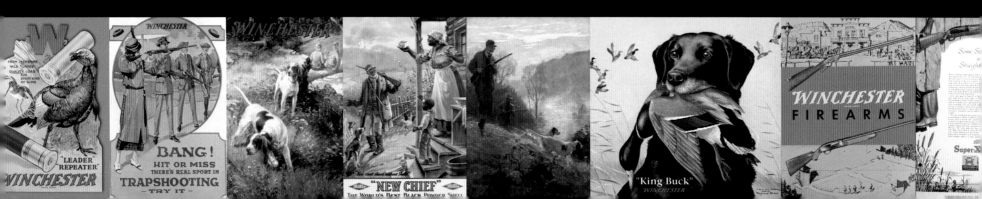

Winchester collectors have more than rifles and shotguns to turn their heads these days. With nearly a century and half of history behind it, the New Haven arms maker has been responsible for some of the finest and most desirable firearms art in the world, without always having to show their product in the illustration. Some have been whimsical, others, such as those depicting the rite of passage between father and son, moving and inspirational, particularly when viewed with today's "politically correct" attitudes towards firearms, while many, most actually, have been simply beautiful scenes that could grace the walls of any room in your home, a hunting lodge, a restaurant, or business. In the end, art is what we make it, and for almost 150 years, Winchester had contributed a body of work that is almost without equal.

Working with collectors and the fantastic Winchester art collection archived by Scott Scheffer and Winfield Galleries, LLC, in St. Louis, Missouri, we have assembled a collection of the most significant Winchester calendar art, sales literature, and advertising for shotguns and shotgun shells. We hope this will be an entertaining, and memorable chapter.

—Dennis Adler

Calendar Art

One of the most famous and desirable prints is from 1913, the calendar which served to debut the all-new Model 1912 Winchester shotgun. The illustration was painted by Robert B. Robinson (1886-1952). (Courtesy of Winfield Galleries LLC.)

WINCHESTER

Repeating Arms Co., New Haven, Conn., U.S.A., Makers of

Winchester followed the 1913 calendar with another shotgun scene, this one depicting upland game hunting. (Courtesy of Winfield Galleries LLC.)

The next shotgun scene appeared in 1918, and this is one of the earliest to depict a father and son hunting. Painted by George Brehm (1878-1966), Winchester believed the image "makes a strong appeal both for father and son." (Courtesy of Winfield Galleries LLC.)

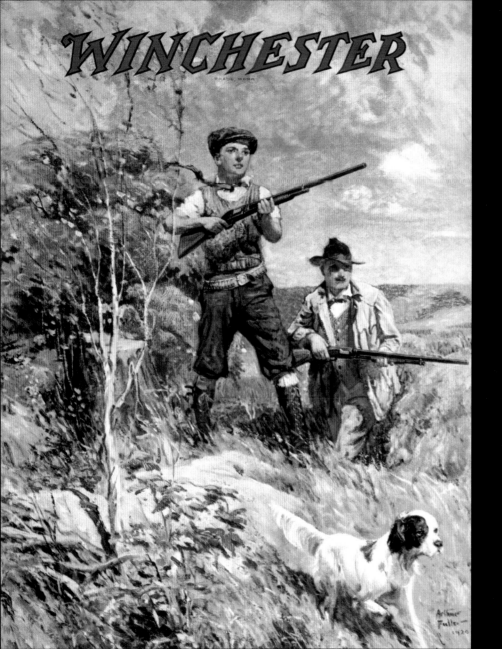

In 1921 Winchester released the second shotgun calendar with a father and son theme. In the interim, there had been a rifle calendar also with a father and son hunting theme. This upland hunting scene was painted by Arthur Fuller (1889-1966) who was best known for his illustrations in *Field & Stream*. (Courtesy of Winfield Galleries LLC.)

The next shotgun calendar was in 1924 depicting a duck hunter crouching in a blind, and did not appear again until this calendar in 1929 painted by Lynn Bogue Hunt, a popular Winchester illustrator. (Courtesy of Winfield Galleries LLC.)

Winchester Poster

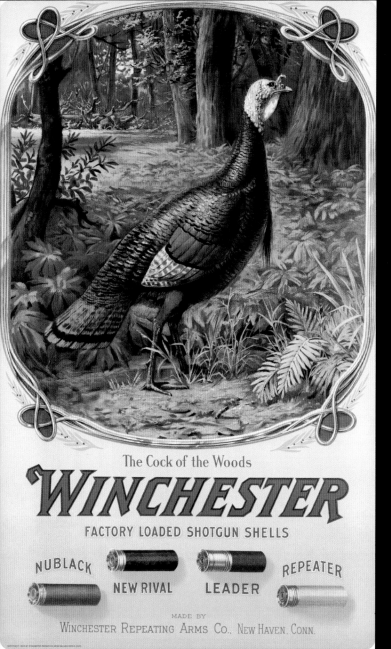

"The Cock of the Woods" poster promoting Winchester shotgun shells dates back to 1905. The artist is unknown. (Courtesy of Winfield Galleries LLC.)

WINCHESTER

A Setter and Pointer were used to promote Winchester 20 Gauge Shotguns in this c.1907-1908 poster. The artist is unknown. (Courtesy of Winfield Galleries LLC.)

This attractive poster was among the most elegant to portray female hunters. It was done in two versions, the one shown titled "Woman in Yellow Hunting Coat" and a second version with the coat and hat rim done in red. The original version was done in 1919 and the red in 1920. The Setter got darker the second time around too. (Courtesy of Winfield Galleries LLC.)

WINCHESTER
20 GAUGE SHOTGUNS
Hammerless, Light and Strong

One of the many cardboard signs supplied to gun stores in the tops of Winchester shotgun shell cases. The signs were intended to be used as window or counter displays. This rare example, of a quail talking flight, was used as a wall or winder hanger. (Courtesy Winfield Galleries LLC.)

WINCHESTER
REPEATING SHOTGUNS

Endorsed by the U.S. Ordnance Board
as being
SAFE, SURE, STRONG and SIMPLE

This dramatic illustration was done in two versions for a Winchester shotguns and shot shells ad. This is the original art without the text as painted by N.C. Wyeth in 1910. In both of the published versions with text, the image was darkened to intensify the look of an early dawn hunt. (Courtesy of Winfield Galleries LLC.)

This is another example that appeared in a variety of tonal ranges beginning in 1912. Some copies used in ads had a warm yellowish tone overall, others had a greenish tint, and still other examples had a cooler tone, such as this copy. Titled "Cartridges, Guns and Green Door" the artist was Alexander Pope (1849-1924). (Courtesy of Winfield Galleries LLC.)

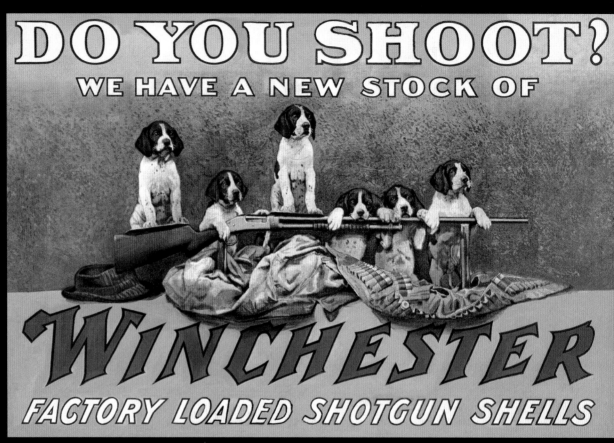

From 1906 "The Hunter's Choice" was an illustration often used for case inserts and cardboard hanging signs in gun shops. "A Drummer" is another illustration from c.1906 used for sales displays. "Do You Shoot" was also from around 1906 and is the only one of the three to feature a Winchester shotgun, a Model 97. The signs were usually shipped to dealers in the top of a case of 12 gauge shells. (Courtesy of Winfield Galleries LLC.)

"Jacksnipe to Wild Turkey" was a die-cut counter sign for
Winchester shot shells c.1926. The scene was painted by Lynn
Bogue Hunt. (Courtesy of Winfield Galleries LLC.)

Counter sign from the 1920s. Winchester frequently featured female shooters, though more often with rifles than shotguns. (Courtesy of Winfield Galleries LLC.)

"On the Scent" was a Winchester shotgun promotional poster. Artist and circa unknown but the style is from the early 1900s. (Courtesy of Winfield Galleries LLC.)

Promoting Western's "New Chief" black powder
shot shells; this ad appears to be from the late
1890s. The artist was A. Russell. (Courtesy of
Winfield Galleries LLC.)

This print used in Winchester promotions was titled
"Upland Morning". The artist is unknown, however, the
style is reminiscent of works by Arthur Fuller and N.C.
Wyeth. (Courtesy of Winfield Galleries LLC.)

Facing page: "King Buck" is one of the most famous
Winchester symbols, and has appeared on everything from
posters to Winchester glassware. He was featured on the
1959-60 Federal Duck Stamp artwork. The painting was by
Maynard Reese, c.1959. (Courtesy of Winfield Galleries LLC.)

"King Buck"

WINCHESTER.

Federal Duck Stamp
1959-60
Maynard Reece

281

A rare, leather bound, 1916 Winchester sales catalog. The book measures 5-3/4 x 9 inches.

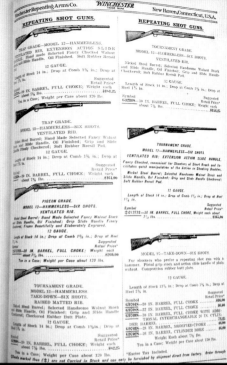

The 1923 *Winchester Product Catalog* listed everything from guns and ammunition to roller skates. Winchester's post World War I products included just about anything the company could put their name on! The section from 1923 shotguns has some rather amazing prices, when viewed from the 21st century!

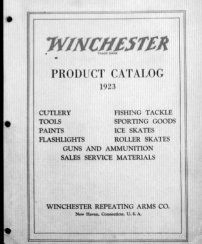

WINCHESTER MODEL 21 -- Standard Grade -- Double trigger -- 12, 16 and 20 gauges

With selective ejection	$69.50
Without selective ejection	59.50

WINCHESTER MODEL 21 -- Standard Grade -- Single trigger -- 12, 16 and 20 gauges

With selective ejection	$79.50
Without selective ejection	69.50

WINCHESTER MODEL 21 -- Trap grade -- 12, 16 and 20 gauges

Double trigger with selective ejection	$99.50
Double trigger without selective ejection	89.50
Single trigger with selective ejection	109.50
Single trigger without selective ejection	99.50

WINCHESTER MODEL 21 -- Tournament grade -- 12, 16 and 20 gauges

Double trigger with selective ejection	$79.50
Double trigger without selective ejection	69.50
Single trigger with selective ejection	89.50
Single trigger without selective ejection	79.50

WINCHESTER MODEL 21 -- With Ventilated Rib

FURNISHED IN EITHER TOURNAMENT OR TRAP GRADE

12 gauge, 32 inch barrels only

Gun as illustrated shows beavertail fore-end, furnished in place of standard fore-end at extra charge.

	Ventilated Rib Standard Fore-end Tournament	Trap	Ventilated Rib Beavertail Fore-end Tournament	Trap
Double trigger, selective ejection	$104.50	$124.50	$122.00	$149.50
Double trigger, non-selective	94.50	114.50	112.00	139.50
Single trigger, selective ejection	114.50	134.50	132.00	159.50
Single trigger, non-selective	104.50	124.50	122.00	149.50

Prices subject to change without notice.

Note--Beavertail fore-end can be fitted to any Model 21 Shotgun if desired at extra charge.

WINCHESTER

"The Greatest of Them All" was the title of this small 15-page brochure from 1932. Measuring only 4 x 9-1/8 inches, it had a double centerfold depicting Winchester's great Model 21 shotguns. The rest of the brochure explained the design and operation of the Model 21. (Thomas E. Henshaw collection)

The "2000-PROOF" WINCHESTER

TRADE MARK

MODEL 21 DOUBLE SHOTGUN

—To Give You the
World's Best Double Barrel Gun

IN building your Model 21 Shotgun, Winchester gives you the benefit of advantages possessed by no other manufacturer of double guns in the world. For almost seventy years Winchester has constantly held world renown for progressive leadership in making guns and ammunition. Producing the first successful repeating rifle, Winchester likewise built the first successful repeating shotgun. No single firearms manufacturer has produced nearly so many successful improvements—or built nearly so many high-grade repeating rifles and repeating shotguns.

Among the earliest manufacturers to adopt modern American standardized precision methods of machine production, Winchester has been similarly foremost in developing their use. It is also Winchester that has led the world for years in searching out and using better firearms steels.

With a world-famous plant covering eighty-one acres—nine city blocks—with superior laboratory and mechanical equipment, and as always a superior-trained and most progressive organization of highly skilled gun and ammunition manufacturing experts, much could be done . . . . Read what has been done—and what to give you the World's Best Double Barrel Shotgun.

Winchester Repeating Arms Company, New Haven, Conn., U. S. A.

WINCHESTER MODEL 21
DOUBLE BARREL SHOTGUN
IN ANY GRADE

1 Is precision built, like your watch or your automobile—*NOT* a product of "cut-and-try" fitting.

2 Has its barrels mechanically interlocked—*NOT* brazed together.

3 Has no extension rib—this gun does *NOT* need it.

Illustration shows a typical Custom Built Winchester Model 21

THE FIRST THREE THINGS TO KNOW ABOUT
THE WINCHESTER MODEL 21 SHOTGUN

WHEN Winchester decided to build a double barrel gun for the host of shooters who prefer this style, Winchester Repeating Shotguns had been world famous for superiority for three decades . . . . as had Winchester Rifles for more than twice as long. The familiar standard style of hammerless double barrel shotgun was as firmly fixed in popular favor as the closed sedan is among automobile styles. Likewise, gauges, barrel lengths, chokes, boring, stock design and dimensions all were established within a clearly defined range of popular demand . . . . What was the new Winchester Double Barrel to be like?

Winchester knew, from its many years of manufacturing World Standard Guns and Ammunition, that the Winchester precision system in gun building—*the modern system*, the same in principle as that used in the large-scale making of modern watches to motor cars. In gun building, it is vitally important to superiority in shooting.

Yet a quite different principle was needed in building double barrel shotguns.

Winchester was well aware that this common method in building double guns had two basic faults, long retained as seemingly "necessary evils". They were, first, the practice of brazing the barrels together; and, second, the use of an extension rib in keeping the gun shut. A third and equally great shortcoming was that these first two faults compelled sticking to the primitive "cut-and-try" methods of the village blacksmith in much of the most important work.

Starting at the bottom, Winchester rooted out the brazing, the extension rib, and "cut-and-try" construction as time-worn.

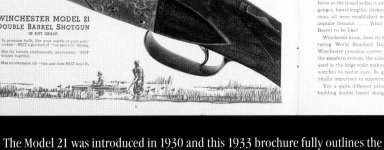

FOUR MODEL 21 SPECIAL FEATURES
AVAILABLE FOR YOUR SELECTION

1 — Ventilated Rib

2 — Single Trigger

3 — Selective Ejection

4 — Beavertail Fore-End

1 — Ventilated Rib

A scientifically designed sighting rib and companion barrel rib, with sliding connections. Permits both ribs to expand or contract independently. Neither can warp the other by heat expansion. The narrow sighting plane, raised above the barrels, assures relief from heat waves in sighting, and a clear, narrow path of vision to the target. The level concave rib, with glareproof matted surface, prevents glare under the hardest sighting conditions. Being raised, it effectively excludes bother from barrel glare.

2 — Single Trigger

The Winchester Single Trigger is made on a new and much improved principle. It will neither balk nor "double". Fully releasing the trigger and again pulling it fires the second barrel. The high lock speed of the Winchester Model 21 is maintained. The selective gold button in the trigger shank tells at a glance, or the slightest touch, which barrel fires first. Can be shifted to either position instantly. For right barrel first, set button to project at right side of trigger. To reverse firing order, push button to left.

3 — Selective Ejection

With Non-selective Ejection, both shells, whether fired or unfired, are pushed part way out of the barrels. The absence of extension rib adds to convenience in removing shells. With Selective Ejection the fired shell is automatically thrown clear when gun is opened, while the unfired shell is pushed well out for easy removal if desired. If both shells are fired, both are automatically ejected. If neither is fired, both are pushed part way out. Both types of ejection are simple, sturdy, dependable for long service.

4 — Beavertail Fore-End

Designed especially for the Winchester Model 21. Has both attractive appearance and high practical value. Gives full protection from barrel heat, greater security and comfort in holding. Increases confidence and precision in handling the gun. Very symmetrical in outline, of moderate width and depth, with high, graceful roll around barrels, flowing into the frame lines in the rear. Hand worked and finished from carefully seasoned best selected walnut. Extensively hand checkered, for any reach.

11

The Model 21 was introduced in 1930 and this 1933 brochure fully outlines the new models and all features of the custom built Winchester double guns. A very handsome opening spread tells potential buyers that "To Give You the World's Best Double Barrel Shotgun..." and then proceeds to explain how the Model 21 is built. On pages 2 and 3 the introduction tells "The first three things to know about the Winchester Model 21 Shotgun" and page 11 of the brochure depicts four special features of the Model 21. (Thomas E. Henshaw collection)

SYMBOL
OF SHOOTING
SUPREMACY

The **WINCHESTER**
TRADE-MARK

MODEL 21 DOUBLE

World's Finest Shotgun

Truly Fine GUNS...

are bought not alone because of need or respect — cost — but chiefly because of desire to own the best.

When you specify an unequalled individual Model 21, YOU and YOUR WINCHESTER Gun will stand out in any gathering of sportsmen and gun connoisseurs. You will have the World's Finest Shotgun. The honest envy of your friends always will attest to this heart-warming fact that you own the best.

Your pipe may become bitter and your bird dog may go lame — but your WINCHESTER Model 21 will continue to give you the best in top performance through the years . . . . a truly fine gun for a discriminating sportsman.

This booklet takes you on a personal tour of inspection in order that you may understand fully the painstaking care with which your WINCHESTER Model 21 is built. A study of the specification pages also will assist you in selecting the style you desire in your Model 21.

World's Finest Shotgun...

THE WINCHESTER MODEL 21 DOUBLE GUN

A Custom Built, DeLuxe Model 21, stocked and ornamented to the purchaser's own needs and wishes—12 gauge.

BRIEFLY SUMMARIZED

Your Model 21 has these features, many of which are exclusive WINCHESTER developments.

1. Exclusive WINCHESTER Proof-Steel barrels capable of withstanding the firing of proof loads which are 50 per cent more powerful than any standard shells you can buy.
2. Exclusive, mechanically interlocked barrels instead of brazed barrels. No distortion or weakening of temper and barrel strength.
3. Exclusive, dovetailed barrels which insure correct alignment.
4. Half lugs which are forged as integral parts of the barrel from the same billet of steel. An exclusive WINCHESTER feature.
5. Exclusive floating barrel stop which protects hinge from damage.
6. Long, deep lug fitting closely in lug slot which prevents lateral shifting of barrels.
7. Broad, deep bolting cut, on correct incline, which insures firm, tight holding throughout long firing of heaviest loads.
8. Set-screw bolt stop which retards bolt and provides adjustment to permit bolt to lock gun firmly shut without sticking.
9. Barrels have walls of supreme uniformity in thickness. No thin spots, AN OUTSTANDING WINCHESTER FEATURE.
10. Frame ("A" in cut at right) is forged from exclusive WINCHESTER Proof-Steel which is capable of withstanding a tremendous force.
11. Exclusive, rugged locking bolt which is held firmly on barrel lug by a sturdy coil spring.
12. Beautiful stock which will fit into frame firmly with long, thick tenons of walnut wedged inside the steel.
13. Long, strong tenon in fore-end which will prevent wood from creeping on stock parts when gun is opened.
14. High-speed locks with short hammer throw. Each hammer ("C" in cut at right) and firing pin is of one piece of exclusive WINCHESTER Proof-Steel.
15. Long sear leverage.
16. Sturdy coiled hammer springs ("D" in cut at right) on long, strong cocking rods.
17. Cocking levers ("B" in cut at right) which act directly on cocking rods, giving especially smooth, easy opening action.
18. Specially long extractor movement and absence of extension rib gives you easier removal of non-ejected shells.
19. Simple, positive-action, powerful ejector. Ejection sear ("E" in cut at right) has dependable motion both ways. Ejection hammers ("F") which work on a roll, have reduced friction and increased ejector power.

Cut-open Standard Grade Model 21, showing left side lock and ejector construction.

20. Absence of extension rib aids quick loading and unloading. An exclusive WINCHESTER feature.
21. Strong, dependable safety—automatic or non-automatic.
22. Positive single trigger that will not "double" or "balk". Another exclusive WINCHESTER design.
23. Gold-plated selector button tells by sight or touch which barrel is set to fire. Can be shifted instantly to either barrel.

12

13

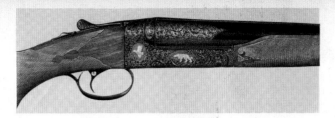

Artistic Ornamentation of . . .
WINCHESTER MODEL 21 SHOTGUN

At the end of your personal tour of inspection, you will find master custom carvers and engravers waiting to put the finishing touches to your Model 21. Controlled only by your tastes and desires in artistic ornamentation, these WINCHESTER master craftsmen will make your Model 21 stand out in any gathering of sportsmen and gun connoisseurs. The finest, most beautiful and elaborate ornamentation can be yours, if you so specify.

Concerning the actual design, WINCHESTER is prepared at all times to furnish appropriate game scenes, monograms or lettering. These designs may be *engraved* or *inlaid* with gold, silver or platinum. Various styles ranging from very fine flat design to very heavy relief can be produced. Game animals, birds, hunting dogs, beautiful floral designs, artistic pattern or scroll work . . . all are done with the highest degree of fidelity and artistic composition.

The frame of your WINCHESTER Model 21 has especially attractive lines which are well-suited to ornamentation. Other parts well adapted to engraving are the trigger guard, barrels at the breech, sighting rib, top lever, tang or strap, and safety slide. Trigger may be checked and either partly or completely gold plated. The Beavertail forearm also lends itself well to inlay work.

The accompanying photographs show two of the standard WINCHESTER designs which are readily available. We will gladly suggest special designs or execute ornamentation in accordance with your own design and specification. There is no limit to our willingness or ability to make your WINCHESTER Model 21 the Finest Double Gun in the World. Our master craftsmen are at your complete service.

Checkered wood butt, standard on all skeet guns.

STANDARD SKETCH NO. 21-1

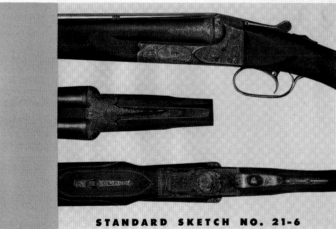

STANDARD SKETCH NO. 21-6

Two examples of the various standard styles of ornamentation available on Winchester Model 21 shotguns. Above, No. 21-1 the simplest style of engraving. Below, No. 21-6, popular elaborate style, combining artistic scroll work and game scenes.

14

15

HOW TO SECURE YOUR WINCHESTER MODEL 21 SHOTGUN

Fill in specifications of the gun you want on this blank. Keep a copy of it. Turn blank over to your dealer, to ascertain price of the gun as you want it. On your approval, he will place your order for your Model 21 in accordance with your exact specifications.

NOTE: No order will exist until you give your dealer definite instructions to order gun for you.

GAUGE.................... BARREL LENGTH...............

BORE—RIGHT...

BORE—LEFT..

RIB ☐ Matted ☐ Ventilated

SAFETY ☐ Automatic ☐ Non-Automatic

SIGHTS Front Middle

Metal ☐ ☐

Ivory Bead ☐ ☐

Red Bead ☐

FORE-END...........☐ Standard...................☐ Beavertail

STOCKS— to any dimensions other than those listed in catalog and also stocks with Monte Carlo, cheek piece or offset, can be furnished at extra charge. Please specify below dimensions desired.

Length of Pull (C to C)..

Drop at Comb (B to B)..

Drop at Heel (A to A)..

Drop at Monte Carlo (E to E)..

Pitch

KIND OF STOCK ☐ Pistol Grip ☐ Straight Grip ☐ Cap on Pistol Grip

☐ Monte Carlo ☐ Offset ☐ Cheek Piece

BUTT ☐ Composition ☐ Checkered Wood ☐ Recoil Pad

SHAPE OF COMB ☐ Thin ☐ Medium (Standard)

Use other side for any additional information you wish to give.

NAME.. DEALER'S NAME..

STREET NO.. DEALER'S ADDRESS..

CITY...................................... STATE..

Printed in U. S. A.

(THIS IS NOT AN ORDER)

Form No. 1988

The Specification Form at the back of the 1948 sales brochure had all of the information necessary to request the price of a custom built-to-order Model 21. (Thomas E. Henshaw collection)

Ad from 1954 for Western Xpert and Super-X shotgun shells. The ad appeared in the September issue of *Field & Stream*, the October issue of *Outdoor Life*, and November issue of *Sports Afield*. (Thomas E. Henshaw collection)

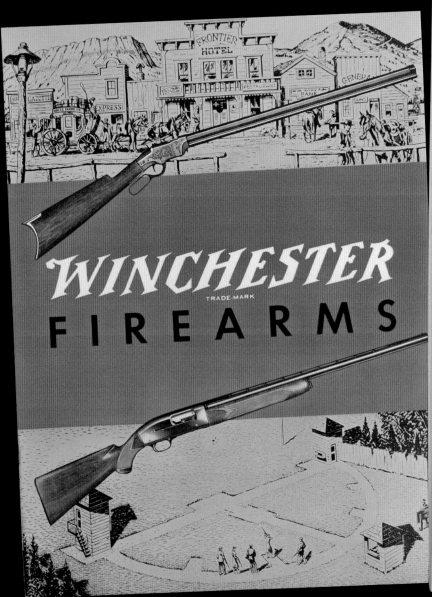

Engravings for Model 50 Shotguns

TASTEFULLY engraved, a good gun assumes an appearance of elegance. The engravings shown here are the skilled results of an art supremely manifested by WINCHESTER craftsmen, accomplishing the difficult task of hand-cutting the chrome molybdenum, proof-steel receivers of a WINCHESTER.

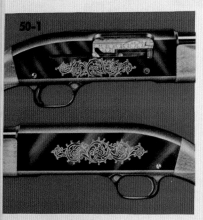

50-1

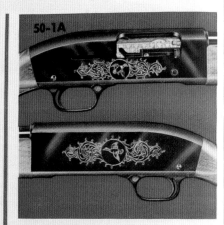

50-1A

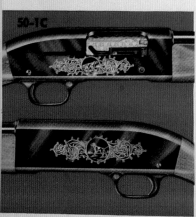

50-1C

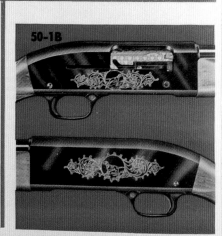

50-1B

A shooter can have any of these engravings duplicated on a Model 50. He may also submit favorite designs of game scenes, animals, etc. for the engravers to copy.

Engravings for
Model 50 Shotguns

For illustrations of stock carvings please see that section under Model 12. Page 49.

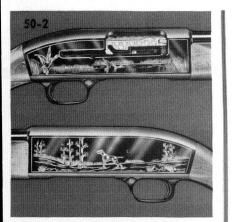
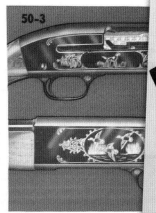

50-2 50-3 50-4 50-5

39

WINCHESTER
MODEL 50

THE WORLD'S FIRST
Automatic Shotgun
WITH NON-RECOILING BARREL

Shoots regular field or high-velocity long-range loads (including 2¾″ Magnum) without any adjustment. Action always works perfectly.

The WINCHESTER Model 50 Automatic* works on a revolutionary and an entirely different principle for shotguns. When the Winchester "Automatic" is fired, the barrel remains stationary, fixed, rigid. The chamber moves back a fraction of an inch and starts the action on its way. Surely and smoothly, the easy-working action flips out the empty and picks up a loaded shell ready for a really-fast second shot. The positive action of the Model 50 does its fast, smooth job every time, regardless of weather, weed-seeds or dirt. Perfect balance and natural ease of pointing will endear the Model 50 to the experienced shooter—and novices alike.

No "double shuffle" to throw you off your target. You don't need to force your shoulder into the stock to make the action work.

The uselessness and compromise that have previously been a part of automatic shotgun construction are eliminated.

The Winchester Model 50 feels and handles beautifully—like you expect a Winchester to handle.

Extra Barrels—No Tools, No Factory-Fitting Necessary. Interchangeable barrels for Winchester Model 50 can be purchased in a variety of lengths and chokes. Easily installed anywhere, anytime and by anyone.

Like other Winchester shotguns, and rifles, the functionally-sound Model 50 has been engineered into a graceful sporting firearm of real beauty.

All parts are correctly proportioned and in a proper relationship to each other, resulting in an arm that's nicely balanced, easy to carry, comfortable to handle, and with natural pointing qualities.

Only the best goes into the making of the Model 50. Receiver, barrel, breech bolt, and other critical parts are carefully machined from Winchester Proof-Steel—a chrome molybdenum alloy steel famous for its strength and toughness. The receiver is milled from a solid block; barrel is bored from a solid bar. There are no metal stampings in the Model 50.

The clean lines of the receiver curve gracefully to meet the nicely shaped pistol grip. Absence of unsightly screw heads, numerous projecting pins and rolled-in inscriptions accentuate its neat and sleek appearance.

With top performance, strength, dependability, handling ease, and graceful beauty successfully combined—at any price, Model 50 is the outstanding value in an automatic* shotgun today.

Model 50 shotguns are made in 12 and 20 gauges. The 12 gauge is available in Field, Skeet, and Trap styles; 20 gauge in Field and Skeet styles. Field guns are offered in barrel lengths and chokes for every shooting requirement.

Pigeon Grade Model 50 shotguns, with many deluxe features are made to special order for those wanting a gun of extra beauty and distinction.

*Self-loading

32

Shot Guns · Self-Loading

MODEL 50 FIELD GUN

WINCHESTER

Fired Position

Initial Unlocking Action

Shell Ejection Position

Shell Reloading Position

Extras For Model 50 Field Gun

• Stocks of other than listed standard dimensions (within manufacturing limits) either straight or pistol grip, no check piece, Monte Carlo or offset (See Page 37)

• For Monte Carlo style stock of special dimensions (within manufacturing limits)

• Winchester Special Ventilated Rib

• Interchangeable Barrels (no forearm) in lengths and chokes listed under catalog symbols Plain or Winchester Special Ventilated Rib

Revolutionary in design, a typical Winchester in streamlined silhouette handling, pointing and shooting the way the finest guns should, the Winchester Model 50 brings entirely new standards in an automatic (self-loading) shotgun in the shooting public.

Capacity is three shells — one in chamber and two in magazine with barrel of Winchester Proof-Steel.

Available in Field, Skeet or Trap grades with plain or ventilated rib barrels and Full, Modified, Improved Cylinder or Winchester Skeet chokes.

Pictures show cross section of M/50 action and chamber.

33

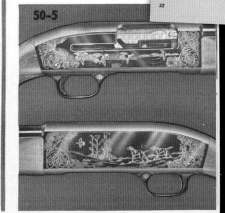

Winchester Firearms celebrated the company's centennial with a beautifully illustrated 80-page catalog in 1955. In January 1954 Winchester had introduced its first all-new (and successful) automatic shotgun, the Model 50. Between 1954 and 1961 nearly 200,000 were produced, the very first of which, serial number 1000, was presented to John M. Olin. In the centennial catalog 8 pages were dedicated to "The World's First Automatic Shotgun with a non-recoiling barrel." (Author's collection)

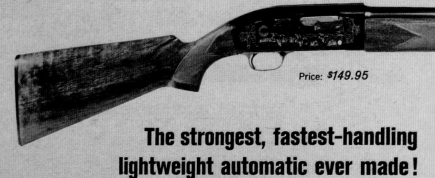
An ad from 1856 for Western Super-X and Xpert shot shells. It appeared in the October issue of *Sports Afield* and the November issue of *Field & Stream*. (Thomas E. Henshaw collection)

WIN-LITE® Barrel

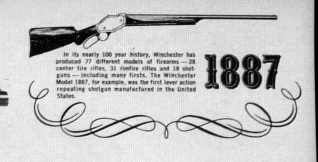

In its nearly 100 year history, Winchester has produced 77 different models of firearms — 28 center fire rifles, 31 rimfire rifles and 18 shotguns — including many firsts. The Winchester Model 1887, for example, was the first lever action repeating shotgun manufactured in the United States.

1887

WINCHESTER Model **59** Pigeon-Grade

The fast, sleek Model 59 is now available in this luxury model. Hand-finished and hand-checkered selected walnut stock, hand-finished internal parts and engine-turned breech bolt and carrier for an extra practical and handsome touch. (Not Illustrated)

From $249.65

SPECIFICATIONS

Pigeon Grade guns will be furnished with any combination of barrel length and choke shown under Model 59 listings and with stock dimensions to individual measure within manufacturing limits.

WINCHESTER Model **21**

The ultimate in the art of gunmaking, the incomparable Model 21 is made especially to your individual measurements and requirements. We have prepared a special brochure containing ... tions. It wi...

The Model ...

By the time this 1962 catalog came out the name on the cover was *Winchester – Western*, the latter being the parent company, owned by the Olin family. Western was the recommended ammunition for all Winchester rifles and shotguns. The cover was a wraparound image (front and back) of 19 Texas Rangers. The photo was taken in the 1890s and all but one of the rangers is holding a Winchester Model 1895 rifle. The fifth ranger from the right was holding a Krag. Among the models featured in the catalog was the Model 59 automatic shotgun with Win-Lite barrel, and the Model 21. The Model 59 was priced from $249.65 while the Model 21 started at $1,000 and went up to the Grand American for $3,500. (Author's collection)

1962 *WINCHESTER - Western* CATALOG

Another handsomely illustrated Winchester catalog, and one of the few to have a shotgun on the cover, was produced in 1970. The cover and interior illustrations were by Hal Frenck. Burlap was the background of choice for catalog photographer Garry Camp Burdick, who created a series of clean, highly-detailed group shots for each section. Among the specially featured models in the 1970 catalog was the Winchester 101 superposed. (Author's collection)

WINCHESTER-*Western*
1970 Sporting Arms and Ammunition

Model 101 hand-engraved receiver.

Hand-checkered,
narrow border forearm.

Combination barrel selector
and safety.

Engine-turned breech.

Model 101s

Quality — Made — by — Professional Shooters

Ever more popular with sportsmen who want lean, handsome styling and superior over-and-under performance. Winchester Model 101. One of the finest sporting arms ever manufactured. Quality you'd expect from hand-crafted shotguns costing far more. Custom-like features you'll value for a lifetime. Engine-turned breech, perfectly machined for a precision feel and substantial appearance. Hand-engraved receiver and trigger guard. French walnut stock and forearm, finished to a hard, high gloss. Crisp narrow border hand-checkering. Chrome-plated bores and chambers. Combination barrel selector and safety button right under your thumb for instant barrel option. Fire either barrel first. Sleek pistol grip with cap. Fluted comb and forearm. Ventilated rib. Single selective trigger. Selective ejection. Superb over-and-under shotguns over and above all others.

1. Model 101 Field Gun: $350.00. Superb one-two punch with a different choke for each barrel. Engine-turned breech. Chrome-plated bores and chambers. Crisp, narrow border hand-checkering. 12 or 20 gauge. Model 101 Field Gun in 28 gauge or 410 bore: $370.00.

2. Model 101 Trap Gun — Over-and-Under, Monte Carlo Stock: $370.00. Regular Stock: $360.00. Middle sight bead. Rubber recoil pad. 30" and 32" barrels available.

3. Model 101 Skeet Gun: $350.00. French walnut stock and forearm. Hand-engraved receiver and trigger guard. Sleek pistol grip with cap. Middle sight bead. Combination barrel selector and safety button right under your thumb. 12 or 20 gauge. Model 101 Skeet Gun in 28 gauge or 410 bore; $370.00.

4. Model 101 Magnum Field Gun: $350.00.

Mixes 3" Magnum and 2¾" standard loads. Great shotgun versatility — shoot waterfowl and upland game with the same gun. In 12 and 20 gauge.

5. Model 101 Trap Gun — Single Barrel, Monte Carlo Stock: $350.00. For the trapshooter who prefers single-barrel competition with Model 101 performance and style.

MODEL 101 TRAP AND SKEET SETS
Complete shooting systems for the claybird sportsman. Versatility, extra value, and instant interchangeability added to Model 101 style and performance. No tools needed to change barrels. Separate forearm with each different set of barrels.

Model 101 Trap Set — Over-and-Under and Two Single Barrels: $735.00. Economy and versatility on one 12-gauge frame.

Full and improved modified chokes on the over-and-under. Single barrels with improved modified and full chokes. All 32" long, chambered for 2¾" shells.

Model 101 Trap Set — Over-and-Under and One Single Barrel: $560.00. Over-and-under: 30" or 32" with improved modified and full chokes. 32" single barrel in improved modified and full or 34" full chokes for handicap shooters. All barrels chambered for 2¾" shells.

Model 101 Skeet Set — Three Barrels, Different Gauges $750.00. Three over-and-under barrels with one 20 gauge frame. 20 and 28 gauge, plus 410 bore. All 28" long with skeet and skeet chokes. 20 and 28 gauge barrels chambered for 2¾" shells. 410 bore takes 2½" shells.

GUN CASES FOR MODEL 101 TRAP, SKEET, AND FIELD GUNS AVAILABLE ON SPECIAL ORDER.

**1981
Sporting Arms
and Ammunition**

Shotguns were in the spotlight when the 1981 *Winchester – Western* catalog came out, with a Model 101 over and under sharing the front cover with a Model 94 XTR lever action and Model 70 XTR Featherweight bolt action rifles. Shotguns covered the entire back cover with a Super-X Model 1 XTR Trap Gun (right) a Model 23 XTR Pigeon Grade (center), and a Model 1300 XTR Slide Action shotgun. (Author's collection)

These B&W ads appeared during World War II in the November 1942 issue of *Hunting and Fishing* and May 1943 issue of *American Rifleman*. The *American Rifleman* ad rekindled the father and son theme so popular in early Winchester ads. The ad went on to explain that "No peacetime products are being made now. We've long been on round-the-clock production of military ammunition and grenades...those semi-automatic rifles which wrote such brilliant pages in U.S. military history at Bataan and Wake Island." The *Hunting and Fishing* ad pretty much told the wartime Winchester story. (Thomas E. Henshaw collection)

EVERY INDIAN'S MOST CHERISHED POSSESSION

Indians everywhere—natural-born hunters—prized Winchester rifles above everything else. Their greatest ambition was to own one and they would do anything to obtain it. If not by trade, by violence or war.

"Dad...what does this little Ⓦ mark mean?"

"THE 'W', son, stands for *Winchester*. The 'P' stands for *Proof*—Winchester Proof. Together they mean that your Winchester and mine are extra strong and safe."

No Winchester gun comes from the factory without that W. P. None can have it without having been proved on the firing range. There, experts load the gun with a powder charge more powerful than any standard load you can buy for that gun—and proof-fire it . . . again and again.

A mark of master craftsmanship—a guarantee of supreme quality—W. P. is the result of 76 years' research into metals and gun-making and many remarkable improvements in shotguns, rifles and ammunition.

No peace-time products are being made now. We've long been on round-the-clock production of military ammunition and Garands . . . those semi-automatic rifles which wrote such brilliant pages in U. S. military history at Bataan and Wake Island. We've done more. When the U. S. Army needed a carbine we pioneered and developed that weapon *from scratch* —the famous Winchester U. S. Carbine M-1 that tremendously increases the fire power of our military forces.

Such things you expect from Winchester leadership. Just as, when peace comes, you'll expect—and get—full supplies of world-famous Winchester sporting arms and ammunition.

Winchester Repeating Arms Co., New Haven, Conn.
Division of Western Cartridge Company

The name WINCHESTER on ammunition stands for the same high perfection of master craftsmanship as the Winchester proof-mark on Winchester guns.

WINCHESTER

TRADE MARK

"*On Guard for America Since 1866*"

COPR., 1943, WINCHESTER REPEATING ARMS CO., DIV. OF WESTERN CARTRIDGE CO.

RIFLES AND SHOTGUNS • CARTRIDGES AND SHOTSHELLS • FLASHLIGHTS AND FLASHLIGHT BATTERIES

"It's Messerschmitts not Mallards today, Bill!"

RAPID FIRE... Winchester was a pioneer in rapid fire—developing the first successful repeating rifle, the forerunner of the modern rapid-fire gun. For years Winchester leadership in sporting arms has included repeating shotguns. First, the sturdy Model 97. Later, the famous Model 12, the world's most popular repeater.

TODAY, when warbirds swoop and circle with deadly menace, America's familiarity with firearms is paying big dividends.

Men who yesterday trained themselves to swing a gun smoothly and accurately at wildfowl—who thrilled at the long range of Winchester Super Speed shotshells—are today the guardians of our safety. For now their peacetime skill is helping to rid the skies of Messerschmitts and Zeros.

Today, while its great reputation lives on in the hearts of sportsmen, Winchester, too, has gone to war—proud that its world leadership in sporting arms and ammunition can now help America to victory. But we are not unmindful that war can teach—as well as destroy. Already our experience in wartime production is bringing to light new methods and developments. And when peace comes, you will benefit. For rest assured that if Winchester Super Speed, Leader and Ranger shotshells and Super Speed and Silvertip cartridges can be improved, they will be.

WINCHESTER REPEATING ARMS COMPANY, NEW HAVEN, CONN.
Division of Western Cartridge Company

IMPORTANT Limited supplies of Winchester shotshells and cartridges are still obtainable. See your dealer.

MORE VALUABLE THAN GOLD. At one point on his 1915-16 Antarctic expedition, Sir Ernest H. Shackleton was forced to reduce the weight of his equipment to the absolute minimum. He abandoned valuable instruments, even gold coin, but he felt he could not dispense with his Winchester .44 cartridges.

WINCHESTER
TRADE MARK
"On Guard for America Since 1866"

COPR., 1942, WINCHESTER REPEATING ARMS CO., DIV. OF WESTERN CARTRIDGE CO.
RIFLES AND SHOTGUNS • CARTRIDGES AND SHOTSHELLS • FLASHLIGHTS AND FLASHLIGHT BATTERIES

16   *Nov. 1942* HUNTING AND FISHING

A trio of vintage Winchester companion booklets. The oldest example, far left, was published in 1917. The other two are from the 1950s. (Author's collection)

Western ad for Xpert shells appeared in *True* magazine and *Country Gentleman*. (Thomas E. Henshaw collection)

In the 1960s the name in small print was now Olin Mathieson, Winchester-Western and the topic in this 1960 advertisement appearing in the November *Guns and Ammo* stating that Winchester has never seen a shotgun that was worn out.

A CARLOAD OF SHOTSHELLS...
WON'T WEAR OUT A WINCHESTER

This season thousands of gamebags will be filled by Winchesters that were young when Hector was a pup. Blueing worn—sure . . . scarred-up stock—maybe, but each one shooting as fast and dependably as the day it came out of the box. In fact, a Winchester is so strongly made that we've never seen *one* that was worn out—no matter how old, no matter how heavily used. Will you shoot better with a Winchester? Absolutely. So will your son. So will your grandson.

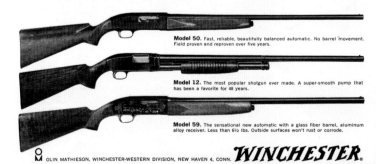

Model 50. Fast, reliable, beautifully balanced automatic. No barrel movement. Field proven and reproven over five years.

Model 12. The most popular shotgun ever made. A super-smooth pump that has been a favorite for 48 years.

Model 59. The sensational new automatic with a glass fiber barrel, aluminum alloy receiver. Less than 6½ lbs. Outside surfaces won't rust or corrode.

OLIN MATHIESON, WINCHESTER-WESTERN DIVISION, NEW HAVEN 4, CONN. **WINCHESTER.**

N. Y. 5220—Guns—November, 1960; Guns & Ammo—November, 1960

Index

(Illustration captions marked with italics)